HEALING STORIES

HEALING STORIES

Picture Books for the Big & Small

Changes in a Child's Life

JACQUELINE GOLDING, Ph.D.

M. EVANS

Lanham • New York • Boulder • Toronto • Oxford

Published by M. Evans
An imprint of The Rowman & Littlefield Publishing Group, Inc.
4501 Forbes Boulevard, Suite 200, Lanham, Maryland 20706

Designed and typeset by Evan Johnston

Distributed by NATIONAL BOOK NETWORK

Library of Congress Control Number: 2006927694
ISBN-10: 1-59077-097-8 (pbk. : alk. Paper)
ISBN-13: 978-1-59077-097-9 (pbk. : alk. Paper)

∞™ The paper used in this publication meets the minimum requirements of American National Standard for Information Sciences—Permanence of Paper for Printed Library Materials, ANSI/NISO Z39.48-1992.

Manufactured in the United States of America.

To Jim, Daniel, and Emily
with love

CONTENTS

PART 9. TRAUMA 281

ACKNOWLEDGEMENTS

My parents shared their love of reading with me from the very beginning.

Jerome L. Singer, Ph.D., laid the foundation of what I know about children's imagination, believed in me at an early stage, and always inspired me to do my best work. Dorothy Anderson, Ph.D., was a wonderful role model, and I hope that some of her warmth and practicality come through in this book.

The Berkeley, Contra Costa, Oakland, and Pleasanton public libraries processed hundreds of holds for me and loaned me hundreds more books. Librarians were kind, patient, and friendly, and several shared my excitement about this book.

My agent, Jim Levine, Ed.D., played a vital role in turning this book from a dream into a reality. My editors at M. Evans and Company, PJ Dempsey and especially Matt Harper, listened to my struggles with writing and provided skilled, thoughtful feedback, much-needed humor, and the collaboration and encouragement that sustained the process of writing this book. Evan Johnston's beautiful design work brought substance to my words. Rick Rinehart, Jen Linck, and Stephen Driver at the Rowman & Littlefield Publishing Group guided this book through a major transition and out into the world with competence, care, and grace

Many people generously shared their ideas, favorite picture books, and resources for finding picture books with me, especially Cathy Aiello; Judith Flory, L.C.S.W.; Fran George, M.F.T.; Judi Hampshire, M.F.T.; Shelly Havrilenko; Charmaine Hitchcox, Ph.D.; Lisa Kahan, Ph.D.; Mary Krentz, Ph.D.; Caroline Peterson, D.M.D.; Susan Scatena, Ph.D.; Patti Turetzky; Linden Van Wert; and Grant Wyborny, Ph.D. Judy Goldstein, L.C.S.W. introduced me to End Note with an enthusiasm that was easy to share. Penelope Burrows, M.F.T. and Helen Savin, L.C.S.W. knew just when to ask about this book to inspire its continued progress. Through her friendship and her unshakeable optimism about this book, Lisa Kahan, Ph.D. made a huge difference. The warmth, encouragement, and wisdom of Katherine Fellner, Ph.D.; Judith Flory, L.C.S.W.; and Mary Krentz, Ph.D., have been enormously important in making this book possible.

Jim, Daniel, and Emily supported me in writing this book in unique, essential ways, and bring joy to my life.

INTRODUCTION

Books allow us to open all kinds of doors. Some doors lead to people, giving us the chance to encounter personalities and characters we'd otherwise never know. Other doors guide us to places and times beyond our own, broadening our sense of what's possible. Perhaps most important, all of these doors lead us to one place: ourselves. Using diverse yet universal examples, books provide us with fundamental truths about ourselves, illuminating parts of ourselves that we haven't developed fully, don't know well, or don't trust yet.

For a long time in my personal and professional life, I've believed in the power of stories to help kids understand themselves and the world around them, so it was a natural progression that led to incorporating them into my work with children. When I was a post-doctoral fellow at the Contra Costa County Child, Adolescent, and Family Mental Health Service, I shared stories with several young clients. My supervisors liked those stories so much that when my fellowship ended, they asked for a written list of books that they might want to use with clients. That list was a little less than a page long. Since then, I've updated and expanded it, first when I happened to run across a picture book that struck me as useful, and then with a growing sense of intention and purpose. I began to share the list with colleagues and with parents in my practice, many of whom told me they found it very helpful. This experience led me to write this book so that this resource would be available to you, wherever you are and whatever your connection to children.

If there is an underlying theme to the picture books listed here, it's that each of these stories opens doors that lead into a secure sense of a strong self in reliable relationships, a capacity to use imagination to work through difficult situations, and a self that can cope positively and creatively with the challenges children face as they develop. These doors take on many forms—from the cute to the serious, from the beautiful to the tragic—but each book contained in this list brings kids to a deeper understanding of themselves, helping them to deal with the demands that they face as they grow up, from the everyday to the traumatic.

HOW STORIES HELP

Even under ordinary circumstances, a child's world is filled with changes. As kids grow, their capacities change, and with this development come changes in their expectations of themselves and in adults' expectations for them, such as when kids begin to go to sleep on their own, learn to use the potty, and go to school for the first time. Development also brings changes in kids' family situations, forcing them to integrate experiences like a new brother or sister or a move to a new house. As children gain the ability to understand situations between people in more complex ways, new questions arise that require more detailed answers about their family, friends, school, and society.

All of these changes require youngsters to expand, adjust, and refine their ways of thinking about different aspects of their lives. Stories can help kids do this by showing new ways of thinking about things. Developmental changes also bring feelings that need to be processed. Children may feel not only proud, happy, and competent, but also sad, angry, worried, lonely, ashamed, or confused. Stories can help them understand and resolve their feelings.

But the healing properties of books aren't limited to the everyday transitions of child development. These stories are also vital tools for helping kids understand some of life's most difficult experiences, such as parents' divorce, the serious illness of the child or someone close to them, the death of a person or pet they love, or exposure to natural disaster. Books can effectively aid in the process of healing from these stresses. Regardless of the how big the trauma may be, children will take comfort and learn from characters' stories that encourage them to confront their complex emotions. Furthermore, normal processing of trauma includes mental reliving of the experience, with an increasing sense of resolution over the course of many relivings. Stories can provide opportunities for reliving painful or frightening experiences within the safe limits of their covers.

Stories allow children to acknowledge distressed feelings and the events that lead to them. Although initially some experiences may seem too painful to talk about, a story about a similar event shows the child that it's possible to discuss the event openly, and over time, it may help the child to talk about the event. Stories may also help kids realize that they're not alone—others have similar experiences and feelings, and there's a name for what they're going through. In this way, stories can function as an extra source of empathy for kids, helping them to feel understood and so allowing them to understand their own lives better through the context of this story. Ultimately, a story in which the problem is resolved may inspire hopefulness in children that their problem, too, can be resolved.

At the same time, stories can give youngsters enough distance on a stressful experience to allow them to get some perspective on it. After all, in stories, the stressful event happens to someone else. It doesn't even always happen to a child. Many stories for small children have animals as their main characters. For example, in *Owl Babies*, owls learn that Mother always comes back. In *A Baby Sister for Frances*, a badger adjusts to having a new baby in the household. In *The Kissing Hand*, a raccoon has to leave his mother to begin school. The sense of "safe distance" may be helpful in allowing kids to approach their own difficult feelings and relive their own experiences in ways that lead to a sense of mastery.

Perhaps the most amazingly universal thing about these stories is that many of them can be useful even when the child hasn't experienced the challenges that the character faces. Most of these tales offer general examples of positive coping, which are helpful regardless of the specific situations of children who are reading them, and a child who eventually has the experience described in the story will have the benefit of a familiar story within which to process the experience.

DISCUSSING BOOKS WITH CHILDREN

Sometimes just hearing a story is a healing experience all by itself. At these times, you and your child may be joined in an understanding of the story that goes beyond words. But often, sharing a story with your child will involve talking about the story together. For books to reach kids most effectively and comfort them about their challenging or painful experiences, it's important to present books in a way that opens, rather than discourages, communication. Sometimes you may find it helpful to talk about the character's experiences rather than your child's, at least at first. For example, reading *Alexander, Who's Not (Do You Hear Me, I Mean It) Going To Move*, you might say something along the lines of, "Alexander is really angry about moving, isn't he?" In many situations, this might be enough to let kids know that their feelings are heard and acknowledged. For other children, or at other times, a story might open more direct discussion about the youngster's feelings. In the face of a child's distress, adults may find themselves wanting to say, "Don't cry." But it's important to let kids know that it's okay to cry, or even, sometimes, that the adult, too, feels like crying. A story in which a character's feelings about the event are acknowledged straightforwardly is a way to acknowledge and accept the child's feelings.

Books are most effective in promoting acknowledgment of feelings, processing of experience, empathy, hope, and self-understanding when these experiences are available to children in their most important relationships. If children take from a story the message that it's okay to feel and talk about strong emotions, that message will be much more believable and reliable in a world where they have the experience of sharing those feelings in an accepting relationship.

Books are *not* ways to avoid talking with your child about experiences or feelings. Please don't send the message that "I'll let you figure out how to solve your problem with this book," or, even worse, "I've given you a book because it's too hard, scary, etc. for me to talk with you about what's happening, or about your feelings." Books can only be helpful if they're used to facilitate, not short-circuit, children's processing of their experiences and emotions.

PRACTICAL TIPS FOR PARENTS WHO READ STORIES

As you probably know, there's more to reading to your child than just choosing how to make funny voices. Here are a few tips to insure that your reading sessions with your child are as enjoyable and productive as possible.

- **Don't force books on a child.** Don't insist that a child read a particular book, or read it at a particular time, even if you think that's when the child most needs it. It may work better to include the book with other reading that's less emotionally loaded. The youngster's own readiness will determine when it's appropriate to read these books. If a child wants to stop reading a story that's related to a stressful experience, it's usually most helpful to stop. You can offer the book later. This process can require patience from adults who are eager to help. It's important not to expect miracles overnight. Go at your child's pace and enjoy the time you're sharing together.

- **Keep your expectations realistic.** Reading, by itself, can't solve all problems. Stories are just one tool for coping with life transitions. Again, they're most likely to be successful when they encourage communication between children and the adults who are important to them.

- **Choose stories you enjoy.** It's a good idea to choose books that you like and whose message you approve of. Kids are perceptive enough to sense your true feelings, and if you read your child a book that you don't like, this won't help the child. You'd also miss an opportunity to convey the message that reading is enjoyable.

- **Choose stories that match your child's stage of development.**
  Developmental readiness should be taken into account when choosing
  books, in terms of intellectual, emotional, and social maturity. I've
  suggested age ranges for each picture book I summarize, but because
  every child is unique and develops at his or her own rate, use these
  age ranges only as a general guide. On the average, kids in the listed
  age range are most likely to benefit from the given book. But because
  your child may be more or less emotionally mature, or more or less
  verbally skilled, at any particular age, only you know and will be able
  to judge whether a book is too simple or boring, or too complex or
  difficult, for your child. If a book is too simple, the child may say so,
  or may criticize the author for not bringing up more complex issues.
  If a book is too difficult, the child may become distracted or be unable
  to tell you what the book is about at all. Using these signals, choose
  stories according to how your child reacts.

- **Choose stories that reflect your child's perspective on the
  situation.** Another consideration when choosing books is the child's
  specific concerns. What about the situation is important to this child
  at this time? For example, when there's a new baby in the house,
  some children may have more intellectual curiosity about how babies
  develop, whereas others may be more focused on worries about
  whether their parents will still love them. Some kids are more literal-
  minded than others about these kinds of issues. One six-year-old, who
  was familiar with several books about losing pets, said there ought to
  be more books about losing a grandparent, because that happens to a
  lot of children. On the other hand, another child proposed sharing *The
  Tenth Good Thing About Barney* with his grandma when his grandpa
  had died. A three-year-old girl who had been adopted from China by
  a European-American mother responded to *I Love You Like Crazy
  Cakes* by telling her own story as she turned the pages and looked
  at the pictures: "Mommy flew on a plane to come get me, there I am
  at the orphanage," and so on. At the same time, for many children, it
  may be more important to match the *feelings* than the details of the
  situation. One seven-year-old who was traumatized by witnessing a
  murder had difficulty tolerating *A Terrible Thing Happened* once, but
  wanted to hear *What Was I Scared Of?* over and over again. She was
  ready to process her feelings of fear, but not the specific trauma. If

you're not sure whether to match feelings or specific events, I suggest that you err in the direction of starting with books that match the child's feelings as well as possible.

ABOUT THE BOOKS

Although I describe over five hundred books in the following chapters, the list is not exhaustive. Rather than include all the picture books I could find on each of the thirty-four topics that follow, I included only those that, in my opinion, have positive value for promoting children's development. I passed over many books because they seemed unhelpful and rejected others that relied too heavily on cultural stereotypes or presented a negative view of girls, women, or gender relations. During the book-selection process, I put a lot of emphasis on the role of story; however, I've also included some nonfiction picture books that offer empathy and reassurance without the use of plot. I didn't exclude books that are out of print, because many are available at public libraries or through used booksellers (often online). I haven't included overtly religious books because your religious leader or spiritual advisor is best qualified to recommend those.

READING IS A SHARED ADVENTURE

Perhaps the most important tip for reading with your children is to join in their journey of discovery. Reading is an amazing experience that will bring you closer to the kids and give you a chance to create memories together. If you aren't involved with the story, they probably won't be either, so just take your time, relax, and don't be afraid to allow yourself to be as caught up in the story as they are.

I hope that you'll benefit from this book by finding picture books that are genuinely helpful to the children in your life, and in this way, by becoming empowered to expand the ways in which you promote their development and healing. I hope that the children in your life will benefit from your heightened ability to empathize with and accept their experiences and, through you, will find more meaningful understandings of themselves. And finally, I hope that you'll both benefit from deeper connections to each other and from the richness that each of these stories has to offer.

HOW TO USE THIS BOOK

I've broken the chapters down into basic categories of childhood issues to help you find the books that are most helpful for your child's immediate needs. As a result, you don't need to read this book from start to finish. It's probably most helpful to start with the part or chapter that best describes the events or feelings that your child is currently experiencing. Each chapter begins with an introduction that points you toward the ways that the event or feeling is addressed in the picture books summarized in that chapter. When it's relevant, this introduction ends with comments about other chapters or books that are often related.

Following these introductions is an alphabetical list of picture-book descriptions on the chapter's topic. The description of each picture book begins with the title, author, illustrator (if not the author), length in pages, publisher, and year of publication. This information is followed by a paragraph describing the story. I recommend that you use these descriptions to choose books to read yourself, so that you can decide which ones you'd like to offer to your child. At the end of each entry is a suggested age range, but because of individual variations in development, these ranges are only a guide; you should take your own child's specific level of development into account when choosing books.

Finally, each listing includes the main character's cultural background and what I have labeled *cultural context.* By *cultural context,* I mean the cultural background of the characters in the story, as a group. For example, if all the characters in the words or illustrations are European-American, then the cultural context for that story is described as European-American. If more than one culture is represented in the characters or illustrations (for example, a classroom includes children who appear to be European-American, African-American, and Latino), I describe that context as multicultural. However, I use the term *multicultural* to refer to an individual only when that person clearly has a heritage that represents more than one cultural background. This occurs in *Hope* (Chapter 22): the main character has one African-American parent and one European-American parent, and so is described as multicultural. If the main character's cultural background is the same as the overall context, then only the cultural context is listed.

Although characters' backgrounds are often apparent from their appearance, sometimes they're less clear, particularly when the illustrations are more abstract, and the illustrators' intent is not always clear. I've sometimes (and probably not consistently) interpreted characters who are shown with medium-light skin tones and dark eyes and hair as European-American (in the absence of other cues), but they often could as easily be seen as Latino, Asian American, or African-American. And some illustrators use colors that have no resemblance to human skin tones (for example, Todd Parr). In stories that have animal (or monster or vegetable) characters, or no characters, I've described the cultural context as "N/A" (not applicable) but even animal characters can represent human cultures; for example, in the children's cartoons *Sagwa* (in which the cats are Chinese) or *Dragon Tales* (in which at least one recurring dragon character is Latino).

Ultimately, the purpose of this cultural information is to help you make the best decisions about how to broaden your child's cultural exposure, so please don't use this information simply to match the character's cultural background with that of your child. By providing this, my goal is not to limit your selections but instead to give you as much information about these books as possible. This way, when it comes time to pick the right books for your child, you will know as much as you can about them and have the added benefit of knowing which ones will widen their cultural horizons.

PART 1

EVERYDAY GROWING:
The Basics

[CHAPTER 1]

Security in Relationship

Every child needs to know that at least one adult will care for him or her, no matter what. From earliest infancy, children's sense of self depends on, and develops out of, their sense of connection to the important people in their lives. One of the major developmental tasks of early life, which continues in other forms throughout kids' lives, is to create and sustain relationships. It's crucial for children to know that the important adults in their life will always love them, even if the adult doesn't always love their behavior. Adults must provide kids with spaces that are both physically and emotionally safe in which they can explore their environments and their feelings. Ideally, as they grow, children learn to care for themselves by keeping a sense of the adult with them even when the adult isn't physically present (see also Chapter 9).

Abuelita's Heart by Amy Córdova. 32 pages
Simon & Schuster, 1997.

Children can experience a deep, sustaining connection even with an adult whom they don't see often. When a girl visits her *abuelita* (grandmother) in the rural American Southwest, Abuelita teaches her about plants that heal and how the heart reaches out to heal other people. The girl has a magical dream in which she, her parents, and Abuelita shine with a special light that connects all beings to one another. The light reminds her that Abuelita is always with her in her heart, and provides a wonderful example of how security from a special adult stays with you.

Ages: 4–8.   **Cultural context:** Native-American and Latino

Blueberries for Sal by Robert McCloskey. 55 pages Viking, 1948.

An important quality of a secure parent-child relationship is the sense that each sees and appreciates what's special about the other. In this classic tale, two mothers, one human and one a bear, take their little ones to pick blueberries. For a little while, Sal and the cub each follow the wrong mother. Upon discovering the mix-up, the two mothers have similar reactions, as each locates her own child by listening for the child's unique and delightful sounds. At the end of the day, both mothers are reunited with their children, and everyone gets all the berries they need. With blueberry-colored line drawings, Robert McCloskey reminds kids that although many people (or maybe, in fiction, a bear) can take care of you, your own personal mother will always recognize and find you.

Ages: 0–3.   **Cultural context:** European-American

Even If I Did Something Awful by Barbara Shook Hazen.
Illus. by Nancy Kincade. 28 pages Aladdin, 1992.

This reassuring story shows that parents still love you even when they're angry with you. When a girl accidentally breaks a vase, she worries that this might make her mother stop loving her. To find out, she asks whether Mommy would still love her if she did "awful" things like getting crayon on the carpet. Of course, the answer is yes, although she'd make her clean up her mess. When the girl finally confesses to breaking the vase, Mommy expresses both anger and love as they pick up the pieces together. Here Barbara Hazen shows children that it's safe to be their imperfect, human selves—they'll still be loved, and with a parent's help, their mistakes won't be out of control.

Ages: 4–8.   **Cultural context:** European-American

Good Job, Little Bear **by Martin Waddell.**
Illus. by Barbara Firth. 32 pages Candlewick, 1999.
To discover and delight in their abilities, children need an adult who will keep them safe. Little Bear experiences this safety while leading Big Bear in an exploration of rocks, trees, and streams. Little Bear shows off his skills proudly to an appreciative Big Bear who watches when Little Bear needs watching and catches when Little Bear needs catching. When Big Bear asks Little Bear afterward whether falling scared him, Little Bear answers that he knew Big Bear would be there, which Big Bear confirms. The pencil-and-watercolor illustrations clearly convey tender protectiveness through Big Bear's body language and excitement, forlornness, relief, and security through Little Bear's. This book reassures children that parents will share their pride in kids' skills and independence, while staying close to help whenever that's needed.

Ages: 2–5   **Cultural context:** N/A

Gotcha, Louie! **by H. M. Ehrlich. Illus. by Emily Bolam.**
32 pages Houghton Mifflin/Lorraine, 2002.
Children can use games such as peek-a-boo to learn about the security of their relationships. A ritual for Louie and his mother is "Gotcha!", in which he runs away and Mommy catches him. When Louie gets tired of grown-up talk at dinner one night, he decides that it's time to play this game, but his mother, who is busy with the grown-ups, doesn't notice he's gone. Upon realizing this, she and the other adults look for him. Eventually, Mommy solves the problem by inviting Louie to catch *her*, and of course, Louie (who is hiding close by) comes running. This hide-and-seek tale shows kids that even when a caring adult seems preoccupied with other people or things, their secure contact with her or him is still present.

Ages: 1–4   **Cultural context:** European-American

Grandmother's Song **by Barbara Soros. Illus. by Jackie Morris. 32 pages Barefoot Books, 1998.**

A loving relationship has the transformative power to help even a fearful child to grow up trusting, trustworthy, brave, strong, and confident. In *Grandmother's Song*, a grandmother holds her granddaughter close and in profoundly empathic moments, imparts these attributes as they have come through generations of grandmothers. As an adult, the granddaughter cares tenderly for her grandmother as she ages. After her grandmother's death, the granddaughter grieves, but soon feels her grandmother's strong, soothing presence. When the girl becomes a grandmother herself, she embodies her grandmother's qualities as she cares for her own grandchildren. An afterword for adults elaborates on the power of grandmothers' touch, particularly within Mexican culture. The luminous, earth-toned watercolors mirror the language's strength and tenderness, creating an overall sense of how to use the support of a deeply caring adult to nurture one's own development.

Ages: 4–8 **Cultural context:** Mexican

I Love You, Stinky Face **by Lisa McCourt. Illus. by Cyd Moore. 32 pages BridgeWater, 1997.**

It's important for children to know that their parents will survive what they imagine to be their own awfulness. In *I Love You, Stinky Face*, the main character's Mama would love her child even if the child turned into a big, scary ape, an alligator with big, sharp teeth, or even a skunk that smelled so bad that its name was Stinky Face. In each case, Mama would take care of the child in ways that best met the child's needs—for example, she would bake a banana birthday cake for the ape-child. The illustrations are gently humorous, full of color, energy, and sweetness without being cloying. They combine with the text to reassure children that parents will tolerate their strong, destructive feelings, and love them regardless.

Ages: 2–4 **Cultural context:** European-American

I'll Always Be Your Friend **by Sam McBratney. Illus. by Kim Lewis. 32 pages HarperCollins, 2001.**

Children need enough room in their relationships with parents to experience and resolve emotions safely, even anger at their parents. In this story, a little fox has fun playing with Mother Fox all day, and when it's time to stop for the night, he doesn't want to. He expresses his anger and frustration by telling her that he isn't her friend anymore. Mother Fox accepts his anger calmly, and he soon decides to be her friend again. She replies that she'll always be his friend. Even if children view their anger as being so out of control that it could destroy the parental relationship, from reading this story, they will know that it's safe to have these feelings because their parents will always be there for them.

Ages: 3–8 **Cultural context:** N/A

Let's Play Rough! **by Lynne Jonell. Illus. by Ted Rand.**
32 pages Putnam, 2000.
An important function of safe relationships is to help children to learn that they can control scary experiences and angry feelings. In *Let's Play Rough!*, a boy asks his daddy to "play rough" with him, pretending he's a bear. When Daddy pretends to be a bigger, wilder bear, this feels overwhelming to the boy, who asks his father to stop the rough play. Daddy stops, reassures the boy that he's Daddy, not a bear, and hugs him, making it clear that the boy is in control of the make-believe, and Daddy is aware of the boy's needs. It's clear that the boy feels safe knowing this, because once reassured, he's ready to play rough again. The illustrations provide the boy's perspective on their human and bear selves so that kids can see the situation as the boy does. Kids can use this story to learn how to use a safe relationship with a parent to regulate their experiences of fear and anger.

Ages: 2–5 **Cultural context:** European-American

Mommy's Hands **by Kathryn Lasky and Jane Kamine.**
Illus. by Darcia LaBrosse. 24 pages Hyperion, 2002.
Everyday interactions demonstrate love between all mothers and their children in *Mommy's Hands*. In this tale, the little ones (one Asian American, one European-American, one African-American) tell about the wonderful things Mommy's hands do: holding the child's hand, preparing food, braiding hair, helping the child write, and taking off Band-Aids. Each Mommy takes care of her child,

teaches him or her, joins with the child in playing and creating, and lovingly tucks the child into bed. Children will find a warm sense of security and comfort in this delightful story.

Ages: 0–5   **Cultural context:** Multicultural

"More, More, More" Said the Baby **by Vera B. Williams. 32 pages Greenwillow, 1990.**
Children's sense of security in relationships develops through everyday interactions. This book contains three stories in which a caregiver (daddy, grandma, or mama) shows love for a child (one boy, one girl, and one who can be understood as a boy or a girl). In each story, the adult playfully catches the running, scooting, or even sleeping toddler, reminding kids that the adult will always create a safe world for the child. Illustrated with beautiful gouache paintings, this remarkable book has a timeless quality that will appeal to all ages, particularly younger children. The warmly affectionate interactions in these stories convey a strong sense of security to kids.

Ages: 0–3   **Cultural context:** Multicultural

Okomi Climbs a Tree **by Helen Dorman and Clive Dorman. Illus. by Tony Hutchings. 24 pages Dawn, 2003.**
Okomi, a young chimpanzee, is able to discover some of his capabilities because his Mama Du gives him room for exploration but still helps him when he really needs help. Okomi bravely struggles to climb a slippery, wet tree to reach some tasty-looking leaves, and after he falls down, Mama Du keeps an eye on him, giving him room to make his own decision about what to do next. When he decides to try again, his mother watches his successful second attempt, supporting him from afar. Once he realizes that he's unable to get down by himself, Mama Du climbs up and holds him in the tree until he can climb down on his own. Reading this story will help children understand that it's safe—and rewarding—to push the limits of their competence and try new things, because a parent will always provide the necessary help.

Ages: 2–5   **Cultural context:** N/A

The Runaway Bunny by Margaret Wise Brown.
Illus. by Clement Hurd. 32 pages HarperCollins, 1972.

In this classic story of a bunny child's requests for reassurance of his mother's continuing presence, the mother not only responds with comforting words, but also shows that she means it by joining him in imagination. When the little bunny announces that he is going to run away from his mother, imagining himself as a fish in a stream, a rock on a high mountain, a flower in a garden, and other things (including a human boy), she follows him by imagining that she's a fisherman, a mountain climber, a gardener, and so on. The charming illustrations show the little bunny as his real and imaginary selves simultaneously—for example, as a bunny-shaped rock on the mountain. In the end, he decides to stay and be the mother bunny's little bunny. Using imagination, he has maintained the reassuring presence of an adult who understands him and keeps him safe.

Ages: 0–5 **Cultural context:** N/A

There's Nothing to D-o-o-o by Judith Mathews.
Illus. by Kurt Cyrus. 32 pages Browndeer/Harcourt, 1999.

Children can expand their possibilities when they're secure in a relationship with an adult, as a calf named Laloo does when she becomes bored with life on the farm. She explores a field and a forest, finally going to sleep in a ravine. Her mother, Mamoo, finds her, and Laloo decides that although she's had a good adventure, she's missed Mamoo and wants to go home. The author's word choices give this story a hilarious, endearing, mooing sound. Children will understand that it's safe to enjoy exploration because a parent will always find them.

Ages: 1–5 **Cultural context:** N/A

The Way Mothers Are by Miriam Schlein. Illus. by Joe Lasker.
32 pages Whitman, 2000.

Although children may behave in disruptive ways, they need to know that this won't sever their connections with their parents. In this story, a toddler-like kitten can't imagine that his mother could love him when he resists getting dressed, screams, or grabs things from his sister. Mother cat acknowledges that she doesn't like those behaviors, but she still loves the kitten. The puzzled kitten guesses that maybe she loves him because he's smart, paints well, sometimes shares with his sister, or is generally well-behaved. Mother cat explains that she does appreciate those behaviors, but she loves *him* all the time, just because he's hers. When kids experience their misbehavior as out of control, but know that their behavior doesn't overwhelm parents, they have a safe place to learn *self*-control.

Ages: 2–5   **Cultural context:** N/A

What Sadie Sang **by Eve Rice. 28 pages Greenwillow, 1976.**
Being understood by a parent goes a long way toward making the world a safe place, something that the character of Sadie shows in this sweet story. Sadie, who is one or two years old, is big enough to walk, but rides in the stroller because she wants to. Sadie's Mama knows she's singing, even when the other people they meet on their walk think she's crying. When children know that parents understand them and appreciate their creations, their sense of security is enhanced.

Ages: 0–3   **Cultural context:** European-American

[CHAPTER 2]

A Resilient Sense of Self

When children like, trust, and believe in themselves, they're more resilient to both everyday stresses and big changes in their lives. This gives them the strength they need to persist in solving difficult problems and to fulfill their potentials. You can use the stories summarized in this chapter to support your efforts to promote your child's resilience. Some of these stories are great for helping all kids develop a healthy sense of self. Others are especially useful for children who feel discouraged about themselves, whether this comes from an internal sense of criticism, a sense of being "different," peer or adult criticism, or an excessively evaluative attitude by others. From these stories, children can learn to regain a positive sense of self by finding inner resources, such as creativity, and using these resources to learn to believe in themselves. They can identify with a character who discovers that it feels best to be who he or she is.

See also *Regina's Big Mistake* (Chapter 3) for a story of a child who feels good about herself when she redefines "mistakes" as creativity.

Geez Louise! (Chapter 21) has a positive message about moving from preoccupation with your limitations to developing your strengths.

A Bad Case of Stripes by David Shannon. 32 pages
Blue Sky, 1998.

When we try to be someone we're not, we become unrecognizable to everyone, including ourselves. Camilla learns this as she goes through a series of bizarre transformations—even becoming striped—in her attempts to please not only other kids, but even the medical experts who are called in to treat her strange disease. It's only by being true to herself—eating lima beans even though other kids might laugh at her because they don't like them—that she resumes her normal shape and color. The illustrations have a surreal quality that may be scary for some kids, but they effectively express the creepiness of Camilla's disconnection from herself when she tries to be what others want her to be. The message comes across loud and clear that you'll be much happier being who you are than trying to be what you're not.

Ages: 5–8   **Cultural context:** Multicultural
Main character's cultural background: European-American

Belinda the Ballerina by Amy Young. 32 pages Viking, 2002.

When criticism focuses on kids' seemingly negative qualities, it becomes hard for them to trust their own capabilities. *Belinda the Ballerina* is the story of a hardworking, competent ballerina whose large feet prevent her from auditioning successfully and cause her to stop dancing, taking up waitressing instead. The restaurant owner and customers like her for the very qualities that made her a good dancer—quickness, lightness on her feet, and ability to work hard. When a band plays at the restaurant, Belinda can't resist dancing, and she becomes very popular. Word eventually reaches a ballet director, who is profoundly impressed and offers her a job as a dancer. No one notices the size of her feet. The importance of believing in yourself comes across in a positive, upbeat way.

Ages: 3–8   **Cultural context:** Multicultural
Main character's cultural background: European-American

The Carrot Seed by Ruth Krauss. Illus. by Crockett Johnson. 32 pages HarperCollins, 1945.

Children may sometimes need to trust their own strengths even when others don't. In this classic, simply worded story, a preschool-age boy plants a carrot seed, and everyone tells him it won't grow. In fact, for a long time, it *doesn't* grow, but the boy tends it lovingly. Eventually it produces a carrot as big as the boy. The boy's self-reliance gives kids a positive message about believing in themselves in spite of what anyone tells them to the contrary.

Ages: 2–5   **Cultural context:** European-American

Chrysanthemum by Kevin Henkes. 32 pages Greenwillow, 1991.

It can be hard for kids to maintain a positive sense of self when others are critical, and this is precisely the problem Chrysanthemum encounters. Chrysanthemum grows up happy, secure, and loving her name—until she starts school. Her classmates tease her cruelly about her name. Although her parents support her lovingly, Chrysanthemum wishes she could change her name. Then everyone's favorite teacher says that not only is her own first name Delphinium, but also, she may name her own daughter Chrysanthemum. Chrysanthemum reclaims her self-confidence, and her classmates consider taking new names that are more like hers. Repetition is used effectively to evoke Chrysanthemum's emotional states, and the author is very skilled at showing how mean kids can be. Chrysanthemum discovers that the other kids' criticism is arbitrary and ephemeral, and that more positive points of view are possible and will make her feel better about herself.

Ages: 3–8   **Cultural context:** N/A

Dog Eared by Amanda Harvey. 32 pages Doubleday, 2002.

There's often more than one opinion about a child's attributes, and their decision about which opinion to believe affects how they feel about themselves. When another dog tells Otis that his ears are big, suddenly, they look too big to Otis. He worries—and has nightmares—about this, and thinks he has to change his ears somehow. The misguided ways that he manipulates them (for example, tying them in a bow) mirror his struggles to feel better. When Otis's human, Lucy, snuggles with his ear and tells him how wonderful his ears are, all is right again. Otis realizes that he doesn't believe the dog at the park; he believes Lucy, who loves him. The illustrations effectively convey Otis's distortions and Lucy's affection for Otis, helping to show kids that there's more than one way to understand their unique qualities. They'll understand the benefits of seeing themselves from the perspective of a loving friend, rather than that of an uncaring stranger.

Ages: 4–7   **Cultural context:** European-American
Main character's cultural background: N/A

Emily's Art **by Peter Catalanotto. 32 pages Atheneum, 2001.**
Excessive evaluation can undermine children's sense of their uniqueness, but books like *Emily's Art* can support kids' sense of self. Emily paints creative, meaningful images, but when there's an art contest at school, she worries about whether her painting will be the "best." The judge misinterprets Emily's painting of her dog as a rabbit (she's painted him with big ears because he hears well) and awards the prize to another picture because she hates dogs. Emily decides that she'll never paint again. Luckily, this doesn't last long, and as the story ends, Emily feels confident about making choices that reflect her own taste. This emotionally truthful story shows children how matters of taste arbitrarily get turned into evaluation as "best." It celebrates their capacity to trust their own preferences.

Ages: 4–8   **Cultural context:** Multicultural
Main character's cultural background: European-American

Happy Birthday to You **by Dr. Seuss. 55 pages**
Random House, 1959.
A birthday is a wonderful occasion to celebrate a child's joy in being who she or he is, an idea reflected in the birthday customs of the imaginary land of Katroo. Accompanied by the Birthday Bird, the birthday child enjoys unlimited snacks, wondrous flowers, a delicious lunch followed by a swim, a new pet, and finally, a party in a special palace, with live music, fish who spell out "Happy Birthday," and a spectacular cake. Finally, the Birthday Bird flies the child home to bed. One special birthday ritual is that the child shouts to the world

that he or she likes him–or herself, and there are several wonderful statements about being glad to be one's own self. A joyful celebration of the uniqueness and value of each individual, this book is perfect as a birthday present.

Ages: 3–9   **Cultural context:** European-American

Happy to Be Nappy **by bell hooks. Illus. by Chris Raschka. 32 pages Jump at the Sun/Hyperion, 1999.**
This joyful book celebrates the soft texture and diverse styles of African-American girls' hair, and the fun of combing, brushing, styling, and playing with it. Hair is seen as contributing to girls' freedom of movement and happiness, regardless of its style. The illustrations, which seem to dance on the page, reflect this sense of motion. This positive approach will help African-American girls to feel good about their hair.

Ages: 3–8   **Cultural context:** African-American

I Like Me **by Nancy L. Carlson. 32 pages Viking, 1988.**
There are several aspects to having a positive sense of self, and the little pig in *I Like Me* shows children many of these. She is her own best friend, enjoying her competence and persisting in the face of inevitable mistakes. The little pig takes good care of herself by eating well and bathing, and expresses a positive body image. She shows kids that self-esteem includes not only enjoyment of one's own company, but also self-care and perseverance.

Ages: 2–7   **Cultural context:** N/A

It's Okay to Be Different **by Todd Parr. 32 pages Little, Brown, 2001.**
Many experiences can support resilience. With a statement of acceptance about one attribute on each page, this book takes a positive, reassuring approach to aspects of self that range from human diversity (in size, color, and place of origin), to feelings and sense of self (feelings of anger, embarrassment, wishfulness, or pride; talking about your feelings; doing nice things for yourself), to making mistakes (finishing last in a race, losing things), to self-protection (saying no), to playfulness (eating macaroni and cheese in the bathtub, helping squirrels gather nuts). It ends with a statement of the specialness

of each individual. The straightforward, charming text and simple, vibrant, engaging illustrations encourage children's self-acceptance.

Ages: 2–7   **Cultural context:** Multicultural

Just Because I Am: A Child's Book of Affirmation **by Lauren Murphy Payne. Illus. by Claudia Rohling. 32 pages Free Spirit, 1994.**

There are many ways to feel good about yourself, and beginning with the statement that we're special and important "just because I am," this book elaborates on these. In the first person, it expresses acceptance and care for one's body, one's emotions, and the process of learning. The text celebrates the child's decision-making capability, including the right to say yes to hugs and touches that feel right, and the right to say no if they feel uncomfortable. It also acknowledges that people have needs, and it's okay for kids to ask for what they need. The boldly colored pen-and-marker illustrations combine a sense of simplicity with elaborate patterns and page borders. This book powerfully presents a positive, accepting view of what it is to be human.

Ages: 3–8   **Cultural context:** Multicultural

The Mixed-Up Chameleon **by Eric Carle. 32 pages HarperCollins, 1984.**

When we don't accept ourselves, nothing about us seems right. In *The Mixed-Up Chameleon*, a chameleon wishes it had attributes of other animals. With each wish, it gets an animal's body part; for example, a flamingo's feet and wings, a fox's tail, a giraffe's neck, an elephant's head and trunk, and a human being's hat and umbrella. These changes leave the chameleon feeling fragmented and unhappy, and ultimately, it wishes to be itself again. This book is illustrated with Carle's unique, strikingly beautiful collages made from hand-painted and -printed tissue paper. Cleverly designed around a rainbow of colors, it uses die-cut pages that help the reader keep track of the many animals the chameleon has wished to become. The end product is a dazzling book that will help children understand that self-acceptance brings a sense of wholeness and satisfaction.

Ages: 3–7   **Cultural context:** N/A

Some Dogs Do by Jez Alborough. 40 pages Candlewick, 2003.

Sometimes it's hard to believe in ourselves when others don't, and Sid, a dog, experiences this after he flies one day. When he gets to school and excitedly tells his teacher and classmates, no one believes him. He tries to fly again, to prove it, and just flops on the ground. His teacher and classmates scold him for lying. At home, dejected, he explains to his dad that he's unhappy because dogs don't fly. His dad lets him in on a secret: *he* flies. So Sid flies with his dad and is happy again. This rhyming story encourages kids to believe in their unique talents, even when no one else does.

Ages: 3–7   **Cultural context:** N/A

Tacky the Penguin by Helen Lester. Illus. by Lynn Munsinger. 32 pages Houghton Mifflin, 1988.

A sense of being "different" can be distressing to children, as it is to Tacky. While the other penguins are polite and debonair, Tacky is boisterous, uncoordinated, "an odd bird." But when hunters threaten the penguins, Tacky outsmarts them with his un-penguinlike behavior, saving himself and his friends. In the end, the other penguins conclude that although Tacky is odd, they're glad to have him around. This funny story will help children see their "different" qualities in a positive light.

Ages: 3–7   **Cultural context:** N/A

Thank You, Mr. Falker by Patricia Polacco. 40 pages Philomel, 1998.

Learning disabilities can make children feel bad about themselves. In this autobiographical story, Trisha grows up in a literate family and loves books, but can't learn to read. When she asks her grandma whether she's "different," her grandma says that uniqueness is miraculous. But kids tease Trisha about being dumb, and she hates school until she meets her fifth grade teacher, Mr. Falker. He protects Trisha from teasing and bullying and praises her intelligence and courage, eventually helping her to read. This moving story helps children understand that a learning disability doesn't invalidate all their other positive attributes. It offers hope that with kindness and appropriate teaching, a learning disability need not limit the child.

Ages: 5–10   **Cultural context:** Multicultural

Main character's cultural background: European-American

Unlovable **by Dan Yaccarino. 32 pages Holt, 2001.**

When children think they're unlovable, they may hide their true selves in the hope that this will make others love them. In *Unlovable*, other animals continually tell Alfred, a pug dog, that he's unlovable. When a new dog, Rex, moves in next door, Alfred and Rex talk through the fence, and Alfred impulsively tells Rex that he's a golden retriever, thinking that Rex will be his friend as long as Rex can't see him. Eventually, Rex digs a hole under the fence, and the two dogs meet— and Rex looks just like Alfred. Alfred stops caring what other animals think when he realizes that Rex, who is his friend, accepts him as he is. From this, kids can see that others' opinions don't make you unlovable and that a friend accepts you just the way you are.

Ages: 3–7   **Cultural context:** N/A

Wings **by Christopher Myers. 40 pages Scholastic, 2000.**

With the pressures for conformity that children face, even a remarkable talent can make them feel strange. This is what happens to Ikarus Jackson, who has wings. Neighbors call him weird. Kids at school whisper about him and laugh at him. The teacher complains about Ikarus's wings, and even a police officer speaks harshly to him. The child narrator realizes how lonely Ikarus must be and tells him his flying is beautiful. She redefines him as not weird, but incredible. Illustrated with striking cut-paper collages, this story shows that what makes a person seem weird can also be seen as extraordinary.

Ages: 5–9   **Cultural context:** Multicultural

Main character's cultural background: African-American

[CHAPTER 3]

Imagination

Imagination is an important resource for coping with big and small challenges, and is available to children at a very early age. Using imagination, whether in the form of make-believe play, making art, fantasy, or dreams, kids can learn to better understand and express feelings, experience a sense of control over their environments, practice social roles, nurture their natural curiosity, relieve boredom, develop physical coordination and cognitive skills, increase their sensory awareness, remember the past or plan for the future (resulting in less anxiety and smoother adjustment to new situations), mentally organize confusing experiences, and try out new solutions to problems. Children who play make-believe tend to be happier than kids who don't. Sometimes the creative process involves transforming an ordinary thing, place, or event into something extraordinary, whereas sometimes it involves envisioning an entirely new world. An important part of imagination is trusting your own creative vision. Creativity can also promote connections between people.

See also *When the Wind Bears Go Dancing* (Chapter 6); *Rosie to the Rescue* and *What If?* (Chapter 7); *The Something* (Chapter 8); *First Tomato* (Chapter 10); *A Koala for Katie* and *Mommy Far, Mommy Near* (Chapter 16); *Elizabeti's Doll* (Chapter 17); *The Trip* (Chapter 18); *Good-bye, Daddy, Missing Rabbit,* and *Priscilla Twice* (Chapter 19); *Best Friends* and *Blue Horse* (Chapter 20); *The Chalk Doll, Nora's Roses,* and *Peter's Patchwork Dream* (Chapter 24); *Chris Gets Ear Tubes* and *Shanna's Doctor Show* (Chapter 25); *Carousel* and *The Lion Who Had Asthma* (Chapter 26); *Dear Daisy, Get Well Soon* (Chapter 27); *The Black Dog Who Went Into the Woods* (Chapter 30); *After Charlotte's Mom Died, Flamingo Dream,* and *Marianne's Grandmother* (Chapter 31); *A Terrible Thing Happened* and *The Tin Forest* (Chapter 33); and *Daisy* (Chapter 34) for stories about using imaginative play, fantasy, art, or dreams to cope with specific stresses.

All I See by Cynthia Rylant. Illus. by Peter Catalanotto. 32 pages Orchard, 1988.

In this tale, a man named Gregory and a boy named Charlie show that the coming together of two imaginative visions can be the foundation of a friendship. Every day, Gregory paints pictures beside a lake as Charlie shyly watches. During one of Gregory's breaks, Charlie paints a picture for him, leading to a friendship in which the two paint together, each painting whatever he sees, whether or not it's literally present. The watercolor illustrations capture the quiet of the lakefront and the growing connection between Gregory and Charlie. By experiencing this friendship through the story, kids will see how imagination flourishes in a relationship where people can safely trust their internal vision.

Ages: 5–8　　　**Cultural context:** European-American

Appelemando's Dreams by Patricia Polacco. 32 pages Philomel, 1991.

Dreams may seem to be of value only to the childlike parts of ourselves, but they also speak to our adult selves in important ways. A boy named Appelemando loves to dream. The adults in his village dismiss him as unintelligent, but other children know better—they can literally see his colorful, magical daydreams, which adhere to wet surfaces. When Appelemando dreams on a rainy day, all the buildings get covered with his dreams, evoking the village elders' anger. They demand that he prove the origin of the pictures. He finds himself unable to dream, and the discouraged children wander away and get lost in the forest. Appelemando sends a dream up into the air that helps the adults find them, teaching the adults to believe in and value Appelemando's dreams. The vitality of the illustrations mirrors the energy of this story, which will inspire children to believe in their own dreams' importance.

Ages: 4–8   Cultural context: Multicultural

Main character's cultural background: European

Bear's Picture **by Daniel Pinkwater. 39 pages Dutton, 1984.**

Using your imagination means attending to what's inside, even if it isn't consistent with what's outside. A bear paints a picture just the way he wants it to be, but afterward, two fine, proper gentlemen—otherwise known as penguins—tell him that he can't paint a picture and that he isn't doing it right. Although they continue to believe this, the bear is happy with his picture, which is just what he wants it to be. Through the character of the bear, kids can see that they are the authority on their own creative process.

Ages: 3–7   **Cultural context:** N/A

Cherries and Cherry Pits **by Vera B. Williams. 40 pages Greenwillow, 1986.**

By drawing pictures and telling stories about them, Bidemmi beautifully illustrates the creative process. She makes three drawings of people who bring their loved ones a delicious treat: cherries. Like the dot that Bidemmi makes with her marker as she begins a drawing, the cherries grow into something beautiful and life sustaining. Bidemmi draws herself buying a bag of cherries and planting the pits in her dilapidated yard. She tends them carefully until finally, the yard is full of cherry trees, covered with ripe cherries. All her neighbors eat the cherries, and the pits from *those* cherries grow into even more trees, eventually creating a lush orchard. Watercolor paintings illustrate Bidemmi, and marker drawings show her drawings. Although they may not be able to articulate it, children will intuitively grasp the message that their imagination can nurture them in a unique way.

Ages: 3–8   **Cultural context:** Multicultural
Main character's cultural background: African-American

Cloudy With a Chance of Meatballs **by Judi Barrett.**
Illus. by Ron Barrett. 32 pages Aladdin, 1982.
One silly event can be the beginning of an entire imaginary world, and when Grandpa accidentally flips a pancake onto Henry's head, it inspires a story about the town of Chewandswallow, where instead of weather, food falls from the skies. For example, at breakfast time, it might rain orange juice, and clouds might be made of eggs and toast. Disaster strikes when enormous food falls from the sky, but the people manage a resourceful escape and are safe in the end. Detailed line drawings enhance this hilarious story, which shows children how to create an entire world out of one unusual—and perhaps embarrassing—moment.

Ages: 3–8   **Cultural context:** Multicultural
Main character's cultural background: European-American

Harold and the Purple Crayon **by Crockett Johnson. 64 pages**
HarperCollins, 1955.
Sometimes all it takes is a crayon and some imagination to create a delightful world. Preschool-age Harold goes for a walk with his purple crayon and draws everything he needs—including a boat for an unexpected ocean, a picnic of nothing but pie, a floating balloon with a basket to jump into in the midst of a long fall, and finally, the way home when he's tired. Illustrated with line drawings in broad, purple strokes, this classic story shows kids both the joy of imagination and its capacity to serve as a resource. Just be careful to keep children away from walls after reading this one.

Ages: 3–8   **Cultural context:** European-American

I Wished for a Unicorn **by Robert Heidbreder. Illus. by Kady**
MacDonald Denton. 32 pages Kids Can, 2000.
Imagination can be a way to make wishes come true, and in this rhym-

ing story, a girl wishes so hard for a unicorn that she finds one. From everything she says about its behavior and appearance, it's a dog, but to her, it's a unicorn. They travel through a magic forest together in her imagination, past mysterious creatures, a castle, and magic wands, triumphing over a fierce dragon and an evil wizard. After their adventure, they fall asleep, and though only her dog is with her when she wakes up, she knows she'll find the unicorn again if she wishes hard enough. The gouache paintings show many nuances of the girl's facial expressions. In this story, kids will see a way to find what they wish for in imagination.

Ages: 3–8   **Cultural context:** European-American

In the Attic by Hiawyn Oram. Illus. by Satoshi Kitamura. 28 pages Holt, 1984.

Imagination can create excitement even in an environment that appears dull. Bored with his toys, a boy climbs up to the attic, where he meets mice and a spider, opens windows to new worlds, makes an old flying machine work again, and makes friends with a tiger. When he returns in time for dinner, his mother says the house doesn't even have an attic. But the boy continues to trust his imagination, which he has used to transcend the physical present and enter the realm of all that can be dreamed.

Ages: 3–8   **Cultural context:** European-American

It Looked Like Spilt Milk by Charles G. Shaw. 32 pages HarperCollins, 1947.

An important aspect of imagination is seeing things in new ways. Based on the premise that a cloud can look like many different things, each page of this classic book suggests a possibility, beginning and ending with "spilt milk." Each suggestion is paired with a white bloblike, but representational, drawing on a dark blue background. It isn't until the last page that the author tells us that the white blob is a cloud as well. The very simple text is accessible to younger children, although you may need to explain to some children that *spilt* means spilled. This book is a great example of how kids can use their imagination to look beyond what is literally there to see many different possibilities. It will also inspire children to look at real clouds and describe what they see.

Ages: 2–5   **Cultural context:** N/A

Mud Is Cake by Pam Muñoz Ryan. Illus. by David McPhail.
33 pages Hyperion, 2002.
In this rhyming book, mud becomes cake if you use, and believe in, your imagination (and you don't really take a bite). The preschool-age girl and boy shown in the illustrations imagine scenes in which animals take human-like roles, showing kids that in imagination, they can try out many ways to be, from strong and fierce, to soft and gentle. Another nice thing about imagination is that it contains choices; for example, the child can choose to be a hero or can choose to run away.
Ages: 2–5   **Cultural context:** European-American

Nose to Toes by Marilyn Baillie. Illus. by Marisol Sarrazin.
32 pages Boyds Mills, 2001.
Although mental and ephemeral, imagination can be strongly connected with kids' literal, physical selves. This book encourages children to make believe that they're different animals to discover their physical abilities—for example, to pull their heads in or out like a turtle, to sniff out a snack like a lamb, or to slurp up spaghetti like a bird eating a worm. An afterword gives child-friendly animal facts and suggests ways to move like different animals. Children will be inspired to link imagination with physical play.
Ages: 3–6   **Cultural context:** Multicultural

Oh, the Thinks You Can Think by Dr. Seuss. **41 pages**
Random House, 1975.
You can think up all kinds of things that no one else has thought of before. Although most of Dr. Seuss's books have a lot to teach us about the process of imagination, this one addresses the issue directly, encouraging children to "think up" exotic imaginary animals, desserts, and countries. It will inspire children to use this process to transform ordinary things into extraordinary ones.
Ages: 4–8   **Cultural context:** N/A

Regina's Big Mistake by Marissa Moss. 32 pages
Houghton Mifflin, 1990.

Critical perspectives inhibit imagination, but an open heart facilitates
it. Everyone in Regina's class has to draw a jungle, but Regina feels
blocked and sees her attempts as being plagued by "mistakes." When
she learns to incorporate these into her drawing, she finds a source of
creativity within herself. She stops forcing the process of creation and
allows the artwork itself to guide her. In the end, she understands that
each child's drawing is unique and beautiful, resulting in an empathic
story that helps children trust their own creativity.

Ages: 4–8   **Cultural context:** Multicultural
Main character's cultural background: unclear

The Salamander Room by Anna Mazer. Illus. by Steve
Johnson. 24 pages Knopf, 1991.

An everyday occurrence can lead to a delightful imaginative process, as
it does when Brian brings home a salamander. As his mother asks questions about how the salamander will have its needs met, Brian's room
becomes transformed in his imagination—and the illustrations—into a
magical-looking woodland where the salamander can sleep on a boulder
next to Brian's bed. Giving kids an opportunity to use imagination to
try out new options, this story appropriately encourages them to enjoy
magical possibilities even while realizing that they aren't realistic.

Ages: 4–8.   **Cultural context:** European-American

The Squiggle by Carole Lexa Schaefer. Illus. by Pierr Morgan.
32 pages Crown, 1996.

Even a very simple thing can metamorphose into a range of creative
possibilities. On a walk to the park with her preschool class, a girl sees
a squiggle, which she imaginatively makes into the motions of a dragon,
the top edge of a wall, the path of an acrobat, and other things. Each image is accompanied by a sound. The girl joyfully shares her images and
sounds with her class. The Asian-inspired illustrations effectively convey
the girl's imaginative process, and the story offers kids the chance to see
how imagination can transform something as simple as a squiggly line.

Ages: 2–6   **Cultural context:** Asian

***You Are Here* by Nina Crews. 34 pages Greenwillow, 1998.**
Children can use imagination to make ordinary objects into the stuff of
adventure. Bored inside on a rainy day, two girls decide to take a trip that
is illustrated with photographs in which the girls appear tiny compared
with household objects. During the trip, they encounter a giant who demands a treasure, but unfortunately, a fierce monster (who looks very
much like an enormous house cat) guards the treasures in this strange
land. The girls dance and chant a spell, which puts the monster to sleep—
on top of the treasures. However, when it wakes up, they trade a shield
(spoon) for a treasure, allowing them to find their way home. With clever
juxtaposition of kids and everyday household objects, this story shows
kids how to create a make-believe world using changes in size.

Ages: 3–7   **Cultural context:** African-American

PART 2

FEELINGS

CHAPTER 4

Emotional Awareness

One important developmental task of childhood is to learn to identify, accept, differentiate, and manage a range of emotions—in short, to develop "emotional intelligence," a skill that's important for understanding oneself and getting along with other people. When children can name and comprehend their own feelings, they're better able to offer empathy and compassion to others. Sometimes children will push aside one feeling when they have another emotion that seems inconsistent with it, which limits their capacity to experience and accept all their feelings, a capacity that is an essential part of feeling alive. The picture books summarized in this chapter show children how to identify and deal with a wide range of emotions, helping them to feel comfortable with all kinds of feelings.

See also *It's Okay to Be Different* (Chapter 2) and *Dinosaurs Alive and Well!* (Chapter 23) for acceptance of feelings and encouragement to talk about them. *Just Because I Am* (Chapter 2) expresses acceptance and ownership of a range of feelings; suggests ways to cope with difficult feelings; and promotes optimism about effective coping. *The Boy Who Didn't Want to Be Sad* (Chapter 7) offers insight into acceptance of feelings. Books about specific feelings are summarized in Chapters 5–7.

Double-Dip Feelings: Stories to Help Children Understand Emotions by Barbara S. Cain. Illus. by Anne Patterson. 32 pages Magination, 1990.

Kids don't always realize that it's possible to have two seemingly contradictory feelings at the same time. The author gives examples from life situations that are common for children; for example, feeling both proud and scared on the first day of school. By inviting children to recall times that they've had more than one feeling at a time, this book will help them acknowledge *all* of their feelings, not just the ones that seem consistent.

Ages: 4–7   **Cultural context:** Multicultural

Feelings by Susan Canizares. 16 pages Scholastic, 1999.

It's important for young children to learn how to name and recognize emotions. Each page of *Feelings* names a feeling and illustrates it using a color photograph of a child. A two-page note at the end defines many of the feelings illustrated and discusses how to cope with difficult feelings and understand what other people are feeling. Reading this book will increase children's awareness of feelings in themselves and others.

Ages: 0–3   **Cultural context:** Multicultural

The Feelings Book by Todd Parr. 26 pages Little, Brown, 2000.

Sometimes naming feelings involves putting words to an experience that you might think no one else has had before. Each page of *The Feelings Book* describes a feeling—from ordinary feelings like crankiness, silliness, and fear, to unique feelings that don't quite have a name, such as feeling "like kissing a sea lion." Illustrated with vividly colored drawings that are childlike yet evocative, the book ends with the excellent suggestion that children share their feelings with someone they love. By showing children how to identify and name even funny-sounding feelings, this book will help them recognize and accept a full range of emotions.

Ages: 2–7   **Cultural context:** Multicultural

Glad Monster, Sad Monster: A Book About Feelings by **Anne Miranda. Illus. by Ed Emberley. 17 pages Little, Brown, 1997.**
Emotions combine uniquely with facial expressions in this colorful book. Each page tells about the kinds of situations in which a monster has a particular feeling—glad, sad, loving, worried, silly, angry, and scary. Each page also invites readers to try on a mask of the monster's face (created using cleverly die-cut fold-out pages) and encourages them to discuss what makes them feel that feeling. Using this book will promote children's awareness of feelings by cultivating their emotional vocabulary.

Ages: 3–7   **Cultural context:** N/A

How Are You Peeling? Foods with Moods by **Saxton Freymann and Joost Elffers. 42 pages Arthur A. Levine, 1999.**
Emotional expressions may be so universal that we can recognize them in foods. The authors have carved remarkably expressive faces in fruits and vegetables, showing a wide range of moods. Color photographs of the produce are accompanied by text that invites children to notice and label their emotions, and encourages them to share their feelings with others. The end result is a delightful book that offers an amusing way to promote emotional awareness.

Ages: 3–7   **Cultural context:** N/A

Lizzy's Ups and Downs: NOT an Ordinary School Day by **Jessica Harper. Illus. by Lindsay Harper duPont. 33 pages HarperCollins, 2004.**
One day can contain a wide range of emotions, as Lizzy shows here while telling her mom about her day in this rhyming story. She was worried that she might miss the school bus. She was scared, and then mad, when another kid startled her with a toy snake. She was sad to watch her friend, who was moving away, leave school for the last time. But after a play date with another friend, and a chance to greet her

dog and cat, she feels fine. Mama assures Lizzy that ups and downs are normal. With a wide range of concrete examples from a child's world, this story will heighten children's awareness and acceptance of the range of emotions they experience on an everyday basis.

Ages: 3–8   **Cultural context:** Multicultural
Main character's cultural background: European-American

Lots of Feelings **by Shelley Rotner. 24 pages Millbrook, 2003.**
Using this straightforward book, even the youngest children can learn to recognize the emotions shown by facial expressions. Each page names an emotion and illustrates it with three color photographs of children's faces. An afterword for parents and teachers suggests ways this book can help children understand feelings better. Practical and fun, this one will enhance children's identification of feelings in themselves and others.

Ages: 0–3   **Cultural context:** Multicultural

My Many-Colored Days **by Dr. Seuss. Illus. by Steve Johnson and Lou Fancher. 32 pages Knopf, 1996.**
One way to think about feelings is to connect them with colors. On each page, a color is connected with an emotion; for example, purple days are sad, yellow days are busy, and black days are angry. Some days are mixed up and confusing, but this doesn't last long. Dr. Seuss wrote *My Many-Colored Days* in 1973, and Steve Johnson and Lou Fancher illustrated it posthumously in 1996 with intensely colored oil paintings. This book will help promote children's emotional awareness in a playful way.

Ages: 3–8   **Cultural context:** N/A

On Monday When It Rained **by Cherryl Kachenmeister. Illus. by Tom Berthiaume. 33 pages Houghton Mifflin, 1989.**
Understanding emotions can be a lot easier for kids if they see the emotions in ordinary situations. A preschool-age boy describes various situations in daily life, each involving a feeling and illustrated by a black-and-white photograph of the boy expressing that feeling. For example, when it rains, the boy is disappointed that he can't play outside. The boy's dad expresses acceptance of feelings as ordinary experi-

ences, making this a simple introduction to feelings that encourages identifying feelings in day-to-day life.

Ages: 1–5   **Cultural context:** European-American

Proud of Our Feelings **by Lindsay Leghorn. 32 pages Magination, 1995.**

Awareness of feelings makes it easier for kids to accept them. Priscilla introduces the reader to several of her friends, each of whom is having a different feeling. Priscilla tells how she knows that each child is having that feeling, sometimes tells what situation led to the feeling, and invites readers to consider that emotion in their own lives. An introduction for adults encourages acceptance of children's feelings and suggests ways to use the book. The watercolor illustrations show facial expressions clearly. This book promotes children's capacity to articulate feelings in themselves and others.

Ages: 4–8   **Cultural context:** Multicultural
Main character's cultural background: European-American

There's No Such Thing As a Dragon **by Jack Kent. 33 pages Golden, 1975.**

If we don't pay enough attention to feelings, they get bigger and more destructive. Such is the case when Billy wakes up to find a dragon in his room, and it seems to enjoy his attention. Unfortunately, Billy's mother tells him that there's no such thing as a dragon, so he ignores it, causing it to grow bigger and bigger, until it fills the whole house. In fact, it lifts the house off its foundation and onto its back, as it follows a delicious-smelling bakery truck. When Billy's mother insists that there's no such thing, Billy now interrupts, saying that the dragon is not only real, but very big. At this, the dragon shrinks down to its original size, as Billy comments that the dragon had grown big just because it wanted to be noticed. Using this humorous metaphor, the story conveys that it's less dangerous to attend to feelings than to push them aside.

Ages: 3–7   **Cultural context:** European-American

Understand and Care **by Cheri J. Meiners. Illus. by Meredith Johnson. 40 pages Free Spirit, 2003.**

Understanding feelings enables empathy, and this non-fiction book explains to children how to understand others' happy, sad, proud, and angry feelings. The illustrations demonstrate ways to care for other people's feelings. An afterword for adults suggests ways to discuss each page of the book and gives ideas for games intended to encourage empathy. Through discussion, this book teaches children how to comprehend other people's feelings and show caring toward them.

Ages: 2-6   **Cultural context:** Multicultural

CHAPTER 5

Anger

Anger is an important feeling, but it presents challenges for many children. While you want them to feel comfortable feeling angry, expression is not enough; it's important to manage anger in constructive ways. Children need to learn that they have the power to make choices between destructive and constructive behavior. Out-of-control anger results in destructive behavior that leaves kids feeling helpless, worried, and, if they've hurt someone, guilty. Conversely, when kids cope with anger successfully, they feel safer and less overwhelmed by their anger, and have a sense of mastery. It's important for kids to know that parents can help contain their angry feelings through acceptance, discussion, and conflict resolution.

See also *I'll Always Be Your Friend* (Chapter 1), *It's Okay to Be Different* (Chapter 2), and *Dinosaurs Alive and Well* (Chapter 23) for examples of acceptance of anger. *Sunshine and Storm* (Chapter 20) addresses the effects of anger on a friendship. For stories about being grumpy about having a bad day, see Chapter 10. Stories that include angry feelings about specific life situations are summarized in Chapters 16, 19, 22, 24, 26, 27, 30, 31, 32, 33, and 34.

Angry Arthur by Hiawyn Oram. Illus. by Satoshi Kitamura.
30 pages Dutton, 1982.
Sometimes anger feels like a storm inside. Arthur is angry because his mother won't let him stay up late to watch a Western. In his imagination, his anger becomes a series of destructive storms, ending with a "universe-quake." Although his parents and grandparents have ideas about when enough is enough, they aren't always right, and the anger has to run its course. At the end, Arthur forgets what he was angry about, allowing him to gain some perspective. This story would be a good choice for children who already have some control over acting out their angry feelings, since those who don't might be tempted to take it too literally and behave destructively.
Ages: 3-8   **Cultural context:** European-American

Don't Rant and Rave on Wednesdays! The Children's Anger-Control Book by Adolph Moser. Illus. by David Melton.
64 pages Landmark Editions, 1994.
There are lots of constructive ways to cope with anger, and this self-help book explains them in a non-judgmental way. The author tells kids that although out-of-control angry behavior can be dangerous and get people into trouble, suppressing anger is unhealthy. He discusses the difference between angry feelings and angry behavior, and offers suggestions and encouragement for controlling one's behavior in healthy ways when one is angry. Practical ideas for understanding and controlling anger are presented in an upbeat, accessible way with cartoonlike illustrations.
Ages: 5–11   **Cultural context:** Multicultural

Hands Are Not for Hitting by Martine Agassi.
Illus. by Marieka Heinlen 35 pages Free Spirit, 2000.
One way children may express anger is by hitting, and this book addresses the problem within the context of what hands do. It discusses the many positive ways to use hands: communicating, making music, caring for ourselves and others. But hands are not for hitting, which hurts both the person who hits and the person who is hit. It acknowledges the *feeling* of wanting to hit someone and gives suggestions for other, safer ways to express that feeling, while discussing ways to re-

solve conflicts without hitting. An afterword for grown-ups elaborates on the role of violence in children's lives, suggests activities related to the book, and provides a brief resource list. This book would be a particularly good choice for reading to a group, though this doesn't detract in any way from its usefulness with individual children. A simpler board-book version, focusing only on positive uses for hands, was published in 2002.

Ages: 3–8 (paperback) **Cultural context:** Multicultural
1–3 (board book)

I Call My Hand Gentle **by Amanda Haan.**
Illus. by Marina Sagona. 33 pages Viking, 2003.
Choices between constructive and destructive expressions of anger can be understood by looking at the different things hands can do. This simply worded, first-person book starts by naming many of these, such as picking flowers, hugging, or throwing a ball. The narrator acknowledges having control over his or her hand, which does what he or she wants it to do. The narrator chooses not to use his or her hand to do hurtful things such as stealing, hurting, or breaking things. With engagingly colorful, retro-style illustrations, this book encourages self-control and positive behavior choices.

Ages: 1–4 **Cultural context:** Unclear

I'm Mad **by Elizabeth Crary. Illus. by Jean Whitney.**
31 pages Parenting, 1992.
Children can learn to choose their behaviors constructively when they're angry. Katie and Dad have planned a picnic in the park, and it's raining. She's mad. Dad acknowledges Katie's anger and disappointment, tells her it's okay to stay mad if she wants to, and invites her to consider what to do if she doesn't want to stay mad. This story has an unusual format that allows your child to choose what Katie will do, and you turn to the page that reflects your child's choice. Often, additional choices follow that page. Katie's dad and aunt give her several ideas, from making up a mad dance to blowing angry feelings into a balloon and letting it blow away. An "idea page" at the end summarizes Katie's ideas and leaves room for the reader's, while a foreword and afterword for adults elaborate on the ideas of the book. Although the

format won't work for every child, this story includes lots of constructive ways to cope with anger and helps kids apply a problem-solving approach to their angry feelings.

Ages: 3–8   **Cultural context:** European-American

The Mad Family Gets Their Mads Out: Fifty Things Your Family Can Say and Do to Express Anger Constructively **by Lynne Namka. Illus. by Nancy Sarama. 48 pages Talk, Trust and Feel Therapeutics, 1995.**

When kids express anger constructively, they often feel less angry. A boy describes the experience of feeling angry. Being mad feels bad to him, and when he shouts, slams his door, punches the wall, and throws toys, the angry feelings ("mads") increase and persist. Also, family members respond with anger, so the whole family becomes angry. A therapist explains that it's okay to feel angry, but the boy needs to learn what to do with angry feelings. She shows him how to use physical sensations to monitor them and how to let them out safely; for example, by drawing pictures of them. He tells her about situations that made him angry (including being spanked) and practices telling toys, "I feel mad when you . . . ," finding that in everyday situations, this reduces his anger. Lists at the end summarize ways for kids and parents to manage anger and provide resources for parents. The story offers empathy around anger; positive, practical ways to express anger; and inspiration in the boy's realistically positive experience of using these behaviors.

Ages: 3-8   **Cultural context:** Multicultural
Main character's cultural background: European-American

Sometimes I'm Bombaloo **by Rachel Vail. Illus. by Yumi Heo. 32 pages Scholastic, 2002.**

Here's a story for children whose anger is already out of control and for kids who are trying to understand out-of-control anger in another child. Katie explains that although she has lots of positive attributes, she sometimes loses control of her anger. At those times, when she kicks, hits, and yells instead of using words, she's Bombaloo. She acknowledges how scary those times are, but it helps Katie to know that her mother understands that her anger scares her. Along with her mother's understanding, humor helps break her cycle of anger. She feels sorry that she's been out of control and is ready to compose herself again. Presenting an empathic picture of what intense anger is like, this story helps children make the connection between this angry state and what's needed to contain it (time-out, an understanding parent, and humor).

Ages: 2–8. **Cultural context:** European-American

Spence and the Mean Old Bear **by Christa Chevalier. 32 pages Whitman, 1986.**

Out-of-control anger can be as scary as a mean old bear. When Spence feels angry because his mother tells him that he can't watch TV until he's picked up his toys, he expresses his anger as a wish that a mean old bear would come after her. In fact, the mean old bear *is* his anger. He draws a picture of the bear, and it gets up and walks off the paper, saying it's going to get his mother. Spence realizes that he doesn't really want the bear to take his mother away. He's frightened by his anger—that is, frightened by the bear. As his mother reassures him that no bear can get her, the bear gets smaller and smaller until it's just a drawing again. Spence doesn't need his anger anymore, so he throws away the picture—and picks up his toys. Even when his anger feels overwhelming, he can use his mother's capacity to tolerate it in order to tolerate it himself.

Ages: 3–7 **Cultural context:** European-American

Teeth Are Not for Biting **by Elizabeth Verdick.**
Illus. by Marieka Heinlen. 24 pages Free Spirit, 2003.

Very young children may express anger by biting. Using words and colorful illustrations that toddlers can readily understand and use, this board book explains that teeth are for chewing food, not for biting people, because biting hurts. It offers suggestions for children (and, in an afterword, for adults) about what to do when they want to bite because they're teething or because they're in an uncomfortable emotional state. Written to help young kids get biting under control, this book resonates through its simplicity.

Ages: 1–3 **Cultural context:** Multicultural

***The Temper Tantrum Book* by Edna Mitchell Preston.**
Illus. by Rainey Bennett. 36 pages Viking, 1976.
When children are angry, it's important to communicate effectively.
The author asks why each of several animals is angry, describing
their furious appearance and behavior in detail. The animal always
answers, "I hate in when . . . " something happens; for example, "you
get soap in my eyes." The last question is why the hippopotamus is
so happy, and the answer is "I love it when you let me play in the
mud." By showing that the words mean the same thing as the animals'
roaring, raging, howling, snorting, and squealing—but are much more
understandable—this story sets a good example for using your words
to say what you're angry about.
Ages: 3–7   **Cultural context:** N/A

***When I Feel Angry* by Cornelia Maude Spelman.**
Illus. by Nancy Cote. 24 pages Whitman, 2000.
It's important for children to learn that they can understand and manage anger. A little rabbit names some of the situations that make her
angry. She discusses the difference between feeling angry and acting
on that feeling. The problem with acting on angry feelings is that it
can result in hurting someone or getting into trouble, but there are
also constructive ways to manage anger. Talking over her feelings can
help her to sort out whether or not the object of her anger can or should
be changed. She closes with a statement of competence about managing anger. A note to parents discusses ways to help children cope with
anger. This resource will empower children and parents to manage
anger constructively.
Ages: 2–8   **Cultural context:** N/A

When Sophie Gets Angry—Really, Really Angry . . .
by Molly Bang. 35 pages Blue Sky, 1999.
Kids can learn to redirect the energy of their anger toward calming
themselves. Sophie becomes angry when her sister grabs a toy from her,
and their mother supports her sister. She screams, kicks, and roars,
feeling as if she could explode. Sophie uses the energy of her anger to run,
which calms her. She runs to her favorite tree and climbs into it, feeling
comforted there. After a little time in the tree, she's not angry anymore

and ready to go home. This colorfully illustrated book empathically depicts what it feels like to be angry, shows the use of time-out to calm oneself (*not* as a punishment), and demonstrates that anger, like other emotions, passes. Like *Sometimes I'm Bombaloo*, it's probably best for children who already show signs of difficulty with controlling anger. Be careful with kids who are inclined to take Sophie's running away literally; you may need to explain that they can "run away" to their room (or wherever you agree is both calming and safe).

Ages: 2–8   **Cultural context:** European-American

[CHAPTER 6]

Fear

Fears of all kinds arise throughout childhood, limiting kids and making everyday situations overwhelming. Children may be afraid of storms, mean-looking dogs, monsters, roller coasters, swimming, flying, heights, getting lost, public speaking, or even clothing with a life of its own. Kids can learn to cope with fear using the protective presence of a trusted adult, a special friendship, or courage within themselves that they didn't realize they had. They can also learn to cope with fear by standing up for themselves, refusing to be afraid, persisting in spite of fear, confronting scary situations, changing their perspective, gaining strength from their anger, making friends with their fears, or using their imagination.

See also *Grandmother's Song* and *Okomi Climbs a Tree* (Chapter 1), and *Nothing Scares Us* (Chapter 20) for stories of children who use special relationships to cope with fear. Other chapters address additional situations that may evoke fearfulness in children (Chapters 8, 9, 13, 25, 28, 32, 33, and 34). For children who worry about almost everything, rather than having a specific fear about something, see Chapter 7 (Worry).

Brave as a Mountain Lion by Ann Herbert Scott.
Illus. by Glo Coalson. 32 pages Clarion, 1996.
Using imagination can help kids cope with fears of public speaking, as it does for a boy named Spider, who qualifies for the spelling bee but is afraid to enter. With his father's help, he copes with his fear by pretending he is the bravest animal he can think of, a mountain lion. His grandmother encourages him to be as clever as a coyote. His brother advises him to be silent, and he realizes he can be as silent as the spider for whom he was named. Spider also uses helpful coping strategies like visiting the room where the spelling bee is to be held. Using all that he's learned, he finds the courage to enter the spelling bee. Inspiring his family's pride, he finishes second and realizes that he wasn't afraid. Children can use this story to learn what they might say to themselves when they face a common fear.
Ages: 5–8   **Cultural context:** Native-American

Fletcher and the Great Big Dog by Jane Kopper Hilleary.
Illus. by Richard Brown. 32 pages Houghton Mifflin, 1988.
Tolerating fears can paradoxically help children to feel less afraid. Fletcher is out riding his tricycle when he meets a very big, red dog. Frightened, he turns around, but the dog follows. In his attempts to escape from the dog, Fletcher gets lost. Once he loses his way, he discovers that the dog just wanted to make friends, and the pair help each other find their way home again. Fletcher has learned the important lessons that scary-looking dogs may not be vicious and that when we "make friends with" our fears, they aren't so scary.
Ages: 3-6   **Cultural context:** European-American

Give Maggie a Chance by Frieda Wishinsky.
Illus. by Dean Griffiths. 32 pages Fitzhenry & Whiteside, 2002.
Hostile teasing can make fears feel worse, but kids can cope with this in positive ways. Maggie, a good reader, finds herself unable to read aloud in class. On the other hand, her classmate Kimberly is eager to read aloud and teases Maggie about Maggie's struggles. Maggie reacts with shame and then rage, expressed in images that carry genuine emotional resonance. When Kimberly extends her teasing to Maggie's friend, Sam, Maggie's feelings are transformed to competence, ex-

pressed in triumphant images. She is able to use her knowledge that Sam believes in her to stop caring about what Kimberly does or thinks, and she reads aloud successfully. In addition to using Sam's support, Maggie also copes in positive, effective ways on her own. Maggie's experience shows children how to transform their own fear, shame, and rage into competence.

Ages: 5–8   **Cultural context:** N/A

Go Away, Big Green Monster! **by Ed Emberley. 32 pages Little, Brown, 1992.**

One way to cope with fear is simply to refuse to be afraid. This clever book uses die-cut pages to add one scary feature at a time to the child narrator's description of a brightly colored monster. "But," the narrator says, "'YOU DON'T SCARE ME!'" Each page then deletes one of the monster's features at a time, until the monster is finally all gone. The narrator also asserts control over whether and when the monster comes back. Children will understand the idea of taking charge of their fears and coping by refusing to be afraid.

Ages: 3–6   **Cultural context:** N/A

Harry and the Terrible Whatzit **by Dick Gackenbach. 40 pages Clarion, 1977.**

Kids may not realize how much control they have over their fears, and this ingenious story demonstrates children's command over their fears. Harry is afraid of the Whatzit that he knows is in the cellar, but when his mother goes to the cellar and doesn't come right back, he takes a broom and follows. What Harry is going to learn is that anger, assertiveness, and support will reduce fear—literally. In the basement, he finds the two-headed Whatzit and gets angry at it. Interestingly, the more assertive Harry is, the smaller the Whatzit becomes, until it's small enough to be ordered away. His mother (who has been in the backyard all this time) is supportive of his courage. Harry's response to his fear shows children that they can find their strength by confronting their fears.

Ages: 3–8   **Cultural context:** European-American

Katie Catz Makes a Splash by Anne Rockwell.
Illus. by Paul Meisel. 33 pages HarperCollins, 2003.
Children need not let their fear keep them from fun activities such as swimming, which can be an important part of their community's culture. Katie Catz, a cat, is afraid to go into the pool, and her embarrassment leads her to avoid her friends' pool party. But Katie's mother has signed her up for swim lessons with gentle, understanding Patsy Polarbear. Katie comes to trust Patsy and finds herself not only learning to swim, but also having fun. Her parents and Patsy are proud of her, and she looks forward to the pool party. The colorful illustrations clearly show Katie's changing emotional states in her facial expressions. This story shows children that even people who, like cats, aren't "naturals" in the water can learn, with the support of another person, to enjoy and feel competent swimming.
Ages: 2–6   **Cultural context:** N/A

My Mama Says There Aren't Any Zombies, Ghosts, Vampires, Creatures, Demons, Monsters, Fiends, Goblins, or Things by **Judith Viorst. Illus. by Kay Chorao. 48 pages Atheneum, 1983.**
Despite reassuring parents, many children have persistent fears of monsters. This is the case with Nick, whose mama says there are no zombies, ghosts, and so on. However, his experience tells him, in great detail, that "even mamas make mistakes," so he's unsure whether to believe her. Eventually, he acknowledges that sometimes mamas *don't* make mistakes. This story is illustrated with black-and-white drawings of fanciful monsters and people with very expressive faces, which combine with an interesting concept to show children that there's an alternative to worrying about "what if."
Ages: 5–8   **Cultural context:** European-American

Oh Yeah! by **Tom Birdseye. Illus. by Ethan Long.**
32 pages Holiday House, 2003.
Kids can show courage even when they can't admit their fears. When the narrator of *Oh Yeah!* and his friend, Jared, camp out in the backyard, Jared accuses the narrator of being afraid of the dark. Trying to forget about "big, hairy, kid-eating monsters," the narrator declares that he could stay out all night. He and Jared one-up each other, add-

ing more and more scary conditions under which they could do this. Finally, something jumps out of the bushes, and the kids run for their tent. They realize that their favorite stuffed animals are out there and rush to save them from the monster, who, curiously, looks a lot like the narrator's dog. Back in the tent, they assure each other that they're both very brave. The illustrations have a retro edge and plenty of scary energy. Overall, this story shows children that even if they're scared, the can do what needs to be done.

Ages: 5-8   **Cultural context:** European-American

Olvina Flies by Grace Lin. 32 pages Holt, 2003.

When fear becomes a hindrance, it's possible to cope with it using a friend's support. Olvina, a chicken, thinks she can't go to a bird convention in Hawaii because, as a chicken, she can't fly there, and she's too frightened to fly in an airplane. When she realizes how many things she's missed because of her fear of flying in an airplane, she decides to go. Encouraged by her friend Will, a pig, she manages to board the plane, in spite of having to unpack all her luggage to find her ticket. Her seatmate, a penguin, is bound for the same convention, where the two birds have a great time. Grace Lin writes this story with genuine humor and a strong sense of empathy for Olvina, who is really able to make use of her friends' reassurance.

Ages: 4–7   **Cultural context:** N/A

Ruler of the Courtyard by Rukhsana Khan.
Illus. by R. Gregory Christie. 34 pages Viking, 2003.

Fears can restrict our behavior and our sense of ourselves. Saba is so afraid of the chickens that she feels as if she doesn't have the right to be in the courtyard. Only venturing outside if it's necessary, on this day, she hurries across to the bathhouse and suddenly notices something that makes her fear of chickens seem trivial: a snake. At first she decides to kill it, but when she finds that she can't, she decides to trap it under a bucket, and pulling together all her courage, she tries—and misses. On her second attempt, she succeeds. Finding herself with irresistible curiosity, she lifts the bucket, and discovers that the "snake" is the drawstring from Nani's pants. She laughs for a long time, and when she goes outside, roars at the chickens, amazed that she used to be scared of them. Now she knows that she has the right to go wherever she wants to, inspiring readers to act courageously even when they're afraid.

Ages: 3–8   **Cultural context:** Asian

Sheila Rae the Brave by Kevin Henkes. 32 pages
Greenwillow, 1987.

One thing that may keep kids fearful is the *idea* that they're not brave. Sheila Rae is unafraid of the things that scare lots of children (the dark, storms, or mean-looking dogs), and even actively seeks out scary situations (for example, attacks monsters in the closet without hesitation). Her sister, Louise, is fearful, or at least that's what Sheila Rae and Louise both think. Then Sheila Rae gets lost, and no matter how hard she tries to hang onto the idea that she's brave, she can't help being scared. Louise surprises them both when she helps Sheila Rae find her way home, causing the pair to conclude that they're both brave. The idea that fearfulness isn't an all-or-nothing quality is an important distinction for kids to learn since they can be brave even if they don't think of themselves that way.

Ages: 3–8   **Cultural context:** N/A

Thunder Cake by Patricia Polacco. 32 pages Philomel, 1990.

Fear can sometimes give kids opportunities to discover their courage. When a girl hears thunder and hides under the bed, her grandma explains that it's time to make Thunder Cake. She teaches the girl how to count the seconds from the lighting until the thunder. Then she brings the girl to gather all the ingredients for the cake from different parts of the farm, where she has to face scary situations, from the mean hen that might peck her, to a dizzying climb up a tomato trellis. While the cake is baking, Grandma compliments the girl for being brave enough to get all the ingredients. At first, the girl doesn't believe she's been brave, but eventually she realizes that Grandma's right. They finish baking just as the storm is directly overhead, and happily eat their Thunder Cake. Based on the author's own childhood fear of thunderstorms, this story will inspire children to courageous acts and help them acknowledge their bravery.

Ages: 3–8   **Cultural context:** European-American

What Was I Scared Of? In **Sneetches and Other Stories**
by Dr. Seuss. 24 pages Random House, 1989.

Adults often tell kids that the object of their fear is "more scared of
you than you are of it," and this whimsical tale illustrates this point.
A child is repeatedly terrified by the sight of a pair of pants walking
around with no one in them. Finally, when the pants seem inescap-
able, and the child reaches a peak of panic, the pants start to cry. The
child realizes that the pants are just as scared of the child as the child
is of the pants, and they become friendly acquaintances. This story
helps children to look twice at scary situations and consider alternative perspectives that aren't so scary. It also gives amusing meaning to
the idea of making friends with one's fears.

Ages: 3–7   **Cultural context:** N/A

When Addie Was Scared by Linda Bailey.
Illus. by Wendy Bailey. 32 pages Kids Can, 1999.

In this empathic tale, Addie discovers her courage in moments of anger
and protectiveness. Time after time, Addie finds herself in situations
that force her to find courage in spite of her fears. Encountering tur-
keys, bulls, a thunderstorm, and a hawk, Addie designs clever solutions
to overcome her fears and function. After each episode, her babcha
(grandmother) comforts her and tells her how brave she is. Although
Addie is still fearful after this, things are different for her because,
having discovered the anger and protectiveness that are connected to
her fear, she has found courage inside herself and knows she can count
on it. Children will understand that even when they feel scared, they
can still have courage.

Ages: 3–7   **Cultural context:** European-American

When I Feel Scared by Cornelia Maude Spelman.
Illus. by Kathy Parkinson. 24 pages Whitman, 2002.

When children understand fear, they're more able to cope with it. In
this sweet, empathic book, a little bear describes some of the situations
in which he feels scared, expresses acceptance of frightened feelings,
and suggests some helpful ways to manage fear. He also remarks that
some fears are useful signals to stay away from danger, and he can
find out which ones these are. A foreword for adults provides informa-

tion about supporting children in coping with fear. In identifying with the bear, kids will feel confident about their ability to cope with fear.

Ages: 2–5   **Cultural context:** N/A

When the Big Dog Barks **by Munzee Curtis. Illus. by Susan Avishai. 24 pages Greenwillow, 1997.**
Support from parents can help kids manage many fears. A girl's parents protect her when scary things happen—from climbing too high in the playground, to strangers' intrusive friendliness, to watching *The Wizard of Oz* on TV. They even protect her from sharing a special toy when she doesn't want to. When they go out, she knows that they always come home, and she can count on them to keep her safe. Ultimately, this story helps kids understand that with an adult they trust, they can feel safe even in scary situations.

Ages: 2–7   **Cultural context:** European-American

When the Wind Bears Go Dancing **by Phoebe Stone. 32 pages Little, Brown, 1997.**
Imagination is a wonderful tool for coping with fear. When the sounds of thunder and wind frighten a girl, she explains that, according to her mommy, these are the sounds of bears dancing by. She knows she can't really go dance with the wind bears, but imagining what this would be like dispels her fear. Eventually, the wild, woolly wind bears get tired and the noises outside calm down. The illustrations are vividly colored and energetic, yet have a soft-edged quality. Using imagination to transform fear, children will be better able to face scary situations.

Ages: 3–7   **Cultural context:** Multicultural

CHAPTER 7

Worry, Guilt, Jealousy, and Sadness

In addition to anger and fear, there are other emotions that may be challenging for children. This chapter summarizes picture books about four of these: worry, guilt, jealousy, and sadness.

WORRY

Some children (and adults) may go through periods of worry, and there are differences among individuals in their propensity to worry. Kids who worry may imagine a seemingly endless string of "what ifs." Even though children's worries may seem unrealistic to the adults around them, they cause children genuine distress and can restrict their choices. The stories summarized in this chapter show children that other people worry, too, and offer ways to cope: using positive thoughts or distraction, doing the things you worry about and seeing that things turn out okay, and separating your sense of self from the worries.

See also Chapter 6 (Fear) for closely related concerns. In *Wallace's Lists* (Chapter 20), a mouse who, although he doesn't overtly worry, does come across as a worrier.

Felix and the Worrier by Rosemary Wells. 34 pages Candlewick, 2003.

Worries can be particularly powerful if accepted uncritically. Felix is happy during the day, but at night, the Worrier (a creature that looks a bit like a tiny Teletubby) comes to trouble him. For example, it makes Felix worry all night about a black spot on Felix's tooth that turns out not to exist. The night before Felix's birthday, although he isn't worried about anything, the Worrier comes up with things for him to worry about. When they hear a noise, the Worrier is worried, but Felix decides that rather than worry, he'll find out what's making the noise. It turns out to be Felix's birthday present, a dog. Felix and the dog become best friends immediately, and the Worrier, who is very worried around dogs, goes away. When children separate themselves from worry, they can control it by seeking information about how realistic it is.

Ages: 4–8   **Cultural context:** N/A

Rosie to the Rescue by Bethany Roberts. Illus. by Kay Chorao. 32 pages Holt, 2003.

Sometimes separation is an occasion for worry, as is the case for Rosie, who is staying with her aunt while she waits for her parents to come home. She worries about all kinds of things that could have happened to them, but each time says she wouldn't let it happen. For example, when she worries that a tiger ate them, she would rescue them by chasing the tiger until it let them go. After she's created several scenarios in her head, her parents come home safe and sound. In the end, this is a tale of how using imagination as a positive response to worries can assuage them.

Ages: 3–7   **Cultural context:** N/A

Something Might Happen **by Helen Lester. Illus. by Lynn Munsinger. 32 pages Houghton Mifflin/Walter Lorraine, 2003.**

Worries that something bad might happen can lead to a state of paralysis, as they do for Twitchly. He won't shampoo his hair, eat cereal, or put on his sneakers because of the long-lasting consequences he fears. His hut has no door because something might try to get in. His friends keep inviting him to come out for parades, marshmallow roasts, and parties, but he politely declines, afraid of what might happen. When his aunt comes to visit, she washes his hair, puts a big spoonful of cereal in his mouth, and demands that he put on his sneakers. To his surprise, nothing terrible happens. Inspired to feel confident, he makes a door and windows in his hut, and goes off to find his friends. From this story, children see that the things they worry about probably won't happen—and even if they do, they probably won't be as bad as they think.

Ages: 4–7   **Cultural context:** N/A

Wemberly Worried **by Kevin Henkes. 32 pages Greenwillow, 2000.**

For Wemberly, worry can be self-perpetuating. She worries all the time about all kinds of things, in spite of her parents' reassurances, generating seemingly endless lists of "what if"s. When she's most worried, Wemberly rubs her doll's ears and then worries that if she worries too much, the doll will have no ears. At the start of school, she worries more than ever. However, her teacher introduces her to another child, Jewel, who also looks fearful and holds a doll whose nose she rubs. Wemberly plays with Jewel and realizes that she isn't worrying any more than usual. When her teacher urges the kids to come back the next day, Wemberly has a reassurance of her own for her. By showing that whether or not you worry, things might go reasonably well, and that distraction can go a long way toward eliminating worry, this story gently breaks the cycle of worry.

Ages: 4–7   **Cultural context:** N/A

What If? **by Frances Thomas. Illus. by Ross Collins. 26 pages Hyperion, 1998.**

Just as worries can be real, they can also be a form of imagination that distresses kids. Little Monster worries about falling forever down a big black hole in the floor, a big, scary-looking spider, and a house fire. Mother Monster acknowledges how scary this would be and encourages him to imagine positive alternatives, including a delicious breakfast, a walk with her on a sunny day, balloons, ice cream, and a story told by Mother Monster. In the end, Little Monster feels better after having learned that if unrealistic worries can make us feel scared, happy thoughts can help us cope by making us feel calm and safe.

Ages: 2–6   **Cultural context:** N/A

GUILT

These stories address what happens when a character does something hurtful to someone else, whether it's mainly by accident, through impulsivity, or because of difficulty in seeing other people's point of view. Often these actions are accompanied by a feeling of guilt. Characters find a way to apologize and to make up for their wrongdoing. These stories all contain an optimistic message that kids can make things right again. They emphasize kids' personal involvement in alleviating their own guilt.

See also *The Black Dog Who Went Into the Woods* and *When a Pet Dies* (Chapter 30) and *Geranium Morning*, *Stacy Had A Little Sister*, and *Where's Jess?* (Chapter 31) for stories in which guilt is a reaction to a death.

***Harriet and the Garden* by Nancy L. Carlson. 32 pages Carolrhoda, 2004.**
Guilt can be a useful signal that we've done something wrong that needs to be righted. While playing baseball, Harriet accidentally tramples Mrs. Hoozit's prize dahlia. Afraid of the consequences, she runs away. She feels guilty for the rest of the day and evening. She doesn't feel like going out, eating, or even watching her favorite TV program. She can't sleep, and then when she does, she has nightmares. The next day, she confesses to Mrs. Hoozit and helps her plant new flowers. Now, having made things right, she feels like herself again. Helping children understand the experience of guilt, this story shows that the way to alleviate it is to acknowledge their wrongdoing and help to put things right.

Ages: 4–8   **Cultural context:** N/A

Jamaica's Find by Juanita Havill. Illus. by Anne Sibley
O'Brien. 32 pages Houghton Mifflin, 1986.
An important factor in guilt is considering other people's perspectives
as well as one's own. Jamaica finds a hat and a toy dog at the park. At
first thinking entirely from the perspective of her own wants, she turns
in the hat (because it doesn't fit) but takes the dog home. Her mother
subtly suggests that she should return it, but in the end Jamaica
makes the decision to do this on her own because she doesn't feel good.
Once she meets the girl to whom the dog belongs, she's happy to see
the two reunited, helping children understand that not only does guilt
feel bad but that doing the right thing feels good.
Ages: 3–7   **Cultural context:** Multicultural
Main character's cultural background: African-American

Lilly's Purple Plastic Purse by Kevin Henkes. 32 pages
Greenwillow, 1996.
Children commonly feel guilty if they've been mean. Lilly admires her
teacher, Mr. Slinger, immensely, but when she can't resist showing off
her purple plastic purse inappropriately at school, he takes it away for
the rest of the day. She expresses her anger with a picture and a note to
him. She then discovers he's left an encouraging, understanding note in
the purse, along with a snack. She feels very guilty about her expression of anger, apologizes, and ultimately makes everything right again.
By portraying Lilly's impulsivity, anger, and remorse empathically, this
story shows children that if Lilly can apologize, they can too.
Ages: 4–9   **Cultural context:** N/A

The Summer My Father Was Ten by Pat Brisson.
Illus. by Andrea Shine. 32 pages Boyds Mills, 1998.
Kids can use guilt in a positive way to learn responsibility. While playing baseball near his neighbor's garden, a ten-year-old boy gets the
idea to pitch a tomato instead of the ball. His friends join him, and
they get so carried away that they ruin the garden. Though the boy
feels terrible, he's unable to apologize. The following spring, for the
first time, the neighbor doesn't plant. When the boy apologizes and
offers to help with the garden, this begins an annual tradition of gar-

dening together. Six years later, the neighbor moves to a nursing home (where he eventually dies), and the boy plants the garden himself. As an adult, the boy still plants a garden every year and tells his daughter, who narrates this book, the story each year. He has learned from his experience of guilt to take responsibility for his actions, to help replace what he's ruined, and to continue telling the story.

Ages: 7–10   **Cultural context:** European-American

That's Mine, Horace **by Holly Keller. 24 pages**
Greenwillow, 2000.
Guilt is an important signal that we've done something we know is wrong. Horace finds a wonderful toy truck and takes it home, but it doesn't make him as happy as he'd expected. First he's afraid to take it out at school, and when he finally can't resist, his classmate, Walter, says it's his. When Horace denies this, their teacher expresses trust in his honesty, a trust that his mother later echoes. He has guilty dreams and is literally sick with guilt. Even his doctor tells him to stay home and play with the truck. Horace's class sends get-well letters, including one from Walter, who tells him he can keep the truck till he gets better and then will have to return it. This is a great relief that enables Horace to return to school, give the truck back, and play with Walter. Through Horace, children will understand that guilt feels bad, and making things right is the way to feel better.

Ages: 3–7   **Cultural context:** N/A

JEALOUSY

Jealousy is a common experience among children. They may wish they had what another child has, whether it's something material, such as a toy, or something more intangible, such as attention from adults. Adults often tell kids that they shouldn't feel jealous or otherwise communicate that it's somehow wrong to have this feeling, but when jealousy is approached empathically, it's much more readily resolved.

See also Chapter 17 and *I Wish I Was Sick, Too!* (Chapter 27) for stories about specific situations that may involve jealousy.

When I Feel Jealous **by Cornelia Maude Spelman.**
Illus. by Kathy Parkinson. 24 pages Whitman, 2003.
A guide to jealousy can be useful for kids who have difficulty with this emotion. In this book, which is illustrated with gentle watercolors that are accessible to very young children, a little bear describes some of the situations in which she feels jealous. Although she doesn't like this feeling, she realizes that it's a universal experience. Talking over this feeling can help her feel better. She can express her needs, although they might not be met right away. When she remembers how to enjoy her own possessions and skills, she can be happy for others' good fortune and no longer jealous. A note for parents and teachers suggests ways to help children cope with jealousy. This constructive, empathic book will help children understand and resolve their own jealousy.
Ages: 2–6   **Cultural context:** N/A

SADNESS

Sadness can be a difficult emotion for children. Because it's painful, children may actively try not to be sad. For the same reason, it can be hard for you, as a parent, to sit with your child's sadness. But understanding and accepting sad feelings makes them more tolerable. When kids can tolerate their sadness, they're safer in the world because they don't have to avoid situations that might make them sad. When sadness is accessible to them, they can use it, like other feelings, as a signal that can help them understand their own needs and make choices.

See also Chapter 4 for books that mention sadness in the context of other feelings, and Chapters 9, 10, 13, 18, 19, 21, 26, 27, 30, 31, 32, 33, and 34 for books about situations that often evoke sadness.

The Boy Who Didn't Want to Be Sad **by Rob Goldblatt.**
32 pages Magination, 2004.
Sometimes sadness makes kids want to withdraw, as it does in this story. A boy decides to get rid of everything that could make him sad. Because bare trees make him sad, he stays inside. He stops playing with toys because they can break or get lost. He stops contact with

his parents and friends, and even kicks out his pets because they'll die someday, and that will make him sad. He finally realizes that "the things that made him sad were also the things that made him happy." Consequently, he embraces life–and all of his feelings, positive and negative. Paradoxically, he has stopped being sad by accepting his emotions, including his sadness.

Ages: 4–8   **Cultural context:** European-American

When I Feel Sad **by Cornelia Maude Spelman.**
Illus. by Kathy Parkinson. 24 pages Whitman, 2002.
Understanding and talking about sadness helps to dispel it. Written from the first-person perspective of a little guinea pig, this book describes what sadness feels like and when a child might feel sad. For example, kids might feel sad when they miss someone, when other children exclude them, or when no one listens to them. The guinea pig says that it feels better to tell someone when you're sad. The story conveys acceptance of feeling and showing sadness, both by the guinea pig him- or herself and others around him or her. It teaches children that while sadness is real and is okay to talk about, it's also temporary. The images of a sad little one moving toward feeling good have real potential to inspire optimism.

Ages: 2–5   **Cultural context:** N/A

PART 3

EVERYDAY STRESS

[CHAPTER 8]

Bedtime Worries

Many children have concerns about going to bed, from fears of the dark, to monsters, to separation from the waking world, to sleeping in an unfamiliar environment. Sometimes this is because their daytime worries are heightened when they're alone, in the dark, with nothing else to hold their attention. It's not unusual for children who have previously slept well to have periods of difficulty with going to sleep, particularly at times of daytime stress. Children can manage their fears by talking to friends their own age and to adults, creating art, having special dreams, finding sources of light, and making friends with the monster they fear.

See also some of the stories about feeling secure in a relationship with an adult (Chapter 1), especially *"More, More, More" Said the Baby*, which ends with a loved, reassured child going to bed. For stories about bedtime worries when parents are away, see *Grandmother's Dreamcatcher* and *Princess Bee and the Royal Good-Night Story* (Chapter 9). *When the Big*

Dog Barks (Chapter 6) reassures children about being fearful at bedtime in the context of discussing other fears.

Can't You Sleep, Little Bear? by Martin Waddell.
Illus. by Barbara Firth. 32 pages Candlewick, 1988.
Some kids have trouble sleeping because, like Little Bear, they're afraid of the dark. Little Bear keeps interrupting Big Bear's reading, which gets a bit exasperating for Big Bear. Nightlights (even big ones) don't help Little Bear feel better; he's scared because there's still darkness outside. Finally, Big Bear takes Little Bear outside to take a good look at the dark, pointing out the beautiful moon and stars. At first, Little Bear is scared again, but when Big Bear holds him, he falls right to sleep. A good choice for children whose fear of the dark keeps them awake, this story shows that parents are comfortingly close even when it's dark.
Ages: 1–4   **Cultural context:** N/A

Clyde Monster by Robert L. Crowe. Illus. by Kay Chorao.
32 pages Dutton, 1976.
In this turn-around of children's fears, Clyde is a toddler-like monster who's afraid to go to sleep because people might get him. His parents do the usual things parents do to calm children in these situations, explaining that long ago, people and monsters made an agreement not to scare each other. Reassured, he's willing to go to sleep in his cave—as long as his mother leaves the rock open a little. Along the way, he acknowledges that he's never heard of a monster scaring a human child, and he is distressed to think that a monster could ever consider doing this to a child. Children will enjoy this story's humor while they learn something about negotiating between their fears and their parents' reality.
Ages: 3–6   **Cultural context:** N/A

Darkness and the Butterfly by Ann Grifalconi. 32 pages
Little, Brown, 1987.
Being small may contribute to children's fear of the dark, as it does for Osa. Although she's brave and curious during the day, she's afraid

that the dark might hide dangerous spirits, and she feels too small to outrun them. The Wise Woman tells Osa that she had similar fears as a child, adding that although the butterfly is even smaller than she is, it flies on. In the Wise Woman's lap, Osa has a magical dream in which she flies like a butterfly and sees the dark as full of beautiful light from the moon and stars. After this dream, she finds that she no longer fears the dark—she has a sense of a light within. The depth of Osa's change is reflected in the intense colors of the illustrations. Experiencing the transformative power of Osa's dream with her, children can use this story to find courage within themselves.

Ages: 3–7   **Cultural context:** African

Dear Bear by Joanna Harrison. 31 pages Carolrhoda, 1994.
Sometimes the bear under the stairs just isn't what you expect, as Katie discovers in this charming story. Katie is happy and busy most of the time, but when she goes to bed, she worries about the bear who lives in the closet under the stairs, waiting to grab her. At her mom's suggestion, Katie writes a letter to the bear, asking him to go away. This begins a correspondence with a surprisingly friendly bear, who eventually invites Katie to a tea party. There she finds tea and cookies, an adorable teddy bear smiling expectantly up at her, and a note asking if the bear can come live with her. Children will see the benefits of using their imagination in a positive, rather than negative, way. You could even invite children to write to the bear/monster/etc. that they are scared of and arrange (eventually) for them to meet a harmless stuffed toy.

Ages: 2–7   **Cultural context:** Multicultural
Main character's cultural background: European-American

Eli's Night-Light by Liz Rosenberg. Illus. by Joanna Yardley. 32 pages Orchard, 2001.
Children who are afraid of the dark sometimes find that it's not as dark as they think. One night, Eli's nightlight bulb burns out, and it's too late to wake his parents to ask them to replace it. At first, his room looks very dark, but as Eli looks around, he sees lots of little lights—from the crack under the door, his clock, and a picture frame. As he looks out the

window, he realizes that the stars will be there whenever he needs them and decides that they can be his nightlights. Illustrated in many beautiful shades of dark, this story provides an excellent example of coping by using the internal and external resources that you already have.

Ages: 1–5   **Cultural context:** European-American

Emily Just in Time by Jan Slepian. Illus. by Glo Coalson.
32 pages Philomel, 1998.
Sometimes bedtime is difficult when it's not at home. In this story, Emily grows up in a lot of ways (for example, she isn't too frightened to slide down a twisty slide any more), but she still feels too scared to sleep at her grandma's all night. Even when she brings her blanket and bears, she still wakes up at night needing to go home. Grandma is extremely patient, assuring her that someday she'll stay easily all night and taking her home when she asks. Eventually that time does come—all by itself, illustrating the importance of kids remaining patient with themselves and accepting that it's okay to need to be at home at bedtime.

Ages: 2–7   **Cultural context:** European-American

Franklin in the Dark by Paulette Bourgeois.
Illus. by Brenda Clark. 32 pages Kids Can, 1997.
For a turtle, being afraid of small, dark places means fearing crawling into his shell. For Franklin, this is compounded by fears that monsters are in there. So instead of getting inside his shell, he drags it behind him. Other animals who have fears offer him solutions, but Franklin isn't afraid of the things that the other animals fear. When he tells his mother about this, she remarks that his friends all had fears. That night at bedtime, he crawls into his shell, even though he's scared. He finds the solution to his own fear: a night-light. Kids who are afraid of the dark will find empathy in this story, along with a role model for courage and a sense of acceptance around the universality of fear.

Ages: 2–6   **Cultural context:** N/A

No Such Thing by Jackie French Koller.
Illus. by Betsy Lewin. 32 pages Boyds Mills, 1997.
Here's a hilarious tale for kids who are afraid of monsters under the bed. Howard worries that there's a monster under his bed, but his

mommy assures him that there's no such thing. Meanwhile, the young monster that *is* under his bed worries that there's a boy on top of his bed, and *his* mommy assures him that there's no such thing as a boy. After several near-encounters (and, unfortunately, threats of punishment from their mommies), Howard and the monster finally meet face to face. Once Howard is satisfied that monsters don't eat little boys, the two dream up a trick to prove each other's existence to their mothers. The story includes some charming made-up words and has energetic ink-and-watercolor illustrations that resemble *New Yorker* cartoons. Acknowledging the reality of children's fears, this story simultaneously helps them get some perspective, all while laughing.

Ages: 4–7   **Cultural context:** European-American

Pip's Magic **by Ellen Stoll Walsh. 32 pages Harcourt, 1994.**
Sometimes when we look for someone else's magic to help us to be brave, we discover magic of our own. Pip is afraid of the dark, so he seeks help from Old Abra, the wizard. But he keeps missing Old Abra— first at the edge of a dark forest, then at a tunnel's entrance, then as night falls. Pip tells himself that he must follow Old Abra through these dark places because he needs magic to overcome his fear of the dark. When he finally finds Old Abra, the wizard tells him he already has magic—he's used it to get through the forest, the tunnel, and the night, leaving Pip with new confidence. The striking cut-paper collages clearly convey both Pip's fearfulness and his curiosity. This story shows children that they have within them the potential to overcome their fear of the dark.

Ages: 1–4   **Cultural context:** N/A

Shadow Night **by Kay Chorao. 32 pages Dutton, 2001.**
Shadows are the source of some children's fears of monsters, as they are for James. His parents not only make the monsters go away, but also show him how to make shadows with their hands. They use these shadow animals to tell a story about courage, which ends with an elephant picking up two spiders, making them feel big. After the story, Daddy holds James high in the air, and he feels big, too. When his parents leave the room, and James feels small and scared, he makes his own shadow figures. Making a shadow monster of his full

silhouette, James has mastered his fears and falls asleep comfortably. The illustrations and an afterword show how to make shadow animals. This story encourages children to see that they have more control over scary things than they might think.

Ages: 2–6.   **Cultural context:** European-American

The Something by Natalie Babbitt. 39 pages
Farrar, Straus and Giroux, 1970.
Even when fears at bedtime are vague, children can dispel them by making art about them. Mylo (a young monster) is afraid of the dark because he is afraid that a vague "Something" will come in through the window. He makes a clay sculpture of the Something. When he finishes the sculpture, he has a dream in which he meets the Something (who strongly resembles a human girl), and finds that he isn't afraid of it. Mylo assertively explains to the Something that he wishes it would get out of his dream. It responds that this is its dream, not Mylo's, and says goodbye in a friendly way. When Mylo wakes up, he finds that he doesn't need the clay anymore, although he keeps the statue so that he'll remember who the Something is. Like Mylo, kids can use art to neutralize fears.

Ages: 2–8   **Cultural context:** European-American

When the Wind Stops by Charlotte Zolotow.
Illus. by Stefano Vitale. 32 pages HarperCollins, 1995.
Bedtime troubles some children because it feels like a loss. In this re-assuring story, a little boy asks his mother at bedtime why the day has to end. She explains that it doesn't really end; it just starts in another place or in another way. For example, although the last days of autumn feel like an ending, they also represent the beginning of winter, and when leaves fall, they don't disappear, but instead become part of the earth that grows new trees with their own leaves. To each of his questions about endings, the mother's answers affirm the continuity of life. The wonderful sense of calm created by this story will promote comfort at bedtime.

Ages: 3–6   **Cultural context:** European-American

CHAPTER 9

Separation and Parents' Travel

Separation from parents can be difficult and painful for young children, yet is a necessary reality brought on most commonly by school, work, or a parent's travel. Parents and children miss each other at these times, but it's important for kids to trust in the parent's eventual return and find ways to keep the parent in their heart even when he or she isn't physically present. Children can cope with separation using imagination, counting days on calendars, arranging special rituals with the absent parent, seeking reassurance and affection from others, snuggling a favorite toy or blanket, and doing things they enjoy.

See also *Abuelita's Heart* (Chapter 1) for a story that shows children a way to stay connected to a special adult when they're apart. Reassurance that a parent will find you when you're lost is a theme of *Blueberries for Sal, Gotcha Louie!,* and *There's Nothing to D-o-o-o* (Chapter 1). *When I Feel Scared, When the Big Dog Barks* (Chapter 6), and *Rosie to the Rescue* (Chapter 7) address fears and worries related to parents going away. Separations from parents related to other situations are addressed in Chapters 13, 17, and 27. For stories about coping with separation from a special friend, see Chapters 18 and 20.

Abel's Moon by Shirley Hughes. 32 pages DK, 1999.

Sharing stories can promote use of imagination to cope with separation. Abel tells his two young sons, Adam and Noah, stories about his exotic travels and writes these stories down for them. When Abel travels again, the kids read his stories many times. They have make-believe adventures that are a lot like Abel's real adventures. Adam imagines flying with Noah in the "moon machine" they've built to visit Abel, and sharing their adventures with him, just as Abel has shared his adventures with them. Adam's story demonstrates how to use make-believe to cope with missing someone.

Ages: 4–8   **Cultural context:** European-American

Always My Dad by Sharon Dennis Wyeth. Illus. by Raúl Colón. 32 pages Knopf, 1995.

The circumstances of a parent's life may prevent him or her from being with children consistently. A girl explains that her dad moves a lot and has had a lot of different jobs. Once, when she and her brothers spend the summer with their paternal grandparents, Daddy comes to stay with them. He reassures the girl that he always loves her and is always her dad no matter where he is. She feels the truth of this inside her. The illustrations are done in a subtly colored, uniquely textured style, and this story offers empathy to children whose family arrangements are similar to the girl's, letting them know that parents love them even when they aren't present.

Ages: 4–8   **Cultural context:** African-American

Daddy, Will You Miss Me? by Wendy McCormick. Illus. by Jennifer Eachus. 32 pages Simon & Schuster, 1999.

Parent and child can use imagination together to cope with separation. Before a boy's daddy leaves on a four-week business trip, he tells the boy that every day, he'll whisper his name to the wind and blow kisses to him. The boy will say good night to Daddy each night, and joining the boy in imagination, Daddy adds that the boy will wake each day to the kisses Daddy has blown him. The boy also plans to mark each day on the calendar and save something each day to show Daddy when he returns. While Daddy is away, the boy misses him and imagines what he's doing until he and Daddy joyfully reunite. Honestly acknowledging the sadness of separation, this story shows that there are ways to cope and that even though we're sad, the separation will come to an end.

Ages: 3–6   **Cultural context:** European-American

Grandmother's Dreamcatcher **by Becky Ray McCain.**
Illus. by Stacey Schuett. 32 pages Whitman, 1998.
Being away from both parents can be particularly difficult. When Kimmy stays with Grandmother while her parents look for a new house, she has bad dreams at first and misses her parents all week. Grandmother reassures her by helping her make a dreamcatcher and telling her the story of its origin. After this, Kimmy has no more bad dreams. Kimmy and Grandmother spend the week making gifts for Kimmy's parents and their new home. Illustrated with colorful, evocative acrylic-and-gouache paintings, this story shows children that they can manage separation by taking care of themselves and keeping the person they miss in their thoughts in a positive way.

Ages 3–8   **Cultural context:** Native-American

If You Listen **by Charlotte Zolotow. Illus. by Stefano Vitale.**
31 pages Running Press Kids, 2002.
A fundamental question about separation is how you know that the person who is away loves you. When a girl's father is away, she explores this idea as she searches for evidence of his love. Her mother poetically explains that you know that someone loves you by listening inside yourself, and together they think of several images that reflect this kind of listening. The girl considers this and responds that she will listen hard, but she wishes that her father would come home. Acknowledging children's sadness in missing someone, this story offers a way to keep that person's love with them all the time.

Ages: 4–8   **Cultural context:** European-American

***I'll See You When the Moon Is Full* by Susi Gregg Fowler.**
Illus. by Jim Fowler. 24 pages Greenwillow, 1994.
Finding concrete ways to track the time till a parent returns, along
with a sense of being together in imagination, can help children cope
with separation. Daddy is going on a trip by himself, and Abe keeps him
company while he packs. He and Abe tell each other how much they'll
miss each other. Daddy explains that he'll be home when the moon
is full, and Abe decides to draw a picture of the moon each day that
Daddy is away. Daddy assures Abe that he's as reliable as the moon.
When Daddy leaves, they know that their shared observation of the
moon keeps them together metaphorically, offering kids a constructive
example for managing separation.
Ages: 3–7   **Cultural context:** European-American

The Magic Box: When Parents Can't Be There to Tuck You In
by Marty Sederman and Seymour Epstein.
Illus. by Karen Stormer Brooks. 32 pages Magination, 2003.
Tangible, creative reminders of an absent parent can promote kids'
coping with separation. While Casey's father is away on a few days'
business trip, his mother gives him a gift from his father, a "magic
box" full of hugs and kisses, along with a picture of Casey and Dad
and a package of new markers. Casey uses the markers to make a
magic box of hugs and kisses that Daddy can take with him on his
next trip. Casey and Dad's special game is hide-and-seek, and as the
story ends, Casey says that he always finds Dad—a sense of certainty
that's all the more meaningful with a dad who goes away at times.
An afterword for parents suggests ways for parents to help children
come to terms with a parent's temporary absence. In the end, this
tale provides validation and reassurance for kids who worry when a
parent travels.
Ages: 3–7   **Cultural context:** Multicultural
Main character's cultural background: European-American

***Mama Will Be Home Soon* by Nancy Minchella.**
Illus. by Keiko Narahashi. 32 pages Scholastic, 2003.
When a parent's absence is hard to tolerate, it seems as if it will never
end. Lili stays with Grandma while her mama is away for a few days.

Although Grandma says that Mama will return soon, it never feels soon enough. Lili asks Mama how she'll find her, and Mama suggests that Lili look for Mama's yellow hat. During Mama's absence, Lili keeps seeing yellow things and thinking that Mama's home, but it's always something other than Mama's hat. When Mama finally comes home, at first Lili is too discouraged by her near-misses to look, but she soon has a joyful reunion with Mama, who has brought her a yellow hat of her own. While giving kids lots of empathy about missing a parent, this story reassures them that parents do come home, even when it feels as if they never will.

Ages: 3–7   **Cultural context:** Multicultural
Main character's cultural background: European-American

Mama's Coming Home **by Kate Banks. Illus. by Tomek Bogacki**
26 pages Foster/Farrar, Straus and Giroux, 2003.
Even though it's a short period of time, kids may miss their parents during an ordinary workday. In this rhyming story, with their father, two boys and their baby brother or sister anticipate their mama's arrival home after a day at work. As the boys play, set the table, and wait for Papa to make pizza for dinner, Mama closes her shop, walks to the train station, rides the train, and walks home. Finally, the family happily sits down to dinner together, creating a reassuring reminder that parents do come home.

Ages: 2–6   **Cultural context:** Multicultural
Main character's cultural background: European-American

Mommy, Don't Go **(2nd edition) by Elizabeth Crary.**
Illus. by Marina Megale. 30 pages Parenting, 1996.
There are many ways to manage the stresses of separation, and using an unusual format, this story emphasizes the roles of discussion and active choice. Matthew's mother is about to leave on a trip, and his baby-sitter will stay with him. Matthew is unhappy because he doesn't want Mommy to go. The child is invited to choose what Matthew can do to feel better, and then you turn to the page that describes the child's choice. Several pages invite children to speculate about how Matthew feels, which can help them anticipate and articulate their own feelings. A foreword for adults is included, and an "idea page" at

the end lists Matthew's ideas and invites kids to add their own. While this format won't be right for every child, the story helps children use a problem-solving approach to their emotional needs related to separation from parents.

Ages: 3–8   **Cultural context:** Multicultural
Main character's cultural background: European-American

My Father Is Far Away **by Robin Ballard. 32 pages**
Greenwillow, 1992.
Imagination can be an important resource for managing separation. A girl imagines the exciting things her father could be doing while he is far away and she is doing ordinary things like drawing pictures and patting her dog. Maybe he's finding treasures or riding a horse in a race. Whatever he's doing, the girl knows that he misses her as much as she misses him, showing children how to keep someone they miss in their thoughts and hearts.

Ages: 2–5   **Cultural context:** Multicultural
Main character's cultural background: European-American

Owl Babies **by Martin Waddell. Illus. by Patrick Benson.**
26 pages Candlewick, 1992.
Even when you know a parent will come home, it can be scary when she's gone. Three baby owls, Sarah, Percy, and Bill, wake up one night to find their mother missing. As they wait for her, Sarah, like the most mature part of a child, makes brave, reasonable statements (for example, that mother will be back), and Percy, though he doesn't think of these things himself, agrees and elaborates. Little Bill, like the part of a child that feels small and frightened, plaintively replies, "I want my mommy!" As soon as Sarah starts to worry, mother owl comes home, reminding them that they'd known she'd come back. Verbal patterns and repetition, along with the owls' body language, communicate effectively. This gentle story acknowledges children's mixed feelings when a parent is away and reassures them that parents always return.

Ages: 0–4   **Cultural context:** N/A

Pilot Mom by Kathleen Benner Duble. Illus. by Alan Marks.
32 pages Charlesbridge, 2003.

Separations can be particularly difficult in military families because of the realistic threat of danger. Such is the case for Jenny, whose mom, an Air Force tanker pilot, is about to leave for a two-week mission. Jenny helps Mom pack the pockets of her flight suit, as she always does. She and her friend K.C. play at being pilots. Jenny, K.C., and Mom talk about the possibility of war, which Jenny tries to avoid thinking about. Jenny is both worried about her mom and proud of her competence, intelligence, courage, and ability to stay calm. Mom reassures Jenny that she thinks of her when they're apart, telling Jenny that she loves being her mom and loves being a pilot, too. Jenny struggles to hold this apparent contradiction, saying that when she grows up, she wants to be a mom, but not a pilot. The empathy conveyed in this story will help children of military families feel that they're not alone.

Ages: 5–10   **Cultural context:** Multicultural
Main character's cultural background: European-American

Princess Bee and the Royal Good-Night Story by Sandy Asher.
Illus. by Cat Bowman Smith. 30 pages Whitman, 1990.

Separation challenges kids to keep the absent person with them in some way, even when that isn't literally possible. When Princess Bee's mum goes to visit her aunt in Goodness-Knows-Where for three days and nights, she misses Mum's bedtime stories. Bee's sister and brother try to tell her bedtime stories, but they're too short and self-centered to help Bee sleep. On the last day, Bee's dad tells her that although Mum isn't there in the usual way, she's present in other ways. That night at bedtime, Bee listens very hard, and "hears" one of Mum's stories about a princess and a queen who missed each other very much until Mum came home with new stories. Now she's able to sleep, having found a way to keep Mum's love with her even though Mum isn't physically present.

Ages: 3–7   **Cultural context:** European-American

***When I Miss You* by *Cornelia* Maude Spelman.**
Illus. by Kathy Parkinson. 24 pages Whitman, 2004.

Separation leads to difficult feelings, but it's possible for children to manage those feelings by talking to others and having other things to comfort them. A little guinea pig explains that he/she misses his/her parents—when they go to work, out for the evening, or on a trip. Evocatively describing what missing a parent feels like, the guinea pig knows that we can't always be with the people we want to be with. He/she copes with missing someone by seeking reassurance and affection from others, snuggling a favorite toy or blanket, reading a favorite story, and drawing a picture to show the absent parent. The guinea pig can have fun while missing a parent, and he/she knows that the parent will always return. A note to parents and teachers suggests ways to help children think about separation. Children will find empathy and helpful coping strategies in this book, as well as a good role model for using painful feelings about separation to remind themselves of constructive ways to cope.

Ages: 1–5　　**Cultural context:** N/A

***You Go Away* by Dorothy Corey. Illus. by Diane Paterson.**
32 pages Whitman., 1999.

This very simply worded book is about going away and coming back. It begins will small departures: peek-a-boo and holding a baby close and far. It progresses to toddlers' adventures in walking across the room on their own—and coming back. Eventually, daddies go away to work, mommies go away while their children are at school, and then they come back. Finally, an adult is going "far away" on an airplane but will come back. This story can help the youngest children understand that although there are many kinds of separation, their adults will always come back to them.

Ages: 0–2　　**Cultural context:** Multicultural

[CHAPTER 10]

Having a Bad Day

At any age, we all have an occasional bad day. Sometimes kids will experience a series of essentially unrelated mishaps, or occasionally a whole day goes badly because of a specific event. Ways to cope with having a bad day include using humor, imagination, acceptance, hopefulness, helping someone else, and the presence of a patient adult. Some of these stories don't explicitly discuss a bad day, but are good choices for times when a child just needs to laugh.

See also *Why Did We Have to Move Here?* (Chapter 18) for a story about a bad day at a new school.

Alexander and the Terrible, Horrible, No Good, Very Bad Day
by Judith Viorst. Illus. by Ray Cruz. 32 pages Atheneum, 1972.
This is a catalogue of all the rotten things that happen to Alexander in one day, from tripping on a skateboard first thing in the morning, to being the only one among his brothers without a prize in his cereal,

to having his best friend decide not to be his best friend anymore, to unintentionally annoying both parents. Alexander wishes to escape from all the mishaps by going to Australia, but he eventually comes to understand that some days are just like that. This book offers humor and empathy to kids who are having a crummy day, while helping them accept that having a bad day sometimes is just part of life.

Ages: 4–8 **Cultural context:** Multicultural
Main character's cultural background: European-American

Can You Make a Piggy Giggle? **by Linda Ashman.**
Illus. by Henry Cole. 32 pages Dutton, 2002.
Sometimes we're in such a serious mood that it seems like nothing can make us laugh. In this story, a boy tries all kinds of silly tricks to get a piggy to giggle, from telling a silly riddle to wriggling like a noodle. All the other animals at the farm are rolling with laughter, but not the serious piggy. It's hard not to laugh when the author concludes that in spite of everything, the piggy probably won't giggle. The rhymes, assonance, and rhythms are wonderfully funny, and with a definite resemblance to Dr. Seuss's brilliant *Oh Say Can You Say*, this story can help a child who's having a bad day to see the lighter side.

Ages: 3–8 **Cultural context:** European-American
Main character's cultural background: N/A

Don't Make Me Laugh **by James Stevenson. 32 pages Foster, 1999.**
Laughter is an excellent treatment for a bad day. Dinosaur-like Mr. Frimdimpny tells readers not to laugh, otherwise they have to go back to the beginning of the book. This is followed by irresistable stories of tickles, a giant sneeze, and uncontrollable dancing that are very hard not to laugh at. At the end, Mr. Frimdimpny comments that the reader's face is very funny, and he can't help laughing—and going back to the beginning of the book. Even if they're having an ordinary bad day, children will have a hard time keeping themselves from laughing and learning that humor helps when things are going badly.

Ages: 2–7 **Cultural context:** N/A

First Tomato **by Rosemary Wells. 25 pages Dial, 1992.**
When things are going badly, sometimes we just need to be someplace else, even if it's just in imagination. Everything goes wrong for Claire (a rabbit), and the author concludes, "Claire needs a visit to the Bunny Planet." On the Bunny Planet, Bunny Queen Janet treats Claire to the kind of day she deserves—instead of a cold, wet, frustrating, embarrassing winter day at school, she has a delicious summer day at home in the vegetable garden with her loving mother. This touching story offers a satisfying example of how useful imagination is for coping with stress.
Ages: 2–8   **Cultural context**: N/A

Franklin's Bad Day **by Paulette Bourgeois.**
Illus. by Brenda Clark. 32 pages Kids Can, 1996.
Sometimes there's a specific reason for a bad day. In this story, Franklin wakes up grouchy, and everything goes wrong for him. In anger, he kicks over his block castle. When his father hears the crash and asks him what's going on, he tells his father that he'd made the castle with Otter, who moved away yesterday. Franklin's father understands that Franklin is sad and angry because Otter is gone. He tells Franklin that he and Otter can still be friends and suggests they share feelings by calling or writing. After Franklin writes a letter to Otter, he feels much better. Children will understand that when something troubles you enough to ruin your day, things will go better once you've addressed the problem directly and constructively.
Ages: 3–7   **Cultural context:** N/A

Grover's Bad, Awful Day **by Anna H. Dickson.**
Illus. by Tom Brannon. 25 pages Western, 1986.
When things go badly, it's easy to get discouraged. One day, everything seems to go wrong for Grover, from the moment he wakes up late. For example, he spills toothpaste off his toothbrush, is late to preschool, forgets the letter after Q, and is rejected by a group of monsters he wants to play with. During preschool, Grover's teacher and his friend comment that Grover is having a bad day. When Grover gets home, he tells his mommy all about his bad day, and she reassures him that everyone has bad days. Grover soon feels hopeful that tomorrow will be better. By showing children that others have bad days, too, that it

helps to talk about it with someone who cares about you, and that it's possible to hope for a better day soon, this story assists children who are confronted with the discouragement of a bad day.

Ages: 2–5   **Cultural context:** N/A

I Love You Just the Way You Are **by Virginia Miller.**
32 pages Candlewick, 1998.
Emotional support is important in coping with a difficult day. Bartholomew, a little bear, is having a very grumpy day, but George, a big bear, takes care of Bartholomew, expressing understanding of his feelings and acceptance of him in spite of his grumpiness. From this simple, yet resonant tale, children will see how a caregiver's love can help them tolerate feeling grouchy.

Ages: 1–3   **Cultural context:** N/A

Mean Soup **by Betsy Everitt. 32 pages**
Harcourt Brace Jovanovich, 1992.
Empathy and humor help Horace feel better when he has a terrible day and comes home from school very grumpy. His mother, who is very tuned in to him and not a bit afraid to be silly, understands his growls and hisses and invites him to make soup with her. She screams into a pot of water on the stove, encouraging him to scream, too. In screaming along with him, she's both empathizing with how Horace feels and showing him how to cope. She tells him that this is called Mean Soup, causing him to see the humor in it and alleviating the frustration from his day. The illustrations are colorful and energetic. This story shows children how to manage a bad day by doing something special that acknowledges their mood, using humor, and making use of the empathy that's offered to them.

Ages: 3–7   **Cultural context:** Multicultural
Main character's cultural background: European-American

Serious Farm **by Tim Egan. 32 pages Houghton Mifflin, 2003.**
When kids are having a bad day, sometimes they just need a laugh. Farmer Fred is a very serious fellow, and so all the animals on his farm have to be serious, too. But after a while, they agree that they need some laughter. They try hard to make Farmer Fred laugh, but

he just won't do it. The animals can't stand living there and decide to leave. When Fred goes to find them, he's mildly amused by the idea of a bunch of farm animals running loose in the woods. Heartened by this display of a nascent sense of humor, the animals decide to return to the farm. They find that the best way to make him laugh is still to bring up the time they were loose in the woods. This story is just the thing for a child who needs a laugh and needs to lighten up a bit.

Ages: 3–7   **Cultural context:** European-American

The Three Grumpies **by Tamra Wight. Illus. by Ross Collins. 32 pages Bloomsbury, 2003.**

Grumpiness can ruin your day if you don't laugh enough. One day, a girl wakes up to find the Grumpies waiting for her—three of them, to be exact, monsters named Grumpy, Grumpier, and Grumpiest. They cause all kinds of trouble, spilling milk, losing shoes and homework, tripping on the school bus steps, and splattering paint on the girl's shirt. Adults have lots of ideas about how to get rid of them: telling them to go away, showing them how she feels, scaring them away with mean faces, and ignoring them, but nothing works. When the girl gets home, she smiles just a little and notices that the Grumpies are starting to look nervous. So she laughs at all the nasty things they do, and with persistence on her part, they walk right out the door. Kids will find the story funny and endearing, while the message that laughter banishes grumpiness comes through loud and clear.

Ages: 4–8   **Cultural context:** Multicultural

Main character's cultural background: European-American

Where's Your Smile, Crocodile? **by Claire Freedman. Illus. by Sean Julian. 26 pages Peachtree, 2001.**

One way to deal with a bad day is to do nice things for someone else. When Kyle wakes up grumpy, his mom isn't worried—she knows he'll find his smile. The other animals try unsuccessfully to cheer Kyle up. Then Kyle meets Little Lion Cub, who has lost his way home. Kyle suggests that they look together for his smile and Little Lion Cub's way home. Kyle tries to cheer up Little Lion Cub in some of the same ways the other animals had tried to cheer *him* up, and it does help.

Not only that, but they find Little Lion Cub's home—and Little Lion Cub finds Kyle's smile, right on Kyle's face where it belongs. This delightful book illustrates that performing acts of kindness can help children to feel good about themselves, which is one way to relieve their own case of the grumpies.

Ages: 3–7   **Cultural context:** N/A

PART 4

GROWING UP

CHAPTER 11

Feelings About Being Little and Growing Up

Children may have many feelings about being little and growing up. Sometimes kids wish they were more grown up and may even feel shame about the "little" part of themselves. At other times, kids may just enjoy being little. There may also be times of conflict between being little and being big. It's helpful to accept both the "big" and "little" parts of each child. Parents can also help kids resolve conflicts about being both little and big by helping them find ways to keep their little self, in a special form, when they get big, by celebrating their discoveries of "big" parts of themselves while acknowledging that they're still little, and by supporting kids' decision that being little is special in some way or is just right for now.

See also *Rosie's Baby Tooth* (Chapter 14) for a story about growing up and keeping a part of the "little" self always, in a different way.

***All by Myself* by Ivan Bates. 27 pages HarperCollins, 2000.**
Sometimes when kids want to be big, they have to find a way to do this while still being little. Maya, a little elephant, wants to pick breakfast leaves all by herself for the first time. She tries very hard and constructively to find a way to do this, but she just can't reach. Finally, her mother lifts her up so that she can reach the leaves, and she picks the best breakfast ever, all by herself, making a satisfying step toward growing up, while remaining little.
Ages: 2–4   **Cultural context:** N/A

***An Egg Is an Egg* by Nicki Weiss. 32 pages Putnam, 1990.**
There are many kinds of change and growth. In this story, an egg becomes a chick, day becomes night, and a seed becomes a flower. A refrain reminds children that change is inevitable. But although a baby grew into a boy, his mother assures him that he can, and will, always be her baby. This tender story offers children reassurance that growing up doesn't have to mean giving up the "little" part of themselves.
Ages: 1–7   **Cultural context:** European-American

***Geraldine's Blanket* by Holly Keller. 32 pages Greenwillow, 1984.**
The part of ourselves that's little can stay with us, in a transformed state, as we become big. Geraldine loves the blanket that Aunt Bessie gave her when she was a baby, and when her parents try to get her to give it up, she refuses. Aunt Bessie gives her a doll, Rosa, and her parents once again say that the blanket must go. Again Geraldine refuses. Instead, she makes the blanket into a dress for Rosa, saying, "Now Rosa has the blanket and I have Rosa." This story shows children that they don't have to give up their "little" self, but can keep it in a different form even as they get older.
Ages: 3–7   **Cultural context:** N/A

***I Like to Be Little* by Charlotte Zolotow. Illus. by Erik Blegvad. 32 pages Crowell, 1987.**
Growing up involves a tension between being little and being big. When her mother asks what she wants to be when she grows up, a girl responds that she just wants to be little for now. Being little allows

her to skip when she's glad, make an imaginary house under the table, draw with crayons, and do other fun things. Her mother says that being a mother makes all these things happen again as an adult. The little girl acknowledges that she thinks of growing up to be like her mother—even though she likes to be little for now. This juxtaposition deftly shows how to take pleasure simultaneously in a little self and grown-up potential, allowing children to realize that if they grow up to be parents (as the little girl imagines she will), they won't have to give up the joys of being little.

Ages: 3–7   **Cultural context:** Multicultural
Main character's cultural background: European-American

Ira Sleeps Over **by Bernard Waber. 48 pages**
Houghton Mifflin, 1972.
Children may be ashamed of showing the "little" parts of themselves. When it's time for Ira's first sleepover, his sister pressures him not to take his teddy bear, saying that his friend, Reggie, will laugh at him and think he's a baby. After lots of indecision, Ira doesn't bring the bear, but when Reggie tells a scary ghost story, Ira finds out that Reggie has a teddy bear, too. Feeling confident that Reggie won't laugh, he goes home to get his own. This story promotes kids' acceptance of their "little" parts while addressing the feeling of embarrassment that the little part can bring.

Ages: 4–7   **Cultural context:** European-American

Little Gorilla **by Ruth Bornstein. 32 pages Clarion, 1976.**
It can be confusing for children when they think that people love them because they're little and cute, or because they're so grown-up. On each page, someone loves Little Gorilla, and this happens both when he's little and when he grows big. Children will understand that they're lovable no matter what size or age they are.

Ages: 0–3   **Cultural context:** N/A

Little One Step **by Simon James. 26 pages Candlewick, 2003.**
Sometimes being little carries a connotation of helplessness. The littlest duckling doesn't think he can walk all the way home and wants Mama.

His brother teaches him a trick to help him keep going: he says "one" as he lifts his foot and "step" as he puts it down. This helps him to literally put one foot in front of the other, until he's finally home to Mama—with a new name, Little One Step. Providing a sense of control, this empowering tale shows that even when a child feels unable to cope because of being little, there's something she or he can do.

Ages: 2–5   **Cultural context:** N/A

The Littlest Wolf **by Larry Dane Brimner. Illus. by Jose Aruego and Ariane Dewey. 34 pages HarperCollins, 2002.**

Children may think that smallness means incompetence. Such is the case for the littlest wolf in the family, who worries that he can't roll in a straight enough line, run fast enough, or pounce high enough. His father, Big Gray, takes the little wolf's concerns seriously, reassuring the littlest wolf that he's just as he should be. He explains that straight lines, faster running, and higher pounces come later in life, and so the little wolf stops worrying and starts feeling good about himself. Big Gray reminds him that the acorns are also just as they should be, and will become big trees. The illustrations reveal the adorable little wolf's tentativeness and the father's gentleness, giving kids the chance to take Big Gray's message to heart and feel comfortable with being little.

Ages: 1–6   **Cultural context:** N/A

One Day, Daddy **by Frances Thomas. Illus. by Ross Collins. 26 pages Hyperion, 2001.**

Exploration is an essential part of childhood, but it's hindered when kids feel that if they're big enough to explore, they have to give up being little. Little Monster explains to Father Monster that someday he might like to be a space explorer. He considers this a problem because he'd have to leave his parents behind. He tells Father Monster about all the planets and other places he'll explore. When Father Monster suggests that Little Monster might be lonely in space, Little Monster wisely responds that some situations require that you tolerate loneliness. He knows that it would be okay to return to his parents after his adventure. From this interesting story, kids can learn about the complex idea of being big enough to explore outer space without giving up the littleness of returning to their parents.

Ages: 3–7   **Cultural context:** N/A

Owen by Kevin Henkes. 24 pages Greenwillow, 1993.
Children can struggle with themselves and adults when they think that growing up means they can't be little any more. Owen has a blanket that he's loved from birth. His parents, with prodding from their neighbor, Mrs. Tweezers, try to get him to give up the blanket, but he'll have none of it. Finally, his mother gets the "positively perfect" idea to make the blanket into hankies. Even Mrs. Tweezers finds it acceptable for a big boy to carry a hankie everywhere, and Owen can always have part of the blanket with him. By transforming this symbolic object, the story offers children a way to grow up without having to give up their "little" self.
Ages: 3–6   **Cultural context:** N/A

Raccoon on His Own by Jim Arnosky. 32 pages Putnam, 2001.
It can be scary and exhilarating to be on your own, but it doesn't mean you have to give up being little. As his mother and siblings dig through the mud, looking for crawfish, a little raccoon—more curious than hungry—climbs into a boat instead. His family's digging allows the boat to float away, and suddenly unable to return to the bank, the raccoon feels alone and frightened. With his family in the misty background, as if in his memory, he finds his own reflection to keep him company. Relying on himself, the raccoon avoids dangerous animals in the swamp and curiously notices harmless ones. Finally, the boat reaches another shore, and he's reunited with his family, showing kids that they can be on their own safely and still return to being little with their parents.
Ages: 2–5   **Cultural context:** N/A

Something From Nothing by Phoebe Gilman. 32 pages Scholastic, 1992.
As we grow up, we can keep our little self with us in an altered form. Joseph's grandfather makes him a special baby blanket. When the blanket gets old, his mother tells him to throw it out. He replies confidently that Grandpa will be able to fix it—and Grandpa does, by making it into a jacket. Each time it needs to be fixed, there is enough material for something smaller—a vest, a tie, a handkerchief, and finally a button. When the button gets lost, there is "enough material" for the story of the blanket. The wisdom of this story is that the changes in the blanket parallel the ways in which a child's need for a

comforting object gets smaller and smaller with maturation, and can finally be met by a story.

Ages: 3–8   **Cultural context:** European-American

Strong to the Hoop **by John Coy. Illus. by Leslie Jean-Bart. 32 pages Lee & Low, 1999.**
Kids can have short periods of being big on their way to growing up. James is considered too small to play basketball with his brother's friends, but when one older player is injured, James gets his chance. In spite of feeling picked on by the opponent he's assigned to guard, with his brother's encouragement, James scores the winning points for his team. The striking illustrations use a unique Polaroid transfer technique that incorporates drawing and collage. By reading this story, kids can use imagination to try out being big even while they're still small.

Ages: 7–10   **Cultural context:** Multicultural
Main character's cultural background: African-American

The Ticky-Tacky Doll **by Cynthia Rylant. Illus. by Harvey Stevenson. 32 pages Harcourt, 2002.**
The thought of giving up your "little" self can lead to genuine grief. A girl has a special doll that her Grandmama made, but she isn't allowed to bring it when she starts school. She's so sad at school that she doesn't learn and won't even eat. Upon hearing the problem, Grandmama makes the little girl a tiny "child" doll that she can hide in her book bag. Knowing that the little doll is with her, the girl is happy at school and begins to learn. This sweet story encourages kids to take part of their little self along as they take on more grown-up challenges.

Ages: 3–7   **Cultural context:** European-American

When You Grow Up **by Lennie Goodings. Illus. by Jenny Jones. 26 pages Fogelman, 2001.**
Part of growing up is using make-believe to experiment with being big. Zachary contemplates lots of possible careers—but after each work-related adventure he imagines, he sees himself as coming home to live with Mom. When they finally talk about Zachary growing up to be a daddy, he decides that his new family will live next door to Mom. There's

room in Zachary and Mom's world for him to imagine himself being big while acknowledging that he's little. Although he realizes that he when he gets *really* big, he won't be able to live with Mom, he understands that being big doesn't mean giving up his connection to her.

Ages: 2–5   Cultural context: N/A

CHAPTER 12

Learning to Use the Potty

Learning to use the potty is an important task of growing up. Using the potty is one of the many things that kids learn to do independently as they mature. Many children learn in a relatively straightforward way when they're ready; others may refuse the potty at first, but eventually accept it out of curiosity or even a wish for grown-up underwear. Because it can take time to learn, and also because it can be difficult for kids to stop doing other things when it's time to use the potty, accidents are a normal part of the learning process. Parents' patience with, acceptance of, and pride in the child are important in helping kids learn to use the potty. This chapter first summarizes books about beginning potty use, and then addresses stories about bedwetting in children who already stay dry in the daytime.

I've identified many of the books about initial potty learning as being appropriate for children one to three years old. Few children are ready to start potty learning before their second birthday, and a great many won't complete the process until well into their three's, so there's probably not much need for these books before a child reaches the age of two. However, it may be helpful for some kids to have exposure to some of these books before that time so that when they do reach a stage of readiness, the stories will be familiar.

POTTY LEARNING

Annie's Potty **by Judith Caseley. 24 pages Greenwillow, 1990.**
At first, Annie refuses the potty that Mama brings home for her. She's not at all swayed by Mama's attempts to tempt her with underpants with bunnies on them, saying that she's a baby and doesn't want to be a big girl. But Annie can't help being interested in adults' and other children's use of the toilet, and tries out the potty on her own. She's proud of her successes with it, but when she has an accident, she gets discouraged and says she's no longer a big girl. Luckily, Mama knows just how to reassure her. Children who aren't quite ready for the potty will benefit from seeing Annie move into a state of readiness, use the potty successfully and proudly, and tolerate accidents.
Ages: 1–3   **Cultural context:** European-American

Everyone Poops **by Taro Gomi. Translated by Amanda Mayer Stinchecum. 27 pages Kane/Miller, 1993.**
Some toddlers who hesitate to use the potty have concerns about poop. The author matter-of-factly comments that different animals' poop differs in size, color, shape, and smell. They also poop in different ways—stopping or moving, anywhere or in a special place, with or without cleaning up. Adults and children poop, and some children use the potty and some use diapers. Although this book says almost nothing about the potty-training process, its straightforward approach to poop will help make pooping less of a big deal to some children. The contrasting pictures of a screaming baby pooping in a diaper and a broadly smiling child flushing convey a positive message about pooping in the toilet.
Ages: 1–3   **Cultural context:** Asian

Going to the Potty by Fred Rogers. Illus. by Jim Judkis.
32 pages Putnam, 1986.
Toilet learning is presented in the context of the many things children can do for themselves now that they are not babies. In this reassuring, empathic book, Mr. Rogers characterizes accidents as a normal part of the learning process. He tells children that learning to use to the potty will please both them and their parents. A reassuring note to parents is included. Illustrated with color photographs, this straightforward book shows children the potty-learning process, providing them with the capability to approach it with self-acceptance and anticipation of pride.
Ages: 1–3   **Cultural context:** Multicultural

I Have to Go! A Sesame Street Toddler Book by Anna Ross.
Illus. by Norman Gorbaty. 20 pages Random House, 1990.
Some toddlers have difficulty stopping what they're doing to use the bathroom. In this story, Little Grover stops riding his choo-choo and declines several invitations to play because he "has to go." As his friends wonder where he so urgently has to go, he runs home, where his mommy proudly helps him use the potty. There's a clear advantage to interrupting play to go potty: kids will feel good about themselves.
Ages: 1–3   **Cultural context:** N/A

KoKo Bear's New Potty: A Practical Parenting Read-Together Book by Vicki Lansky. Illus. by Jane Prince. **32 pages Bantam, 1986.**
As children grow up, they learn to do more things independently, including using the potty. KoKo learns about the difference between the ways wet and dry diapers feel, and is pleased when PaPa brings home a just-right potty chair. KoKo enjoys trying out the potty, and MaMa is proud when KoKo first pees in it. Having learned about flushing and washing hands, KoKo gets to wear Big-Bear pants. Soon KoKo learns to use an adapter seat on the toilet. MaMa Bear reassures KoKo when an accident occurs, reminding KoKo that it isn't time to wear the Big-Bear pants at night yet. This story has a gentle feel, and KoKo's parents are patient, proud, and loving. There is a brief introduction for parents, and each page includes text for

parents about helping children with potty learning. Through the character of KoKo, children will gain a clear, positive understanding of the entire potty-learning process.

Ages: 1–3   **Cultural context:** N/A

My Big Boy Potty **and** *My Big Girl Potty* **by Joanna Cole. Illus. by Maxie Chambliss. 24 pages HarperCollins, 2000.**

These two books are the same except for the gender of the main character (and the inclusion of a sentence about Daddy teaching the boy to pee standing up). Using a matter-of-fact, reassuring approach, they describe how a child learns to use the potty. The first few "potty times," nothing comes out; when something does, the child's parents are proud. After some practice and skill acquisition, the child picks out big-kid underpants. The parents are reassuring when the child has an accident and children are encouraged to anticipate feeling proud when they've learned to use the potty. Suggestions for parents are included. One possible limitation is that pee and poop are described as going "into pipes under the house"; children may wonder whether they stay under the house indefinitely. But, in general, these books give children a clear, encouraging introduction to potty learning, and the watercolor illustrations have real charm.

Ages: 1–3   **Cultural context:** European-American

On Your Potty **by Virginia Miller. 26 pages Greenwillow, 1991.**

Many kids are in a "no!" phase around the same time as potty learning. Ba, a little bear, generally responds "Nah!" to big bear George's questions. When George asks whether Ba needs his potty, Ba responds with several emphatic "nah"s, but George firmly tells him to sit on the potty. Ba complies, but nothing comes out. George sends Bartholomew out to play, and while playing, Ba suddenly recalls George's command to sit on the potty, using George's words to describe his own sensation. He races home just in time. He's proud, and George gives him a big hug. The illustrations charmingly and simply and convey the characters' emotions. Ba is a good role model for using the potty when you need to, even if your favorite word is "nah."

Ages: 1–3   **Cultural context:** N/A

Potty Time by Guido Van Genechten. 26 pages
Simon & Schuster, 2000.
For some children, the appeal of the potty is that it's "just right" for them. In this simple, funny, story, Joe announces that it's time for potty. Each of the animals, from an elephant to a mouse, has a potty that's just right for its own kind of bottom, and Joe finds his own potty for his bottom. When Joe has used the potty, he compliments himself, giving this story a nice emphasis on the sense of pride that toddlers get from using the potty.
Ages: 1–3   **Cultural context:** European-American

Sara's Potty and *Max's Potty* by Harriet Ziefert.
Illus. by Emily Bolam. 18 pages DK, 1999.
Some kids seem to linger in a transition between playing with the potty and using it for its intended purpose. Like their toy animals, the children in these stories don't sit on the potty yet; they play with it and put toys in it. As the story goes on, the children pee and poop in the potty, and the author compliments them. The children then wash their hands, and on the next page, wear big-kid underpants. The author cheers for the children, who no longer wear diapers. These books might be a good choice for a child who is somewhat reluctant to try the potty, and who already plays with it rather than sitting on it or peeing and pooping in it. The characters model a transition from wearing diapers and playing with the potty to using the potty appropriately and not needing diapers anymore.
Ages: 1–3   **Cultural context:** European-American

Time to Pee! by Mo Willems. 34 pages Hyperion, 2003.
This story tells kids what to do when they get "that funny feeling" (and you'll know exactly what feeling from the kids' body language). They can use those times as an opportunity to demonstrate their increasing maturity by going to the bathroom. Detailed instructions are given, assuring children that it won't take long and that everything will still be there when they're done. Kids are encouraged to be proud, and are reminded that if they aren't successful the first time, they'll have other chances. A chart and stickers are included. Overall, this story offers children information and encouragement in a good-humored context.
Ages: 1–3   **Cultural context:** Multicultural

What to Expect When You Use the Potty **by Heidi E. Murkoff.**
Illus. by Laura Rader. 26 pages Harper Festival, 2000.
Cheerful, chatty, matter-of-fact Angus the Answer Dog narrates this
book, telling children not only about using the potty, but where pee-pee
and poop come from and where they go after you flush. It includes an
enormous amount of detail about subjects such as what poops look and
smell like, and why you should wipe and how to learn (Angus suggests
putting jam on a doll's bottom to practice). Accidents are addressed
supportively, and there's also encouragement along with all the information. For a child who likes lots of details, this book would be an
especially good choice.

Ages: 2–4   **Cultural context:** Multicultural

You Can Go to the Potty **by William Sears, Martha Sears, and**
Christie Watts Kelly. Illus. by Renée Andriani. 32 pages
Little, Brown, 2002.
This book introduces potty learning by explaining in an encouraging
tone that when you were a baby, you needed your parents' help with
a lot of things, but now you can do a lot for yourself. The authors describe the stages of potty learning in a way that expresses confidence
in the child's ability; for example, "When you feel the pee-pee coming,
just say, 'Go pee-pee!'" The book both acknowledges parents' pride in
the child's growing independence, and reassures the child that the parents are still there to help when that's needed. The illustrations have
a sweet, but not fussy, quality, and the text includes a note to parents
about potty learning and sidebars that answer some of children's more
complex questions about toileting. In a warm, accepting tone, this book
gives children lots of helpful information about potty learning.

Ages: 1–3   **Cultural context:** European-American

Your New Potty **by Joanna Cole. Illus. by Margaret Miller.**
40 pages Morrow, 1989.
Illustrated with color photographs, this book follows Steffie and Ben as
they learn to use their new potties. Using the potty is presented as one
of many things that kids learn to do independently as they grow from
babies into children. It's fun and a source of pride. Both children have
occasional accidents and help clean up when that happens. Parents

are shown as patient and accepting. A note to parents is included. Children will understand what happens during potty learning in a matter-of-fact, self-accepting, positive way.

Ages: 1–3   **Cultural context:** African-American, European-American

BEDWETTING

Do Little Mermaids Wet Their Beds? **by Jeanne Willis.**
Illus. by Penelope Jossen. 30 pages Whitman, 2001.
Cecelia is a smart, capable four-year-old who wets her bed. She has a dream of playing with a mermaid, who reassures her that she, too, used to wet her bed. The mermaid adds that bed-wetting does not last forever, and besides, a small puddle is insignificant compared to the ocean. Cecelia wakes up in a dry bed from this dream, although, mysteriously, her coat and hat are wet. A note for parents is included, and this empathic story lets kids know that bedwetting is temporary and not a big deal.

Ages: 3–7   **Cultural context:** European-American

Dry Days, Wet Nights **by Maribeth Boelts.**
Illus. by Kathy Parkinson. 32 pages Whitman, 1994.
Little Bunny (LB), who uses the potty during the day, decides that he's ready to sleep without a diaper. But after many nights of wetting the bed, LB feels ashamed of being a "baby." His mama reassures him that he just isn't ready to stay dry at night, and his papa reminds him that lots of other bunnies his age wet the bed. One night, LB is finally dry and very proud. A note for parents is included. This book is a good choice for families who are willing to get up at night and change wet sheets and pajamas repeatedly. Children will get lots of reassurance that bedwetting is normal, and they'll stay dry at night when their bodies are ready.

Ages: 3–6   **Cultural context:** N/A

CHAPTER 13

Starting School or Day Care

Starting kindergarten or day care is an important event in a child's life. Stories about kindergarten, preschool, and day care are grouped together in this chapter because of the similarities in the child's experience: being away from home in a group setting, usually with peers and a new adult in charge. Children will have a range of reactions to this experience, including curiosity about what school is like, excitement about being more grown-up, worries about whether they'll be able to get their needs met, sadness about separation from parents and home, and a sense of stress about changes in their routines.

See also *Chrysanthemum* (Chapter 2), *Wemberly Worried* (Chapter 7), *Owen* and *The Ticky-Tacky Doll* (Chapter 11), *Stand Tall, Molly Lou Melon* (Chapter 21), *Marianthe's Story* (Chapter 22), *Bill and Pete* (Chapter 28), and *The Color of Home* (Chapter 33) for other stories about starting school.

Adam's Daycare by Julie Ovenell-Carter. Illus. by Ruth Ohi.
32 pages Annick, 1997.

Readers follow Adam, a preschooler, as he spends a day at a home-based day care. The kids are shown as cooperative and friendly, and day care is depicted as a fun, safe place. The children play firefighters, make crowns, walk to the mailbox, make sand pies, and listen to a story. They look for slugs on the sidewalk and watch a worm in the sandbox. When the caregiver's dog eats another child's cupcake, Adam shares his. Parents and children are shown in loving relationships, as Adam gives his mom a big hug and lots of kisses when she drops him off and jumps into her arms when she comes to pick him up. Adam's attachment to his caregiver is also acknowledged as he waves to her on his way home at the end of the day. Letting children know that their feelings about separation are understood, this book reassures them that home-based day care is a fun place where their needs will be met.

Ages: 2–5 **Cultural context:** Multicultural
Main character's cultural background: European-American

Beginning School by Irene Smalls. Illus. by Toni Goffe.
32 pages Silver Press, 1996.

School can be so full of interesting things to do that kids may adjust while they're busy doing other things. Readers follow Alicia as she begins school, through the first, second, and third days, the second week, the second month, and winter holiday time. The emphasis is mostly on what Alicia sees and does at school and how she adjusts, with less on separation from home. Class activities include hearing stories, eating snacks and lunch, learning songs, playing, coloring shapes, writing letters, watching the class snake shed its skin, going on field trips, celebrating birthdays and holidays, and having class pictures taken. By the second month, Alicia feels almost as if she's always been at school, helping children anticipate feeling comfortable later on even if they don't at first. Educating children about what school is like, this story encourages positive expectations.

Ages: 4–6 **Cultural context:** Multicultural
Main character's cultural background: African-American

Billy and the Big New School by Laurence Anholt.
Illus. by Catherine Anholt. 32 pages Whitman, 1997.
This story is less about starting school for the first time than about starting a new school. Billy, a little boy who loves birds, is both excited and worried about this. A little sparrow in his yard who is picked on by other birds needs some gentle care, and Billy makes it a safe indoor nest out of a shoebox. When the sparrow is ready to fly off into the world, it's time for Billy to go to the new school, and with the help of Billy's mom, both meet their challenges. Billy's teacher is nice and helps make sure all his needs are met, and he makes friends at his new school. This leaves him feeling stronger and happier. Through the joined image of Billy and the sparrow, children will see that even though a new school can be intimidating, it may not be as scary as they expect, and in the end they'll find the strength to be successful there.

Ages: 3–7   **Cultural context:** Multicultural
Main character's cultural background: European-American

Bye, Bye! by Nancy Kaufmann. Illus. by Jung-Hee Spetter.
26 pages Front Street, 2003.
In this simply worded story, the separation involved in starting school also brings new attachments. When Daddy tries to leave a little pig at preschool, the little one is hesitant, running after him at first but then joining the other animal children in playing, held safely by the teacher. The end of the day comes quickly, and the little pig rides home on Daddy's shoulders, waving bye-bye to the teacher. This story offers reassurance that even if you worry about separation around the start of school, you can have fun without your parents and make new connections with your teacher and classmates.

Ages: 1–3   **Cultural context:** N/A

Don't Go! by Jane Breskin Zalben. 32 pages Clarion, 2001.
Separation can be a difficult part of starting school. When Daniel goes to preschool for the first time, he's scared and doesn't know any of the children. He cries and asks his mother not to go. He declines his teacher's invitations to participate in class activities. When his mother gives him a photo of the two of them together, she assures him that she'll always come back. With this security, he's able to say a special goodbye

to her and sit with the other children while she waits at the door. Other children invite Daniel to play, and his mother waves goodbye. Daniel has fun with his new friends, and the class bakes cookies. When he's sad at nap time, he keeps the photo close to him, and this helps him feel better. This book includes a checklist for the first day of preschool, a note about ways to help kids prepare, and a recipe for the cookies that Daniel's class made. Children who worry about separation will find both realistic empathy and much reassurance in this gentle story.

Ages: 2–5 **Cultural context:** N/A

First Day, Hooray! **by Nancy Poydar. 32 pages Holiday House, 1999.**

Ivy Green vividly expresses the excitement and worries that many kids feel on the first day of school. What if she misses the bus? What if someone forgets to bring lunch? What if she can't find her classroom? Meanwhile, the school bus driver, custodian, principal, and Ivy's teacher are also getting ready for the big day. Everyone dreams about their first-day worries. Finally, the big day dawns, and everything happens as it should. Ivy listens to stories, eats crackers, stacks blocks, paints pictures, and writes her name, offering a calm reminder that the anticipation does end and things go well.

Ages: 3–7 **Cultural context:** Multicultural

Main character's cultural background: European-American

Going to Day Care **by Fred Rogers. Illus. by Jim Judkis. 32 pages Putnam, 1985.**

When they start day care, children have a range of feelings and questions. Mr. Rogers explains that day care is when "other grown-ups . . . take care of their children" at times "when moms and dads have to be away from home at the same time." The book shows various day care activities and facilities. Mr. Rogers reassures children that their needs will be met at day care, while acknowledging that it may be hard to adjust. Using direct questions, he encourages children to think about their wishes and feelings. From both practical and emotional perspectives, this book helps children anticipate what day care will be like and prepare for it.

Ages: 1–5 **Cultural context:** Multicultural

How Did You Grow So Big, So Soon? **by Anne Bowen.**
Illus. by Marni Backer. 32 pages Carolrhoda, 2003.
Starting school is a step in growing up, and when children reach this stage they've already grown up in many ways. On the night before a boy's first day of school, he and his mama remember how little he used to be and recall the many steps he's taken in growing up: learning to talk, sing, tell stories, walk, ride a bike, and swing high on the swings. Mama tells the boy what he'll do at school and assures him that if he's scared, his bear, who has helped him with other fears, can come with him. She also assures him that she won't be alone while he is at school, because he'll be with her as she thinks of him. Although some readers might find this story sentimental, it's helpful for conveying to kids that they've already coped successfully with lots of new, challenging situations that they can use to cope with starting school.

Ages: 3–6   **Cultural context:** European-American

I Am NOT Going to School Today! **by Robie H. Harris.**
Illus. by Jan Ormerod. 32 pages McElderry, 2003.
Unfamiliarity can be a difficult part of starting school, and this book deals with how this scary notion can cause doubts. The night before the first day of school, a boy sets out school clothes and packs his backpack, but when he goes to bed, he decides that it isn't a good idea to go to school the next day after all because it will feel too new and strange. He decides to wait until the second day to go, because on the second day, everything will be familiar. The next morning, he protests that his stuffed animal, Hank, needs him to stay home. Mommy points out that Hank can go to school with him, and Hank will be okay there because he knows the boy. At this, the boy agrees to go. When he gets to school, all his questions are answered without his having to ask, and he finds that he likes school. Addressing concerns about the newness of the school experience, this book is a good choice for kids who worry about unfamiliar places.

Ages: 2–6.   **Cultural context:** Multicultural
Main character's cultural background: European-American

The Kissing Hand by Audrey Penn. Illus. by Ruth E. Harper
and Nancy M. Leak. 32 pages
Child Welfare League of America, 1993.
Like Chester, kids may be afraid to go to school, anticipating missing
their mother, friends, and familiar surroundings. Chester's mother
responds empathically to these fears and points out some of the good
things about school. Most important, she shares a secret called the
Kissing Hand. She gives Chester a kiss on his palm and tells him that
whenever he misses her, all he has to do is press the kissed hand to
his cheek and remind himself that she loves him. Feeling very safe,
Chester gives his mother a Kissing Hand, too, and easily goes off to
school. By showing children that their parents' love goes with them
wherever they are, this warm story will help children manage the
separation involved in going to school.
Ages: 2–6   **Cultural context:** N/A

Look Out Kindergarten, Here I Come! by Nancy Carlson.
32 pages Viking, 1999.
Children's feelings about starting school may fluctuate, with periods
of excitement and periods of worry. Henry is very excited about all
the fun he'll have when he starts kindergarten, but when he and his
mom arrive at school, he's apprehensive. However, once he's seen some
familiar sights and made a new friend, he's ready to stay and enjoy
school. The colorful, cheerful artwork adds to the positive tone of the
story. Helping kids understand that their worries are temporary, this
tale will allow them to be comfortable with the idea that although they
might worry, it won't last.
Ages: 4–6   **Cultural context:** N/A

Pete and Polo's Big School Adventure by Adrian Reynolds.
25 pages Orchard, 2000.
Many kids will have mixed feelings about starting school. When it's
time for Pete's first day at preschool without Mom, he's excited about
this adventure, but his teddy bear, Polo, who carries Pete's vulnerable
feelings, is apprehensive. When another child makes a remark that
could hurt Polo's feelings, Pete stands up for Polo, and readers feel
confident that Pete can take care of his own scared feelings. Although

Polo starts the school day feeling different because he's the lone white bear among the other brown ones, his color turns out to be an advantage when it's time for Pete to find him. At the end of the day, Pete and Polo agree that school is a great adventure. This story demonstrates to kids that even if they feel scared at school at first, they can not only find strength to cope, but also can have fun.

Ages: 2–5   **Cultural context:** European-American

Sumi's First Day of School Ever by Soyung Pak.
Illus. by Joung Un Kim. 32 pages Viking, 2003.
Sumi, who is from Korea, starts school in the United States. Her mother has taught her how to recognize and respond when people ask her name in English. At first, Sumi experiences school as a lonely, scary, mean place. One child shows behavior that seems racist, "squishing" his eyes, but after the teacher talks to him, he says something to Sumi that sounds nice to her. When her kind teacher hangs Sumi's drawing on the wall, school doesn't seem so scary, and she's even able to use the few words of English that her mother has taught her to make a friend. Children can use Sumi's example to tolerate the initial discomforts of school long enough to discover its positive aspects. Children who are starting school where a language other than their own is spoken will especially identify with Sumi's experience.

Ages: 3–7   **Cultural context:** Multicultural
Main character's cultural background: Asian American

What Will Mommy Do When I'm at School?
by Dolores Johnson. 32 pages Macmillan, 1990.
Although starting school brings separation, it also brings new people and experiences. When a girl starts school for the first time, she worries about how her mom will manage on her own while she's at school. Her worries have a remarkable resemblance to the worries children have for themselves; for example, she worries that Mom might get scared or lonely without her. This resourceful girl thinks of solutions to these problems—telling Mom all about what she's learned, bringing home her artwork, and introducing her new friends to Mom—that will help with her own fears as well. At the end, Mom tells the girl

that she's starting a new job, and they look forward together to how much they'll have to tell each other when they get home each day. The girl has learned something important about her ability to maintain a connection with Mom even when they're in different places, doing different things.

Ages: 4–6　　　**Cultural context:** African-American

When Mommy and Daddy Go to Work **by Joanna Cole. Illus. by Maxie Chambliss. 24 pages HarperCollins, 2001.**

When her daddy goes to work teaching school and her mommy goes to work selling cars, preschooler Carly stays at day care with her toy horse, Oatis. Although she's sad to say goodbye in the morning, she's soon having fun doing lots of interesting things with her friends. She keeps her parents with her by thinking about what they're doing at work, and there's lots of reassurance that parents always come back. A generally useful page of "tips for parents" is limited by the statement that "children who have had quality child care turn out fine," as if parents were assuming that this might not be the case. Children can take from this story a good model for coping with workday separation from parents, while gaining an understanding of what happens at day care and reassurance that it's an enjoyable place.

Ages: 1–5　　　**Cultural context:** Multicultural

Main character's cultural background: European-American

[CHAPTER 14]

Losing a Tooth

L osing a first tooth can carry important meanings related to growing up. Like other aspects of growing up, it involves both a loss of
part of a younger self and a transition into a new, more mature, sense
of self. Although many children happily look forward to losing their
first tooth —often with real impatience—it's also common to have
mixed feelings about losing a tooth, and some kids just don't want to.
Losing a tooth is a physical change that involves unique sensations.
There are also interpersonal aspects to the process. Sometimes a child
is very excited to have a loose tooth, but no one seems to share the
child's excitement. On the other hand, kids who lose teeth late may
feel different or left out, and other children may tease them until they
finally lose a tooth.

See also *It's Okay to Be Different* (Chapter 2), which assures
kids that it's all right to have a tooth—or a few teeth—missing.
Sam's Science: I Know Why I Brush My Teeth (Chapter 28) gives
kids information about dental anatomy, physiology, and hygiene in
the context of a conversation between a boy with a loose tooth and
his mother.

Arthur's Tooth by Marc Brown. 32 pages Little, Brown, 1985.

It's hard to be the last one in your class to lose a tooth, as Arthur is at age seven. Although he does have a loose tooth, he's discouraged. It doesn't help that his classmates are mean, teasing him about being a "baby" and excluding him from games. Arthur's dentist assures him that he's good at waiting and that everyone's timetable for losing baby teeth is different. When a classmate bumps into him by accident, his tooth finally falls out. This story will provide reassurance for kids who are later than average to lose teeth and subjected to other kids' nastiness as a result.

Ages: 4–9   **Cultural context:** N/A

Dear Tooth Fairy by Pamela Duncan Edwards.
Illus. by Marie-Louise Fitzpatrick. 26 pages
HarperCollins/Katherine Tegen, 2003.

Anticipation of losing a first tooth can be both worrisome and exciting. Six-year-old Claire can hardly wait to lose her first tooth, but she doesn't even have a loose one yet. She writes to the tooth fairy, expressing her worry. Soon the tooth fairy writes back, assuring Claire that she'll definitely lose her teeth, explaining that some kids don't lose their first tooth till they're older than Claire, and encouraging her to take good care of her teeth. When Claire has her first loose tooth, she excitedly shares the news with the tooth fairy. Soon after she starts to wonder whether it will ever come out, it does. The tooth fairy writes to her, telling her how beautiful, clean, and special her tooth is. Offering children empathy with the anticipation of losing a first tooth, this story reassures them that it will happen eventually, and when it does, it will be as wonderful as they imagine.

Ages: 4–8   **Cultural context:** Multicultural
Main character's cultural background: unclear

Franklin and the Tooth Fairy by Paulette Bourgeois.
Illus. by Brenda Clark. 32 pages Kids Can, 1995.

Kids can mistake losing a tooth for not just one aspect of growing up, but the *only* sign of maturation. Franklin feels different from his friends because he hasn't lost any teeth yet, but because he's a turtle, he doesn't even have teeth. When Franklin learns that losing teeth means that you're growing up, he sadly wonders whether this means he'll never grow up. His friends tell him about the tooth fairy, and he tries to fool her. That doesn't work, but instead, his parents give him a present to celebrate his growing up so he doesn't feel different from his friends. Although losing teeth means that they're growing up, with this tale, kids see that they can still be growing up even if they haven't lost teeth.

Ages: 5–8   **Cultural context:** N/A

I Have a Loose Tooth **by Sally Noll. 32 pages**
Greenwillow, 1992.
When children have their first loose tooth, they often want to share the excitement. Molly wakes up with her first loose tooth and tries to tell everyone about it. To her dismay and frustration, everyone misinterprets what she's said; for example, one lady thinks she's introducing herself as "Luce Ruth." Finally, she writes her message on her Nanny's birthday card, and Nanny acknowledges the importance of Molly's good news, offering empathy for children who feel that others aren't sharing their excitement about a loose tooth.

Ages: 4–7   **Cultural context:** Multicultural
Main character's cultural background: European-American

Jane vs. the Tooth Fairy **by Betsy Jay. Illus. by Lori Osiecki.**
32 pages Rising Moon, 2000.
Sometimes losing a tooth feels like a loss. Jane definitely does *not* want to part with her first wiggly tooth, which she's had all her life. She wishes for dentures like Grandma's, only to find out that she has to grow her teeth back. When Grandma tells Jane that her teeth fell out because she hadn't brushed them enough, Jane concludes that brushing a lot will keep from losing her tooth, but the tooth falls out while she's brushing. Although she's heard that the tooth fairy will give her $1, she wants $3.50 to buy an art set. Grandma helps her decorate the tooth to make it "fancy" and worth $3.50—and the tooth fairy apparently agrees. The illustrations add to the humor of this story. Children who have mixed feelings about giving up their baby teeth will find

empathy with Jane and, if they're knowledgeable, will find humor in her many misconceptions. But only choose this one if you're willing to pay more for a "fancy" tooth.

Ages: 5–8   **Cultural context:** European-American

Little Rabbit's Loose Tooth **by Lucy Bate.**
Illus. by Diane DeGroat. 32 pages Crown, 1975.
Children sometimes have mixed feelings about giving up their baby teeth. When Little Rabbit loses her first tooth while eating ice cream, she has a new "window" in her mouth. She's unsure whether there's a tooth fairy, and whether she wants to give the tooth to her. She offers some charming speculations about what the tooth fairy will do with her tooth: give it to a baby rabbit, use it to make stars, or say a magic spell to turn it into a dime. She decides to leave her tooth for the tooth fairy, but, still unsure about the fairy's existence, asks Mother Rabbit to leave a present under her pillow if the tooth fairy hasn't done so. Little Rabbit wakes up to find a dime under her pillow, just as Mother Rabbit had predicted. In the context of an encouraging ending, this story both acknowledges some of the sensations children experience with a lost tooth and some of the fairly complex emotions they might have.

Ages: 4–7   **Cultural context:** N/A

Loose Tooth **by Lola M. Schaefer. Illus. by Sylvie Wickstrom.**
32 pages HarperCollins, 2004.
The anticipation of losing a tooth can be both exciting and frustrating. A boy is excited to wake up with a loose tooth, wiggling it for everyone in the family, including the dog, but the boy is frustrated that his tooth won't come out, even when he eats apples, nuts, and carrots. His brother suggests pulling it out, but it falls out on its own. As the story ends, the boy has a hole where the tooth had been. This story assures children that teeth will come out when they're ready, and many children around the age to be losing their first tooth will be able to read this book themselves.

Ages: 5–7   **Cultural context:** European-American

The Lost Tooth Club by Arden Johnson.
33 pages Tricycle, 1998.
When you're the only one among your friends who hasn't lost a tooth, it can feel as if you're excluded from an exclusive club. This is what happens to Olivia, whose friends literally have a club for kids who have lost a tooth. The club plans a soft-food party, wears special badges, and draws pictures of how they lost their first tooth. Olivia tries to trick these kids into believing she's lost a tooth, but the tricks don't work. While stomping over to the clubhouse to tell them that she's starting her own club, she trips over her dog and her tooth falls out. Her friends finally welcome her to the club. Children will realize that although they feel left out if they haven't lost a tooth, at least kids' lives don't revolve around that fact as they do in this story. They'll also understand that eventually they will lose that first tooth.

Ages: 5–8   **Cultural context:** Multicultural
Main character's cultural background: European-American

My Tooth Is About to Fall Out by Grace Maccarone.
Illus. by Betsy Lewin. 32 pages Cartwheel, 1995.
Kids may wonder what to expect when they lose a tooth. In this story, a girl's loose tooth falls out while she's eating. In very simple language, the story describes the sensations of a loose and then missing tooth. The girl happily anticipates the tooth fairy's visit. She enjoys her new "big-kid smile" and looks forward to how great her permanent teeth will look. With a straightforward, positive approach to losing a tooth, this story conveys real understanding of how it feels, preparing readers who may be apprehensive about the physical sensation.

Ages: 3–6   **Cultural context:** European-American

The Real Tooth Fairy by Marilyn Kaye. Illus. by Helen
Cogancherry. 32 pages Harcourt Brace Jovanovich, 1990.
This story gives a satisfying answer to children's questions about who the tooth fairy *really* is. Elise wants to see the tooth fairy, so she stays awake and sees her mother put a quarter under her pillow. She's thrilled to have a mother who has such a special occupation, but her friend Ben claims that his father is the tooth fairy—he's seen him.

Elise brings the question to her mother, who explains that once a child was frightened because the tooth fairy was a stranger, so after that, she magically appeared looking like someone the child knows. When Elise loses another tooth, she has a wonderful dream of a tooth fairy who looks just like her mother but is momentarily transformed into a beautiful winged being. In the end, the tooth fairy looks like Elise's mother again, but is no less beautiful. This sweet story will allow children to hold both their belief in the tooth fairy and their logical knowledge that it's their parents.

Ages: 4–8   **Cultural context:** Multicultural

Main character's cultural background: European-American

Rosie's Baby Tooth **by Maryann MacDonald. Illus. by Melissa Sweet. 32 pages Atheneum, 1991.**

Losing a tooth can feel like losing a part of yourself. When Rosie loses her first baby tooth, her friend tells her to leave it for the tooth fairy, but she doesn't want to lose it. Her sense of loss is also expressed in her experience of feeling that she looks different without the tooth, and her decision that she doesn't want to lose any more teeth. Rosie writes the tooth fairy a letter saying that the tooth came out, but is gone. The tooth fairy writes back, offering to put the tooth on a necklace for her, so she can wear it always. Gentle and empathic, this story offers acceptance to children who are experiencing the loss of teeth as the loss of a part of themselves.

Ages: 5–8   **Cultural context:** N/A

Throw Your Tooth on the Roof: Tooth Traditions From Around the World **by Selby B. Beeler. Illus. by G. Brian Karas. 32 pages Houghton Mifflin, 1998.**

While in the United States (and some other English-speaking countries) children put a lost baby tooth under their pillow and wait for the tooth fairy to leave money, there are other traditions in other countries. Arranged by continent, these brief first-person vignettes describe childhood tooth-loss traditions around the world. Some traditions feature a mouse or rat that takes away the tooth and leaves money. Many countries have traditions that include throwing the tooth on the roof.

In some cultures, traditions emphasize the wish for the permanent teeth to grow in straight, or for an animal to bring the child a tooth that is better than the one that fell out. An afterword explains the difference between primary and permanent teeth, shows the composition of teeth, and describes the different kinds of human teeth. This book celebrates the universality of losing teeth and (nearly always) acknowledging the importance of this event.

Ages: 5–10   **Cultural context:** Multicultural

Trouble on the T-Ball Team **by Eve Bunting.**
Illus. by Irene Trivas. 32 pages Clarion, 1997.
Losing teeth can seem like a mysterious process. Linda begins this story by telling the reader that her T-ball teammates are inexplicably losing something. She tells about the circumstances under which each kid loses "one." Not until the almost end of the story does she reveal that she's talking about teeth. She expresses mixed feelings about losing teeth, although being last among her teammates makes her feel left out. While hitting a home run, she finally loses a tooth, making her excited and proud to be part of the team. Kids who like mysteries will enjoy this story, which gives reassurance that everyone does eventually lose that first tooth.

Ages: 6–8   **Cultural context:** Multicultural
Main character's cultural background: European-American

PART 5

FAMILIES AND FAMILY CHANGES

CHAPTER 15

All Kinds
of Families

There are lots of kinds of families; for example, large and small families, families of different cultural backgrounds, and families formed by birth, adoption, remarriage, or foster care. When families include children, different kinds of adults act as parents to them; for example, straight or gay couples, single parents, stepparents, other relatives such as grandparents, and foster parents. But all families share commonalities in loving and caring for each other.

***Families* by Ann Morris. Illus. by various photographers. 32 pages HarperCollins, 2000.**
Illustrated with photographs of families from many different cultures and countries, this simply worded book introduces children to diverse families. It shows families working, playing, cooking, eating, and celebrating together, and loving one another "even on bad days." Kids see that families come in many sizes, and that children may live with a

mother and father, one parent, stepparent(s), grandparents, or foster parents. Adoptive families are also mentioned. Overall, this leaves readers with a sense that all families belong to a world community.

Ages: 2–6   **Cultural context:** Multicultural

The Family Book by Todd Parr. 32 pages Little, Brown, 2003.
Although they're universal, there's a lot of variability among families. Families can be big or small, may or may not include stepparents or stepsiblings, may bear and/or adopt children, and may have a mother and a father, one parent, or two same-sex parents. Families may live near or far from each other, may be quiet or noisy, and neat or messy. Even within the same family, people may be the same color or different colors, and may have the same or different tastes in food. But, universally, family members share affection, celebrate together, grieve losses, and support one another. The author tells children directly that no matter what kind of family they have, it's special. Vividly colorful, this book will help children understand the diversity of families and to feel good about all kinds of families.

Ages: 2–7   **Cultural context:** Multicultural

Who's in a Family? by Robert Skutch.
Illus. by Laura Nienhaus. 32 pages Tricycle, 1995.
There can be lots of different kinds of families, both human and animal. This book introduces several examples: families with a mother, father, or both, and their child or children; families with two mothers or two fathers (referred to as the parent and parent's partner) and their child or children; one with a grandmother, mother, and children; one with a man and woman; one child who has two families, one with his mom, and the other with his father, stepmother, and half-sister. Some of these descriptions are accompanied by descriptions of animal families that have similar composition. Some families look different from other families, and some people within the same family look different from each other. The last page answers the title's question: "the people who love you the most!" A page for children to draw their own family is included. There's a clear message of acceptance for many kinds of families.

Ages: 1–7   **Cultural context:** Multicultural

BLENDED FAMILIES

Children may have many complex feelings and concerns about living in blended families. Children may have stepparents through divorce or the death of a parent. Children may worry about "losing" the newly married parent to the new stepparent. They may be concerned about whether it's permissible, or even possible, to love both the birth parent and the corresponding stepparent. Sometimes children may have similar concerns about the person a parent is dating.

See also *Dinosaurs Divorce* (Chapter 19) for information about having a stepparent and stepsiblings.

The Memory String by Eve Bunting. Illus. by Ted Rand.
33 pages Clarion, 2000.
When the child's birth parent has died, accepting a stepparent is inextricably linked with grief. Laura remembers her mother, who died three years before this story takes place, in a special way: she uses buttons, strung on a "memory string", that go back to her great-grandmother. She tells her cat about each button's significance. But the restless cat grabs the string, scattering the buttons all over the grass. Laura, Dad, and stepmom Jane find all the buttons except the one that had been Mom's favorite. That night, Laura overhears Dad proposing to substitute another (identical) button and Jane rejecting this idea because she understands the genuine meaningfulness of each button. Although Jane finds the button, she anticipates that Laura would have difficulty with this, and she leaves it for her to find instead of returning it to her directly. Having overheard all this, Laura begins to make a connection with Jane. This moving story offers children empathy in this difficult situation and hope of establishing a true connection with a stepparent.
Ages: 4–9   **Cultural context:** European-American

My Mother's Getting Married by Joan Drescher. **32 pages Dial, 1986.**
When a parent remarries, children often worry about losing a special relationship with the parent. Katy's mother is getting married, and Katy is concerned about losing the special times she and Mom have to-

gether. She expresses resentment and frustration. No one around her seems to understand how she feels. When it's time for the wedding, she appreciates her mother's happiness and feels better for a little while. Then, when Mom and Ben get ready to leave for their honeymoon, she's angry again and able to express her deepest fear: that Mom will love Ben more than her. Mom reassures her that she loves Katy *and* Ben, and that not only will she still have special times with Katy, but also, the three of them will have fun together, too. Through this story, children will feel reassured that they'll continue to have a special place in their parent's heart even after the parent remarries.

Ages: 4–8   **Cultural context:** Multicultural

Main character's cultural background: European-American

The Not-So-Wicked Stepmother by Lizi Boyd. 32 pages
Viking Kestrel, 1987.

Children sometimes worry that a stepmother will be mean and wicked like the stepmothers in fairy tales. When she leaves to spend the summer with her father and stepmother for the first time, Hessie fully believes this. In spite of her expectations, stepmother Molly is nice, and Hessie can't help having fun and forgetting to make horrible faces. It's soon clear that Hessie's ideas about a wicked stepmother are mixed up with feelings of missing Mommy. When she's able to talk to Mommy on the phone, she feels happier. She has an idyllic summer with Daddy and Molly and looks forward to future summers with them. This is very much a "summer vacation" story, without the annoying realities of day-to-day life, but it shows children that it's possible to like and feel close to a stepparent, even when you don't think you will.

Ages: 4–8   **Cultural context:** European-American

Room for a Stepdaddy by Jean Thor Cook.
Illus. by Martine Gourbault 32 pages Whitman, 1995.

A stepparent relationship means negotiating complex new roles. As this story begins, Joey wishes that his mommy and daddy still lived together. Stepdaddy Bill is nice, but he misses Daddy and is afraid Daddy will forget him. Joey visits with Daddy, who continues to be part of his life in important ways. Back at Mommy's house, Bill cares for Joey with kindness. When Joey disobeys Bill, Bill sets limits with firmness and humor. Joey comes to understand that he can count on Bill and can have room in his heart for all three parents. With this story, children will see that it's okay to take your time getting to know a stepparent, and that it's possible to be secure with both parents and stepparents.

Ages: 4–8 **Cultural context:** Multicultural
Main character's cultural background: European-American

Room for Rabbit **by Roni Schotter. Illus. by Cyd Moore**
32 pages Clarion, 2003.
When their parent remarries, children often wonder about their place in the new family. As this sequel to *Missing Rabbit* (Chapter 19) begins, Kara is leaving Mama's house to go to Papa's, bringing her special toy, Rabbit. Rabbit has the important job of voicing Kara's feelings. Papa's house is full of his new wife's things, and Kara tells Papa that Rabbit feels there isn't enough room for him, and no one cares about him now that Papa and Peggy are married. Listening sensitively, Papa reassures Kara that not only is there room for her, but that Peggy brings love for her, too. When the family has worked together to find places for Peggy's things, Kara feels more secure and accepts Peggy more. Returning to Mama's house, Kara says that Rabbit wonders whether there will be enough room for him if Mama remarries, prompting Mama to reassure Rabbit—and Kara, too—that there always will. This warm story will help children to feel secure in their place in their stepfamilies.

Ages: 4–8. **Cultural context:** European-America

She's Not My Real Mother **by Judith Vigna. 32 pages**
Whitman, 1980.
Some children react to a stepparent with anger. Miles is very straight-forward about disliking his stepmother, saying that she isn't his real mother. Openly disrespectful, he refuses to thank her for the balloon she buys him, but he begins to soften a little when she looks sad about his rejection of her. He worries that if he's "too nice" to his stepmother, Mommy might leave him, just as Daddy did. When Miles finally decides to be his stepmother's friend after all, he realizes that this isn't a threat to Mommy, because his stepmother really isn't his mother. By showing these two different perspectives on what it means to be "not my real

mother," this story offers empathy with some of kids' complex, difficult feelings about stepparents, along with hope for a good relationship.

Ages: 4–8   **Cultural context:** European-American

Stepfamilies **by Fred Rogers. Illus. by Jim Judkis. 32 pages Putnam, 1997.**

Many changes (both practical and emotional) occur when stepfamilies are formed, and there are both positive and negative aspects of becoming a stepfamily. Acknowledging these, Mr. Rogers gently reassures children about their capacity to adapt to change and provides helpful suggestions for coping. He also validates kids' ability to love more than one person, including parents *and* stepparents. A brief introduction for adults acknowledges the complexities of stepfamilies and children's need to maintain old bonds while forming new ones, encouraging adults to talk with children about the children's feelings and worries. An empathic guide to managing a difficult transition, this book supports kids' sense of competence and their emotional reality.

Ages: 2–6   **Cultural context:** African-American, European-American

Totally Uncool **by Janice Levy. Illus. by Chris Monroe. 32 pages Carolrhoda, 1999.**

Although a parent's partner may seem "weird" at first, a positive relationship with her or him can still be possible. A girl tells about the ways in which her dad's girlfriend, whom he calls Sweet Potato, is "totally uncool." For example, she plays the tuba, eats green stuff, and wears skirts with sneakers. Not only that, but Sweet Potato isn't a bit interested in a lot of the things the girl enjoys, like soccer and video games. Once the girl has named all these things, she's able to acknowledge what she likes about Sweet Potato; for example, she's good at keeping secrets, appreciates the girl's performance at the school play, and respects the girl's grumpy moods. She can even acknowledge the possibility that Sweet Potato might be okay. This story conveys the message that it's okay to feel conflicted about a parent's partner. It also shows children that their relationship with a stepparent figure can be positive in ways that aren't always obvious at first.

Ages: 4–8   **Cultural context:** European-American

When We Married Gary by Anna Grossnickle Hines.
24 pages Greenwillow, 1996.
Although a parent's remarriage changes the whole family, recognizing the complexities involved can facilitate the transition. The author tells the true story of her remarriage in the first-person voice of her younger daughter. Five-year-old Sarah comments that her older sister, Beth, sometimes misses their father because she's old enough to remember him, but Sarah feels that Gary fits with their family better than their daddy did. When Sarah and Beth participate in the wedding, it feels as if the four people are becoming a family. Acknowledging that the children already have a daddy, Gary invites them to call him Papa. This story gives children a positive model of accepting a stepparent.

Ages: 3–7   **Cultural context:** Multicultural
Main character's cultural background: European-American

GAY AND LESBIAN FAMILIES

This section summarizes picture books about families that include gay or lesbian adults. Families with lesbian or gay adults are described as one of many diverse family forms, emphasizing that it is love that makes a family. Children of gay or lesbian parents may encounter disbelief from other children or adults when they move outside their families' social circles; for example, at school. They can cope with these experiences by having a strong sense of the meaning of family and the diversity of families, and by using support from parents.

   See also *Daddy, Papa and Me* and *Felicia's Favorite Story* (Chapter 16), *Saturday Is Pattyday* (Chapter 19), and *Too Far Away to Touch* (Chapter 27) for more stories that include lesbian and gay family members.

Asha's Mums by Rosamund Elwin and Michele Paulse.
Illus. by Dawn Lee. 25 pages Women's Press, Ltd., 1990.
Not everyone knows that you can have two mothers. Asha's teacher tells her she can't go on a field trip unless her permission slip is completed correctly. The slip indicates both mums' names, and her teacher believes she can't have two mothers. Mum Alice reassures Asha, who

ultimately goes on the field trip. When Asha shows her class a drawing of her family, they insist that you can't have two mummies. Asha replies confidently, "we're a family because we live together and love each other." This positive story helps kids understand that although some people may not understand at first about families with lesbian mothers, it's possible to overcome this. They will also see that children of same-sex parents are not so different as others may think.

Ages: 3–7   **Cultural context:** Multicultural
Main character's cultural background: Asian American

Heather Has Two Mommies **by Lesléa Newman.**
Illus. by Diana Souza. 38 pages Alyson, 2000.
Children of lesbian mothers may find it confusing to learn that other kids have fathers. Heather has two mommies, and when she first goes to a playgroup, she discovers that other children have daddies, and is distressed that she doesn't. Her child-care provider comforts her, telling her that each family is special, and that what's important about families is the love they share. The children say who's in their family and draw pictures of their families, each of which is different in structure. When her mommies pick Heather up, she enjoys sharing her picture with them. I strongly recommend this tenth anniversary edition over the original 1989 version, which had limitations both in form (too much text and detail for children in the intended age group) and content (details about Heather's conception that are not developmentally appropriate for this age group, regardless of parents' gender(s)). The 2000 edition gives children a positive understanding of lesbian families in particular and diverse families in general.

Ages: 2–6   **Cultural context:** Multicultural
Main character's cultural background: European-American

Is Your Family Like Mine? **by Lois Abramchik. Illus. by Alaiyo Bradshaw. 36 pages Open Heart, Open Mind, 1993.**
When children from nontraditional families are exposed to more traditional families, they may wonder why their family is different, which can lead to questions about what a family is. When Armetha starts kindergarten, she has always had a mom and a mommy and has never

thought twice about it. After her friend asks why her daddy isn't coming to school, she begins to wonder why she doesn't have a daddy. She discovers that each of her friends has different people in their family, but like hers, all the people in each family love each other. All of these questions cause her to ask her mothers why she doesn't have a daddy, and they explain that because two women can't make a baby, they asked a man to help create Armetha. Providing an explanation that resonates with readers, they tell her that she has a daddy who helped create her and two mommies who love and care for her.

Ages: 3–7   **Cultural context:** Multicultural
Main character's cultural background: African-American

Molly's Family **by Nancy Garden. Illus. by Sharon Wooding.**
32 pages Farrar, Straus and Giroux, 2004.
Children of lesbian or gay parents may encounter confusing disbelief when they describe their families. When kindergartener Molly draws a picture of her family—herself, Mommy, Mama Lu, and their puppy—a classmate says that can't be a family and she can't have two mommies. Other kids describe the composition of their families, which are quite diverse. Molly's teacher asks if Mama Lu is a visitor or an aunt, and when Molly says no, she agrees that she must be a mommy. When Molly tells her parents about this discussion, they explain that before they had her, they loved each other so much that they wanted to share their love with a baby. So Mommy became Molly's birth mother, and Mama Lu became her adoptive mother. When Molly thinks about the many different kinds of families her classmates have and how much Mommy and Mama Lu love her, she's comfortable with, and proud of, her family, offering children an age-appropriate understanding of families with lesbian mothers as one of many possible kinds of families.

Ages: 2–6   **Cultural context:** Multicultural
Main character's cultural background: European-American

My Two Uncles **by Judith Vigna. 32 pages Whitman, 1995.**
This story addresses homophobia as it occurs within a girl's family. Elly, who lives with her parents and grandparents, loves her Uncle Ned and his partner, Uncle Phil. She can't understand why Grampy

refuses to allow Phil in their home. Her daddy explains that being gay means to love someone of the same gender in much the same way that a married man and woman love each other. He also explains Grampy's prejudice, saying that some people think it's wrong to be gay, and adds that he thinks that it's wrong to be prejudiced against gay men and lesbians. When Ned clearly expresses both his anger toward Grampy and his love for him, Grampy begins to acknowledge his own "stubborn" attitudes and Phil's presence. Children who don't have prior experience with gay people will understand, in an age-appropriate way, what it means to be gay. This story can also help kids make sense of homophobia and to feel hopeful that it can change.

Ages: 3–7　　**Cultural context:** European-American

CHAPTER 16

Adoption

Adoption occurs under a range of circumstances and can be related to a range of feelings, including curiosity about birth parents, loss, fear of abandonment, anger, and a sense of being "different." As with other issues that come up for kids, it's important for parents to encourage children to talk about their feelings and to listen to them. Parents should give honest, age-appropriate answers to their children's questions and should reassure kids that adoption is permanent. The picture books summarized in this chapter address many of the concerns of children who have been adopted.

See also *It's Okay to Be Different* (Chapter 2), which validates adoption among other personal characteristics. In *Aunt Minnie and the Twister* (Chapter 32), a family of nine children adopted by their aunt survives a tornado and feels secure in knowing they will always have a home.

Adoption **by Fred Rogers. Illus. by Jim Judkis. 32 pages Putnam, 1994.**

Children belong in their families whether by birth or adoption, and they can have all kinds of feelings about being in a family. Mr. Rogers gives reassuring and practical suggestions for coping with confusing feelings, such as talking with family members, drawing pictures, or playing pretend games. A note for parents encourages them to use this book to open discussions with their children about adoption. Attesting to the deep sense of connection within families, this lovingly worded book offers adopted children a solid feeling of belonging.

Ages: 2–7   **Cultural context:** Multicultural

All About Adoption: How Families Are Made and How Kids Feel About It **by Marc Nemiroff and Jane Annunziata. Illus. by Carol Koeller. 48 pages Magination, 2004.**

Adoption is complicated, and this book explains in detail how it occurs, starting with the birth parents' decision to adopt the child out and the adoptive parents' search for a child. They explain that the legal aspect of adoption means that it is "for keeps." They acknowledge the different ages at which children can be adopted, the existence of international adoptions, and the diverse feelings that children have as the adoption occurs, including worries that people close to them might leave, anger that leads to "testing" their parents, and feeling different from other kids. The authors suggest answers to questions that people sometimes ask adopted children, while a note for parents describes the emotions that adopted children often have and suggests ways to manage them. If you suspect that your child may have some confusing feelings about his or her adoption and your child likes lots of details, this book could be a good fit.

Ages: 4–8   **Cultural context:** Multicultural

The Best Single Mom in the World: How I Was Adopted **by Mary Zisk. 32 pages Whitman, 2001.**

In this loving story, girl and her mom joyfully tell the story of how they became a family through the girl's international adoption. The mom's explanation of adoption is simple, positive, and just enough for the child. The girl enjoys living, playing, talking, and gardening with her mom. Although she sometimes wishes for a dad, her grandpa and her friend's dad meet many of her needs. There's a clear sense of how special this child is to her mom, and of the child's deep, loving attachment to her mom. Children adopted by single moms, especially those adopted internationally, will find a positive sense of identification in this story.

Ages: 2–6   **Cultural context:** Multicultural
Main character's cultural background: European-American

The Coffee Can Kid **by Jan M. Czech.**
Illus. by Maurie J. Manning. 24 pages Child & Family, 2002.
Adoption can involve creating continuity between a birth mother's love and adoptive parents' love. Six-year-old Annie was adopted from Korea by an American father and mother. Annie's Daddy tells her the story of her birth to a single mother too young and poor to take care of her, who loved her and named her Dong Hee, meaning Shining Hope. Annie's parents keep her first baby picture and a loving letter from her birth mother in a coffee can because an adoption worker told them this would prevent fading. With the security of these items, this story reassures adopted children that they have been loved since the beginning of their lives. Annie is a highly resonant character, especially with internationally adopted children.

Ages: 4–8   **Cultural context:** Multicultural
Main character's cultural background: Asian American

Daddy, Papa and Me **by Andrew R. Aldrich.**
Illus. by Mike Motz. 24 pages New Family, 2003.
Adoption means becoming part of a loving family. A boy describes his adoption by his daddy and papa, who wanted a baby just like him, and got him when his birth mother was too ill to care for him. He tells how Daddy and Papa filled out papers with a social worker. When they finally met the boy, who was a toddler, they loved him immediately and brought him home a few days later. In his new, permanent home, he feels loved and cared for, family members love each other, and there are women who help raise him (teachers and grandmother). His friends have all different kinds of families. The boy's family, though not perfect, is loving, and is more similar to other families than differ-

ent, giving an important sense of identification for children adopted by gay fathers.

Ages: 2–6   **Cultural context:** Multicultural

Main character's cultural background: African-American

Felicia's Favorite Story **by Lesléa Newman.**
Illus. by Adriana Romo 24 pages Two Lives, 2002.
Adoption involves love of the child by both the birth mother and the adoptive parents. Felicia, whose two American mamas adopted her in Guatemala, asks for her favorite story at bedtime—the story of her adoption. Felicia and Mama Linda joke affectionately as they tell this delightful story. Mama Linda explains that when a woman is unable to take care of her baby, adoption is a loving act. She tells Felicia how she and Mama Nessa flew in an airplane to adopt her when she was as small as her teddy bear. They named her Felicia because it means "happy," since Felicia was a happy baby, and they were happy to have her. This story offers a positive, loving perspective on adoption, especially for children adopted by lesbian mothers.

Ages: 3–6   **Cultural context:** Multicultural

Main character's cultural background: Latina

A Forever Family **by Roslyn Banish with Jennifer Jordan-**
Wong. 48 pages HarperCollins, 1992.
Sometimes children are adopted well into their childhood, after foster care. *A Forever Family* is a first-person, non-fiction account of eight-year-old Jenny Jordan-Wong's adoption at age seven, after placement with two foster families since age three. Jenny, an ordinary child, explains that her birth parents were unable to take care of her because they "had lots of problems." She introduces her social workers, who make sure that kids are well cared for. Although initially scared to meet her adoptive parents, she got to know them and wanted them to be her family. She describes the adoption ceremony in court and the party afterward. Jenny truly feels she's a part of her "forever family," but still has questions about her birth mother. The book is illustrated with black-and-white photographs of Jenny and her family. Children who have been adopted under similar circumstances will identify with

Jenny and appreciate her straightforward acknowledgement of her experiences and feelings.

Ages: 5–9   **Cultural context:** Multicultural

Main character's cultural background: Asian American and European-American

Heart of Mine: A Story of Adoption by Dan Höjer and Lotta Höjer. Translated by Rabén Bokförlag and Sjögren Bokförlag. Illus. by Lotta Höjer. 28 pages R&S, 2000.

The loving connection between adopted children and their parents is every bit as real as a biological relationship This book charmingly explains that Tu Thi grew both physically, in her birth mother's tummy, and also in her adopting parents' hearts and thoughts. The parents are so excited when she's born that they can hardly eat or sleep—they can only think of Tu Thi and how the world seems different now that she's in it. After weeks of preparations, they fly to a faraway land to adopt her. The three spend time getting to know one another and growing to love one another before traveling home. This story poetically acknowledges both the love between the parents and the baby, and their connection to the country of her birth. Based on the authors' experience adopting a daughter from Vietnam, this sweet story shows adopted children how deeply their parents love them and offers a special sense of identification to internationally adopted children.

Ages: 2–6   **Cultural context:** Multicultural

Main character's cultural background: Asian European

How I Was Adopted: Samantha's Story by Joanna Cole. Illus. by Maxie Chambliss. 48 pages Morrow, 1995.

Adoption is a unique experience for every child and family. Samantha, a regular kid who likes her guinea pig and loves her parents, tells the story of her adoption as if talking to another adopted child. She explains that before she was adopted, she was born, and she didn't grow in Mommy's uterus. Some things about her are inborn and others come from her experiences in her family. She describes how hard it was for her parents to wait for her, their excitement when they finally adopted her, and how much they loved to care for her. Sam loves her own special adoption story, acknowledging how unique each adopted child's story is. An introduction for parents is included. Providing kids with an upbeat story and a sense of specialness about themselves and their adoption, this story also gives clear, age-appropriate information about how adoption occurs.

Ages: 3–6   **Cultural context:** Multicultural

Main character's cultural background: European-American

I Love You Like Crazy Cakes **by Rose A. Lewis.**
Illus. by Jane Dyer. 32 pages Little, Brown, 2000.
One thing that makes an adoptive family special is the sense of being "just right" for one another. The author (illustrated as a European-American woman) describes in the first person her adoption of a baby daughter from an orphanage in China, to whom she speaks directly. She emphasizes the sense of an immediate and perfect match between the two—over and above the baby's need for a mother and the mother's need for a baby—and her experience of falling in love with her child. The mother expresses hope that the birth mother knows somehow that the baby is happy and safe. Offering empathy to the many American children adopted from China, this story depicts a warm, positive image of the attachment between the child and mother.

Ages: 2–7   **Cultural context:** Multicultural

Main character's cultural background: Asian American

A Koala for Katie: An Adoption Story **by Jonathan London.**
Illus. by Cynthia Jabar. 24 pages Whitman, 1993.
Some kids struggle to come to terms with their adoption and to understand what it means to be a mommy. When Katie is in this situation, she goes to the zoo with her parents and notices a baby koala clinging to her mama. She asks her parents what would happen if the mommy koala couldn't take care of the baby any more. Her parents understand that the question is about her own adoption, acknowledging both the sadness of separation from the birth mother, and the happiness with and love of the adoptive mother. They buy her a toy koala at the zoo store, and Baby Koala becomes Katie's adopted baby, whom she feeds and protects. Through this make-believe, Katie comes to understand

and feel good about her adoption. A note for parents is included. Taking an empathic approach to children's struggle with what adoption means, this story offers a satisfying way to reach resolution.

Ages: 3–6   **Cultural context:** Multicultural
Main character's cultural background: European-American

The Little Green Goose **by Adele Sansone. Translated by J. Alison James. Illus. by Alan Marks. 30 pages North-South, 1999.** Understanding adoption means, in part, taking on a relatively abstract concept of who's in a family. Mr. Goose, who longs for a chick of his own, finally gets an egg. Out of the egg hatches a green goose—or at least, it's a goose in Mr. Goose's eyes; it strongly resembles a dinosaur. Mr. Goose loves his baby, but the other chicks tell the green goose that he isn't a real goose and that Mr. Goose can't be his real mother. Deeply hurt, he looks for his real mother in a frog, a fish, and a lizard. He worries about whether anyone in the world looks like him. But when he considers who would feed him and love him, he realizes that Mr. Goose really is his mother. Mr. Goose lovingly explains that he's the green goose's father, which the green goose accepts easily. Children will understand that you don't have to look like your parents for them to be your real parents. This story is particularly validating for children adopted by a single father.

Ages: 3–7   **Cultural context:** N/A

Mommy Far, Mommy Near **by Carol Antoinette Peacock. Illus. by Shawn Costello Brownell. 32 pages Whitman, 2000.** A developmental task for some adopted children is making sense of having a birth mother and an adoptive mother. Elizabeth, who was born in China and adopted by a European-American mother and father, describes learning about her adoption and the fact that she has two mothers. As Elizabeth and Mommy recall together how Elizabeth's parents had adopted her, using special words with which Mommy vowed to be Elizabeth's mother always, Elizabeth asks her mother to adopt her again and again, and again Mommy says those special words. This story movingly evokes Elizabeth's feelings about both mommies and describes her use of play to process them. She talks on the toy telephone to her mommy from China and "adopts" her stuffed animals using the words with which her mommy adopted her. Seeing a Chinese mother and daughter, she feels a sense of loss of her own Chinese mother. Mommy helps her articulate this and comforts her. Elizabeth's Mommy accepts Elizabeth's feelings and the differences between herself and Elizabeth, offering a way to discuss the potentially confusing feelings that some children have about adoption in the context of a loving, secure family.

Ages: 3–7   **Cultural context:** Multicultural

Main character's cultural background: Asian American

A Mother for Choco **by Keiko Kasza. 32 pages Putnam, 1992.**

Some adopted children have concerns about whether they look like their parents. When Choco the bird looks for a mother, he can't find one. All the possible mothers he meets reject him because, although they look like him in some respects, they don't look like him in other ways. Understandably, he gets the idea that a mother has to look like him, so he's sure that Mrs. Bear can't possibly be his mother. But Mrs. Bear listens to him, loves him, and cheers him up just like a mother would. He's very surprised when she suggests that she could be his mother. It turns out that none of her other children (a hippo, and alligator, and a pig) look like her either, but they're all very happy, making it clear that love and caring make a family, not physical resemblance.

Ages: 2–6   **Cultural context:** N/A

Over the Moon: An Adoption Tale **by Karen Katz.**
28 pages Holt, 1997.

The connection between adopted children and their parents can begin before birth. The night a baby is born, her adoptive parents dream of her. The next night, they receive a phone call saying that she has been born, and with great excitement, they fly far away to adopt her. On their first night together, they tell the baby the story of her adoption, and there's a feeling of a family tradition beginning. When they arrive home, many people welcome them. The parents assure the baby that they will be her parents forever. The illustrations, which are reminiscent of folk art, have bright colors and patterns that mirror the family's joy. This story was inspired by the adoption experience of the author and her husband. Adopted children, particularly those adopted internationally, will feel the strong sense of love and connection in this story.

Ages: 3–7   Cultural context: Multicultural

Main character's cultural background: Latina

***Through Moon and Stars and Night Skies* by Ann Turner.**
Illus. by James Graham Hale 32 pages Harper & Row, 1990.
It may take some time for children to feel secure in their adoptive families. A boy tells the story of his adoption, including his travel on an airplane with an adoption worker from what appears to be an Asian country to North America. He recounts his fears, anticipation, and the process of feeling secure with and loved by his momma and poppa. It's especially important to him that he's had pictures of them, their house, their dog, and his new room before this journey. This story lets children in similar situations know that there are others like them and will validate their experience of feeling safe and loved in their families.

Ages: 2–7   **Cultural context:** Multicultural

Main character's cultural background: Asian American

CHAPTER 17

Arrival
of a Baby

Having a new sister or brother changes a child's life profoundly. Children often feel excited about having a new brother or sister, look forward to their unique role as older sibling, feel special because they can do "big kid" things that babies can't, and identify with their parents. At the same time, they may also feel displaced or excluded, wonder whether their parents have enough love for them and the baby, worry how they'll get their needs met when their parents have to meet the baby's needs, too, and find it hard to tolerate the baby's crying. The experience will be different in some ways depending on whether there is one baby or more, whether the baby comes by birth or adoption, and whether a birth is full-term or premature. Children need reassurance that their parents still love them and that they have an important, unique place in their family. It helps to know who'll take care of them during the delivery or adoption and what life with a baby is like. Often kids enjoy looking at their own baby pictures, helping choose baby names, helping dress, burp, or bathe the baby, or talking or singing to the baby. Older kids need some special time with just their parents, too. Many children feel a stronger connection to their "baby self" when a new sibling is born (see Chapter 11).

Baby on the Way **by William Sears, Martha Sears, and Christie Watts Kelly. Illus. by Renée Andriani. 32 pages**
Little, Brown, 2001.
This warm, accessible book describes the changes of pregnancy, the older child's experience of delivery (being cared for by adult friends or family members, doing something special), and, briefly, life with a new baby. The authors encourage children to talk to and hug the baby before birth. They explain how pregnancy feels to a mommy and suggest ways to help her feel more comfortable, while reassuring children that they're always special to their mother. The book includes a note for parents and caregivers, and ideas for things older children can do to prepare for the pregnancy and birth (for example, "draw a picture of what the baby might look like"). Sidebars provide more details about delivery and newborns' characteristics. Illustrations show a family of pregnant mother, father, sister, and brother, all of whom look happy and loving, and eventually, a peaceful-looking newborn. Child readers will be well informed about pregnancy and delivery and will feel they're being taken seriously.

Ages: 2–6 **Cultural context:** Multicultural
Main character's cultural background: European-American

A Baby Sister for Frances **by Russell Hoban.**
Illus. by Lillian Hoban. 31 pages Harper & Row, 1964.
The presence of a new baby can bring feelings of deprivation and confusion about one's role in the family. When there's a new baby in Frances's household, Frances doesn't feel she's getting quite enough from her parents. She decides to "run away"—to a cozy spot under the dining room table. While Frances is under the table, her parents talk about how much they miss her and how it just isn't a family without her. She "comes home" to a chocolate cake baked by her mother in honor of her return. Some of the language and details come across as a bit dated (for example, Frances can't wear the dress she wants because her mother

hasn't ironed it). However, this story addresses real feelings that children have without any loss of control over feelings on Frances's part.

Ages: 2–6 **Cultural context:** N/A

Buster **by Denise Fleming. 34 pages Holt, 2003.**
Children may experience a new baby as an invader. Buster is a happy dog who has everything he could wish for until a cat named Betty joins his household. Buster is afraid of cats and keeps hoping Betty will disappear. He tries to ignore her as she plays with his toys and uses his other things, until he can't stand it anymore, running away to a park. But when he's hungry and lonely and wants to go home, he realizes that he's lost. He finally finds his way home when he sees Betty in the tree in their yard. Betty is happy to see him, and Buster realizes that he does have everything he wants and that Betty's presence only adds to this. The illustrations are vividly colored and beautifully textured. While keeping a safe distance from children's literal experience of a new baby, this story offers empathy with the experience of someone new in the house and the possibility of resolution.

Ages: 2–5 **Cultural context:** N/A

Darcy and Gran Don't Like Babies **by Jane Cutler. Illus. by Susannah Ryan. 32 pages Farrar, Straus and Giroux, 2002.**
Here's a story for a child who consistently expresses dislike for a baby brother or sister. Darcy tells all the adults she meets that she doesn't like her baby brother. When she tells her gran, she finds out that Gran feels the same way. Gran takes Darcy to the park, where they enjoy big-person activities together, like swinging on the big swings and playing on the seesaw. Because of the bond they develop in doing this, Darcy is able to talk with Gran about her unhappiness with the baby and to receive validation and support from her. This allows her to accept her parents' statements that she used to be a baby like her brother and will like him better when he's older. This story offers children reassurance that it's okay if they don't like the new baby in their house, and at the same time, that they don't have to hold onto this opinion rigidly.

Ages: 3–7 **Cultural context:** Multicultural
Main character's cultural background: European-American

Elizabeti's Doll by Stephanie Stuve-Bodeen.
Illus. by Christy Hale. 32 pages Lee & Low, 1998.
One important feeling that may surface when there's a new baby in the family is an older child's sense of identification with parents. Elizabeti has a new baby brother, Obedi, and wants a baby of her own to care for, just like her mother. She finds a rock that makes the perfect doll and names it Eva. She takes care of Eva in the same ways that Mama takes care of Obedi, only Eva is easier to care for (for example, her diaper never gets dirty). One day Eva disappears while Elizabeti is getting water from the well. She's inconsolable, as no other rock can take Eva's place. She's relieved to find Eva, unhurt but dirty, in the fire pit. This story clearly evokes Elizabeti's sense of identification with her mother and her feelings about growing up to be a good mother someday. These good feelings about herself provide Elizabeti with a connection to Mama that allows her to claim a unique place in her family.
Ages: 3–7   **Cultural context:** African

Franklin's Baby Sister by Paulette Bourgeois.
Illus. by Brenda Clark. 32 pages Kids Can, 2000.
Children often feel joy in anticipating the birth of a sibling. Franklin, a turtle, can hardly wait to become a big brother in the spring. He even knows a little about how to take care of babies, having practiced with his friend Bear's baby sister. But it seems to take forever for spring to come. He calls for spring, but it doesn't answer, so he makes lots of noise to try to wake the earth up. When his baby sister is finally born, Granny takes him to visit her at the hospital. It's Franklin who thinks of the baby's name, Harriet, after their special great-aunt. The story ends as Franklin greets baby Harriet warmly. With Franklin, kids have a good role model for relishing the role of big brother or sister.
Ages: 2–6   **Cultural context:** N/A

Geraldine's Baby Brother by Holly Keller. **24 pages Greenwillow, 1994.**
Here's a story for a child who is persistently expressing anger about having a baby brother or sister. At the beginning of the story, Geraldine is angry about her baby brother, Willie, his crying, and the attention he gets from their family and friends. He cries all day long, and she

resents him all day long. But at night, when she hears him rustling in his bassinet, she goes to see what's going on, and she can't help laughing at a silly face he makes. Since he doesn't cry, she reads to him, beginning to feel warmth and nurturance toward him. Geraldine shows kids that it's okay to let go of an angry response to a new baby.

Ages: 2–7   **Cultural context:** N/A

Hello Benny! **by Robie H. Harris. Illus. by Michael Emberley. 32 pages McElderry, 2002.**
This book describes the first year of a joyful baby named Benny. It doesn't address the feelings of an older sibling (although Benny's cousin Lizzie seems to enjoy him a great deal), but describes developmental milestones in detail, starting from birth. These include not only language and motor development, but also emotional development. With additional text on each page for older children or those who want more information, this book will ease the transition to becoming a big sister or brother by giving kids detailed information about what to expect from babies and how to understand them.

Ages: 3–9   *Cultural context:* Multicultural
Main character's cultural background: European-American

I'm a Big Sister **and** *I'm a Big Brother* **by Joanna Cole. Illus. by Maxie Chambliss. 24 pages Morrow, 1997.**
In each of these two books (with identical text except for the older child's gender) the older child expresses pride in being able to help with bottles and diapers, in being gentle and caring with the baby, and in being able to do "big kid" things that babies can't. Parents' attitudes toward the baby are kind and sensitive; for example, they say that crying is how babies communicate their needs. The older child also says that he/she is special to his/her parents because he/she is unique and is now special because of being an older sibling, as well as all the ways he/she was special before. An afterword for parents is included. These upbeat stories join with children in celebrating their new identity as an older sibling.

Ages: 2–6   **Cultural context:** Multicultural
Main character's cultural background: European-American

The New Baby **by Fred Rogers. Illus. by Jim Judkis.**
32 pages Putnam, 1985.
When a new baby is born, children have complex feelings. Mr. Rogers reassures children that they still have a special place in their family. He explains that "Just as you can have plenty of love for both your mom and dad, they can have plenty of love for both you and the new baby." He also acknowledges the feelings of being left out that older children often have, pointing out that it's possible to express the resulting anger and resentment safely. Mr. Rogers tells about many of the ways the baby will need the older child, such as teaching her or him how to smile, play peek-a-boo, and share. A note to adults is included. Children will feel understood and validated by this book.

Ages: 1–5   **Cultural context:** Multicultural

On Mother's Lap **by Ann Herbert Scott. Illus. by Glo Coalson.**
32 pages Clarion, 1992.
When there's a new baby, children may wonder whether their parents can love and care for both them and the baby. Michael is rocking in his mother's lap, bringing his puppy, his doll, his toy boat, and his blanket there with them. But when the baby cries, Michael says there isn't enough room for her to rock with them. He finds out that there is always enough room on Mother's lap, reassuring children that their parents always have enough love for them and a baby.

Ages: 2–6   **Cultural context:** Native-American

Oonga Boonga **by Frieda Wishinsky.**
Illus. by Carol Thompson. 32 pages Dutton, 1999.
This is a wonderful story about the unique bond between siblings. Baby Louise is crying, and none of the adults can get her to stop. Finally, when her big brother, Daniel, says "oonga boonga" to her, she not only stops crying, but smiles. No one else's "oonga boonga" will do. When people express excitement about the new baby, this book can help kids understand why it's special to be the baby's older sibling—an understanding that will help them to feel secure in a situation when they might otherwise feel displaced.

Ages: 2–7   **Cultural context:** European-American

**Rosie and Tortoise by Margaret Wild. Illus. by Ron Brooks.
32 pages DK, 1999.**

A new baby's prematurity can interfere with the establishment of a relationship with the older child. Rosie can't wait till her baby brother is born—and she doesn't have to wait, because Bobby is born prematurely. His small size and sickly appearance frighten Rosie, who avoids him. When she's able to express her fearfulness to her dad, he tells her a story in which a tortoise finally comes out of the woods by slow, steady progress and a little help from a hare. After that, Rosie understands that Bobby is as slow and steady as the tortoise, and she's ready to get to know him. Children who have similar experiences will also benefit from Dad's story and use Rosie as a good role model for resolving their fears.

Ages: 3–7   **Cultural context:** N/A

**Seeds of Love: For Brothers and Sisters of International
Adoption by Mary E. Petertyl. Illus. by Jill Chambers.
32 pages Folio One, 1997.**

Adoption may involve a longer separation from parents than birth would. Carly is excited to find out that she's going to have a baby sister. Her mommy explains that she and daddy are going to adopt the baby, and so they will have to take a plane trip to her. Carly is scared about who will take care of her, and Mommy assures her that Grandma will do a good job. She gives Carly a sticker to put on the calendar for each day that they're away, and they plant seeds, which will sprout when it's almost time for them to come home. Carly is sad when her parents leave, but she puts stickers on the calendar, waters the seeds, and has fun with Grandma until her parents return with her new sister, Anna, whom Carly loves as soon as she meets her. In its empathic approach to children whose new sibling is adopted internationally, this story offers hope for tolerating the separation and loving the new baby.

Ages: 2–6   **Cultural context:** Multicultural
Main character's cultural background: European-American

***Twinnies* by Eve Bunting. Illus. by Nancy Carpenter.
32 pages Harcourt Brace, 1997.**
Even more than having one new baby, having twins may raise worries
for older children about deprivation and about their place in the family. When a girl's twin sisters are born, she wonders who'll be left to
take care of her and feels "overwhelmed" about the time, energy, and
attention they require. When she tells Dad about her concern that
she's no longer special now that the twins are part of the family, he reassures her that she'll always be special to him. The girl finds herself
"overwhelmed" by the rudeness of a neighbor who complains about the
babies' crying at night. When they cry the next night, their parents
take them into their bed, and the girl gets in with them. Her secure
sense of her place in the family is reflected in an illustration of her between the twins, who are between their parents. She is "overwhelmed"
with love for the babies, showing that even with twin babies, there can
be a special place for children in their family.

Ages: 3–7   **Cultural context:** European-American

***We Have a Baby* by Cathryn Falwell. 32 pages Clarion, 1993.**
Very young children need simple explanations of the changes that
come with a new baby. The very simple text and attractive illustrations in this story show an older child and a baby in loving interaction
with their parents and becoming a family together. This book doesn't
address the negative feelings that may be involved in having a new
baby in the house. Even the youngest children will be able to take a
sense of positive anticipation from this story.

Ages: 0–3   **Cultural context:** Multicultural

CHAPTER 18

Moving House

Moving to a new house can involve change, loss, and new beginnings. Whether the child moves or a close friend moves away, the child is faced with separation from the friend and a need to make new friends. When the child's own family moves, there are the additional stresses of leaving a familiar environment and adjusting to a new one, often not only at home, but also at school and in the neighborhood.

WHEN YOUR FAMILY MOVES

I suspect that a minority of children spend their entire growing-up years in one home. When children move to a new home, they face challenges in saying goodbye to all that's familiar, adjusting to a new home, neighborhood, and school, and making new friends. They may even find new ways to have fun along with new perspectives and ideas. Children benefit from knowing as much as possible about the planned move, visiting the new house, school, and neighborhood before the move (and if not, seeing pictures of them), and talking about their feelings about moving. Be sure to eliminate any misconceptions kids may have about what's happening to the things that are being packed up in boxes and try to maintain normal routines as much as possible. Also, when thinking about the feelings of loss that can come with a move, children sometimes feel better remembering that they're still with the people who are most important to them—their family. Children can also cope with the changes using imagination and symbols, maintaining contact with people from their old home, and keeping their memories of the old house with them. In addition, they'll have a greater sense of control if invited to participate in designing or furnishing their new room.

See also *Dinosaurs Divorce* (Chapter 19) for comments about moving when your parents divorce. In *Blue Horse* and *Friends* (Chapter 20), children who have recently moved find ways to make new friends.

Alexander, Who's Not (Do You Hear Me? I Mean It!) Going to Move by Judith Viorst. Illus. by Robin Preiss Glasser.
32 pages Atheneum, 1995.

Some children vehemently oppose a move. Alexander insists he isn't going to move. There's too much that he'll miss, and he's sure he'll never get used to it. He remembers the special things that happened in his old neighborhood, and says good-bye, contending that it isn't a final good-bye. When it's finally time for him to move, his friends give him gifts and his parents find ways to ease the stress of moving. Although he still doesn't like the thought of moving, Alexander finally starts to pack. Children who feel angry or worried about leaving old friends and their neighborhood will feel understood when they read this story. If even Alexander can tolerate moving when he doesn't want to, they can, too, while his parents' assurances about eventually becoming comfortable in the new neighborhood offer hope.

Ages: 4–8   **Cultural context:** European-American

Good-bye, House by Frank Asch. 32 pages Simon & Schuster, 1986.

As this sweet story shows, saying goodbye to the house is an important part of moving. Just as the moving van is ready to leave their old house, Baby Bear has the feeling that he's forgotten something. When he looks inside the house, it looks empty until his parents remind him that it contains their memories. Together, they remember how the house used to be when they lived there, with shadowy drawings representing their memories. Baby Bear says goodbye to each room and to the whole house, and then he's ready to leave. The act of saying goodbye to the rooms allows him to realize that this farewell is what he was forgetting earlier. As a whole, this story sensitively acknowledges children's very real need to say good-bye when they move.

Ages: 1–7   **Cultural context:** N/A

I'm Not Moving, Mama **by Nancy White Carlstrom.**
Illus. by Thor Wickstrom. 32 pages Macmillan, 1990.
The separation involved in moving can be difficult for children. A little mouse tells his mama that he isn't moving, as she packs his things. As far as he's concerned, his mother can take his things, but he isn't going. To each of these expressions of separation, Mama replies with an assurance of togetherness in the new house. The little mouse finally acknowledges that she can make him go, but he doesn't like moving. The mother mouse replies that she doesn't like moving either, but that when they go someplace new, they'll be together and they'll remember the good times at the old house together. Calling attention to children's reluctance to move, this story shows that although moving involves many separations, it maintains their most important connections.

Ages: 3–8   **Cultural context:** N/A

The Leaving Morning **by Angela Johnson.**
Illus. by David Soman. 32 pages Orchard, 1992.
Although it's sad to say goodbye when you move, it's possible to cope with the sadness. In this poetically told story, a brother and sister say good-bye to their friends, cousins, and neighbors as they prepare to move from their apartment. They even kiss the apartment window good-bye. Their parents are a reassuring presence. When the moving truck comes, the children watch the movers. This story conveys an acceptance of the sadness of saying goodbye, and an impression that the children are able to use their parents' support to cope with this, while suggesting positive anticipation of the family's new home.

Ages: 3–7   **Cultural context:** African-American

The Lost and Found House by Michael Cadnum. Illus. by Steve Johnson and Lou Fancher. 32 pages Viking, 1997.

A move to a new house is a process of transition. A boy and his parents watch the movers pack the truck and leave with their belongings and experience the emptiness of their old house, which contains only memories and light. While driving away, the boy mentally says good-bye to parts of the neighborhood. Although at first the boy forgets where he is at night, he also makes friends with kids who live nearby. As the story ends, he feels hopeful, knowing that the aquarium from the old house will soon be set up in the new house, a symbol of the life the family has brought with them from the old house to the new one. This story has a quiet feel to it and is evocatively told and illustrated. Children will feel validation of their experiences of loss and change, and hopeful about both continuity from their old homes and positive aspects of the change.

Ages: 5–8   **Cultural context:** Multicultural

Main character's cultural background: European-American

Maggie Doesn't Want to Move by Elizabeth Lee O'Donnell. Illus. by Amy Schwartz. 32 pages Four Winds, 1987.

Some kids show their feelings about a move by attributing them to someone else. Simon expresses his concerns about moving by telling his mother, readers, and everyone else he meets that his little sister, Maggie, doesn't want to move. His mother sensitively talks with him about "Maggie's" feelings about moving. After watching the movers at both houses and visiting the new neighborhood, Simon decides that Maggie doesn't want to move—from the *new* house. Children will understand that even when they don't want to move, the move might have positive aspects, and even when they miss people and things, they may like the new people and things in their new home.

Ages: 4–8   **Cultural context:** Multicultural

Main character's cultural background: European-American

Moving by Fred Rogers. Illus. by Jim Judkis. 31 pages
Putnam, 1987.

In this gentle book, Mr. Rogers describes both the sense of loss that
can accompany moving and the excitement of a new house and neighborhood. He reassures children that they don't have to get used to
the new house all at once, encouraging them to maintain contact with
and memories of old friends. In a very child-friendly way, he also explains why families move, what things come along when you move (not
bathtubs!), and how things are packed and moved (cars, small trucks,
or moving vans). A foreword for adults identifies some of the issues
children face when moving and suggests ways to help children cope.
This complete guide for young children addresses both the practical
and emotional aspects of moving.

Ages: 2–6   **Cultural context:** Multicultural
Main character's cultural background: European-American

The Trip by Ezra Jack Keats. 34 pages Greenwillow, 1978.
Imagination is an important resource for coping with a move. Lonely
in a new house, Louie uses his imagination and creative artwork to
remember his old neighborhood. He imagines scary beings who turn
out to be his old friends, costumed for Halloween. Once he's had this
reunion in imagination, he's able to join new kids for trick-or-treat.
Strikingly illustrated with vivid, textured art, this story shows kids
that an imaginative connection to their old life can support them in
their transition to their new life.

Ages: 4–7   **Cultural context:** Multicultural
Main character's cultural background: European-American

Why Did We Have to Move Here? by Sally J. K. Davies. 32 pages
Carolrhoda, 1997.

Even when moving brings frustrations and disappointments, things
can get better. William resents having moved to a new house in a new
area. Nothing seems to go right at home or at school, and he wants "to
go back where they like me." He feels better when he finds that in his
new environment, he has new ideas and realizes that his old friends
were new to him at one time, too. This story will help children who have

already had frustrations and disappointments related to moving to see that things can get better.

Ages: 5–8   **Cultural context:** Multicultural
Main character's cultural background: European-American

Yoko's Paper Cranes **by Rosemary Wells. 30 pages**
Hyperion, 2001
Even though moving involves loss, important connections can maintained. Early in life, Yoko and her *obaasan* (grandmother) feed the cranes in Obaasan's garden in Japan. Yoko is sad to see the cranes go in winter, but her grandmother knows they will always come back. Yoko's *ojiisan* (grandfather) teaches her how to make origami cranes. Later, when Yoko and her parents move to California, she knows that it's winter in her grandmother's garden and sends Obaasan origami cranes for her birthday. She writes that like the cranes, she will come back to Japan. This book is beautifully illustrated using paint, rubber stamps, and cut paper. It shows children a way to keep their connection with people they miss after even a long, cross-cultural move.

Ages: 3–7   **Cultural context:** N/A

WHEN A FRIEND MOVES AWAY

Having a good friend move away can be difficult for children. They may feel sad, lonely, bored, and angry. They may worry that the friends will stop being special to each other. Kids may even feel as if all friendship is gone forever. These losses can be partly alleviated by the possibility of visits with the old friend or the thought that they can live near each other when they both grow up, but also by making new friends.

   See also *Franklin's Bad Day* (Chapter 10).

The Best-Ever Good-Bye Party **by Amy Hest.**
Illus. by DyAnne DiSalvo-Ryan. 32 pages Morrow, 1989.
Kids' sadness and resentment about a friend's move may be expressed as irritability. When Jessica's best friend, Jason, is moving across town to a new apartment building, she feels sad and resentful, especially

when he says anything good about the new apartment. She invites him to a goodbye party for just the two of them, hoping that will cheer them up. At the party, they're both irritable, and they argue until Jessica finally tells Jason that she wishes he weren't moving. When she worries that he'll find a new best friend, he reassures her. She gives him a note to read the next day, which expresses his uniqueness and irreplaceability in her life. This story shows children both a way to say good-bye and a way to carry their friend in their hearts.

Ages: 4–8   **Cultural context:** European-American

Ira Says Goodbye **by Bernard Waber. 40 pages**
Houghton Mifflin, 1988.
When a friend is moving, children can worry that they'll lose the friendship. Ira is sad when he finds out that his best friend, Reggie, is moving. At first, Reggie is sad, too; when he later decides he's glad about the move, Ira is even more hurt and resentful. On moving day, both boys grieve. They give each other meaningful going-away presents. The boys' comments about their pet turtles—whom they've put in one tank, because they're friends—parallel the boys' own story. At the end, Ira is excited about an upcoming visit to Reggie at his new house. Sensitively acknowledging children's feelings about a friend's move, this story offers hope for maintaining friendships after a move.

Ages: 4–8   **Cultural context:** Multicultural
Main character's cultural background: European-American

Janey **by Charlotte Zolotow. Illus. by Ronald Himler.**
24 pages Harper & Row, 1973.
Sometimes it's important to simply acknowledge sadness when a special friend has moved away. A girl lovingly and sadly remembers her best friend, Janey, recalling the everyday moments they shared. The two girls walked home from school together, sometimes said the same thing at the same time, called each other after dinner, gave each other the same book one Christmas, and had sleepovers. Janey has a special, unique place in the girl's life. She ends with the wish that when they grow up, they can live near each other again, offering empathy to children who are feeling the loss of a friend who has moved away.

Ages: 5–8   **Cultural context:** European-American

My Best Friend Moved Away **by Nancy Carlson.**
32 pages Viking, 2001.
Making new friends can help resolve the feelings of loss that children experience when a special friend moves away. In this simply worded book, a girl remembers her best friend, who has moved away. She remembers the fun they had and the times they argued but always made up. She feels that she'll always be bored without her friend. When a girl about her age moves into her friend's old house, she begins to think that although she'll miss her best friend, maybe she and her best friend will both make new friends. Offering acknowledgement of kids' sense of loss when a friend moves away, this story promotes hope that even though no one can replace the old friend, the loss won't be total.

Ages: 3–7.   **Cultural context:** Multicultural
Main character's cultural background: European-American

We Are Best Friends **by Aliki. 32 pages Greenwillow, 1982.**
Kids may worry that it would be disloyal to have new friends when their best friend has moved. Robert's best friend, Peter, moves away, and at first, Robert is lonely and angry. When he meets a new kid, Will, at first he dislikes everything about him (his freckles, his glasses, even his name). After he gets a letter from Peter saying that he has a new friend but that Robert is still his best friend, he's able to make friends with Will and have fun with him. This story reassures children that they don't have to give up their loyalty to a best friend who moves away in order to enjoy new friends.

Ages: 3–7   **Cultural context:** Multicultural
Main character's cultural background: European-American

CHAPTER 19

Parents' Conflict and Divorce

When children live in two-parent households, harmony between their parents is important to their security. Kids experience a range of emotional reactions when parents have significant difficulty getting along. This chapter summarizes picture books about conflicts between parents that may not lead to divorce, as well as picture books about divorce.

CONFLICT BETWEEN PARENTS

Sometimes parents have disagreements that may not lead to divorce and don't include physical violence (see Chapter 34), yet are emotionally charged and distressing to children. All parents will feel angry at each other on occasion, and these times can serve as opportunities to show children how to express anger appropriately and show them that people can work through their conflicts. But when parents have frequent conflicts, kids usually feel frightened, confused, and often, angry themselves. They may have diffuse worries that their world is falling apart.

See also *The Mad Family Gets Their Mads Out* (Chapter 5), which acknowledges children's fear, confusion, and anger when their parents fight, and the need for children to take care of themselves and to let their parents solve these adult problems.

Something's Different by Shelley Rotner and Sheila Kelly. Illus. by Shelley Rotner. 32 pages Millbrook, 2002.

Conflict between parents can bring up complex, confusing feelings for children. A boy describes how things feel different with his parents, who seem angry at each other. They tell him that they have problems that aren't his fault, that they're trying to work out their problems (in part by going to couples' therapy), that they're not getting divorced, and that they'll always love and care for him. The boy tries not to think about it, but he's worried, scared, angry, and confused. He realizes that some of the important parts of his life are still the same and appropriately concludes that kids can't fix adults' problems. This story offers empathy to children whose parents are experiencing conflict, reassuring them that it's not their fault and they'll always be loved and cared for.

Ages: 3–8　　　**Cultural context:** European-American

When They Fight by Kathryn White. Illus. by Cliff Wright. 27 pages Winslow, 2000.

Parents' feelings about each other can strongly affect how a child feels. A little badger describes his/her experience of his/her parents' fighting, in terms of emotions and using analogies such as darkness, cold, and being lost in a storm. When the parents are friends again, the little badger feels happy, strong, competent, safe, and sure of his/her parents' love. Simply worded and evocative, this story validates children's feelings about conflicts between their parents, offering the hope of feeling better when the conflicts stop.

Ages: 3–6　　　**Cultural context:** N/A

DIVORCE

Divorce leads to major changes in a child's life and to many complex emotions, including sadness, loss, guilt, anger, and confusion. Kids may worry that their parents will leave them, as they've left each other. Children need to know that divorce is never a child's fault and that their parents will always love them, care for them, and be their parents. It's often helpful if parents tell their child together about the divorce, discussing it in a simple, straightforward way far enough in advance so that kids have time to prepare emotionally.

See also Chapter 15 (All Kinds of Families) for summaries of related books.

As the Crow Flies **by Elizabeth Winthrop.**
Illus. by Joan Sandin 32 pages Clarion, 1998.
Children often feel pulled apart when their parents are divorced. Second-grader Michael lives with his mother in Arizona, and his father lives in Delaware. During his father's annual weeklong visits, Michael stays with him at a hotel. Michael straightforwardly acknowledges that he hates it that his parents don't talk to each other except to make plans about him. He's happy during his time with his father and sad when it's time for his father to leave. At the end of the story, his father tells him the exciting news that he'll be old enough to visit him in Delaware the next summer. With an understanding voice, this story offers validation of the strain of always missing a parent while loving them both.
Ages: 5–8   **Cultural context:** Multicultural
Main character's cultural background: European-American

At Daddy's on Saturdays **by Linda Walvoord Girard.**
32 pages Whitman, 1987.
When parents divorce, children may worry that they'll lose a parent. Divorce seems to Katie like throwing someone away, and when Daddy moves out, she worries that he'll throw her away, or at least stop loving her. Her parents explain that they can't live together anymore because they make each other unhappy, that it isn't her fault, and that the divorce is permanent. Katie initially struggles with sadness, empti-

ness, distraction, and irritability, but when she can call Daddy on the phone, she begins to feel better. She talks openly with both parents about her worries and wishes related to the divorce, and they answer in clear, reassuring ways. Eventually, Katie understands that Daddy will always be her daddy and is truly reliable. In some ways, her parents are actually more pleasant to be around now, and she has special times with each. This book's special strength is in the way it addresses worries that the child will lose the noncustodial parent.

Ages: 4–8   **Cultural context:** European-American

The Days of Summer by Eve Bunting. Illus. by William Low. **32 pages Harcourt, 2001.**

As this book beautifully illustrates, grandparents' divorce affects children. When Nora and Jo-Jo's grandparents tell the family they're getting divorced, the children are shocked. Jo-Jo thinks that people their age don't divorce, worries that they hate each other, and wishes they would reconcile, while Nora worries about being able to see both grandparents. Nora notices changes in her mom's behavior, prompting the children to help with her sadness. As the family says good-bye to the summer, there's a sense that they're saying good-bye to the grandparents' marriage, too. When the family visits Grandma, although there are bittersweet moments, she matter-of-factly acknowledges both the sense of loss and her happiness that she and Grandpa are better off apart. The new phase of the girls' relationship with Grandpa also contains both loss and positive anticipation. This story offers children a way to see both negative and positive aspects of a divorce and hope that they, like Nora, will learn to cope with it.

Ages: 4–9   **Cultural context:** European-American

Dinosaurs Divorce: A Guide for Changing Families by Laurene **Krasny Brown and Marc Brown. 32 pages Little, Brown, 1986.**

This nonfiction guide addresses practical matters and feelings related to parents' divorce straightforwardly and reassuringly. Right from the start, the authors tell children that a divorce is not their fault. They give kids lots of helpful ideas about managing everything from feelings (with encouragement to express them safely), to different rules in each parent's house, to telling your friends about your parents' divorce, to parents' dating, to issues that come up around having stepparents and stepsiblings. They integrate children's emotional reactions—including ambivalent ones—into discussions of their day-to-day lives. A glossary for children is included (with terms such as *divorce, child custody, child support,* and *visiting rights*). The illustrations are charming and down-to-earth, especially in the way they show facial expressions. In one illustration, a child and stepfather are making peanut butter sandwiches, the child's with banana and the stepfather's with pickle—demonstrating having to get used to a new person's way of doing things. In a supportive, affirming way, this book tells kids what they need to know to adjust to their parents' divorce.

Ages: 4–8   **Cultural context:** N/A

Divorce **by Fred Rogers. Illus. by Jim Judkis.**
32 pages Putnam, 1996.
This gentle, reassuring book gives children lots of permission to have feelings and to talk about them. Mr. Rogers tells kids that their parents will continue to meet their child's needs after a divorce. He acknowledges the enormous amount of change involved and encourages children to ask whatever questions they have about the changes, reminding them that some things stay the same, the primary one being that each parent will always be the child's parent. Mr. Rogers also tells kids that they didn't cause their parents' divorce and can't make them get back together again, although many children wish they could. The color photographs show children and parents in situations common in divorced families. With a nice introduction for parents, this book offers children lots of reassurance and validation while promoting the hope that they'll eventually feel better.

Ages: 3–7   **Cultural context:** Multicultural

Good-bye, Daddy! **by Brigitte Weninger. Illus. by Alan Marks.**
24 pages North-South, 1995.
Imagination can be a resource for coping with divorce. When Tom's father drops him off at his mother's house, he's so hurt and angry that he doesn't want to say good-bye. His teddy bear tells him the story of a young bear who feels the way Tom does. At the end of the story, the mother bear talks with the young bear about how it's better that the

two adult bears don't live together anymore because it's not good to live together when you're always arguing. She reassures the little bear that the father bear loves the little bear very much, cheering up the little bear and making Tom calm enough to fall asleep. This story will help children cope with their anger about divorce.

Ages: 3–7　　　**Cultural context:** European

Grandma Without Me **by Judith Vigna. 32 pages Whitman, 1984.**

Sometimes a divorce can mean the loss of people other than parents. In this story, a boy who lives with his mother misses his paternal grandma very much after his parents' divorce, especially at Thanksgiving. He recalls how Grandma was his main source of support during the divorce, reassuring him that it wasn't his fault. Grandma sends him a loving letter with a scrapbook for keeping in touch with her. As a way to be with her on Thanksgiving, the boy makes a life-size drawing of himself, which he sends to her, and at the end of the story, Mommy promises that he'll be with Grandma next Thanksgiving. Children can use this story to find ways to keep connections with people they miss after a divorce. Grandma's understanding of the boy's sadness, and her firm statement that he's not to blame, will also be helpful to children.

Ages: 3–7　　　**Cultural context:** European-American

I Don't Want to Talk About It **by Jeanie Franz Ransom. Illus. by Kathryn Kunz Finney. 32 pages Magination, 2000.**

Children can have difficulty tolerating their feelings about their parents' divorce. This story begins tense, stormy, and full of a girl's overwhelming emotions as her parents tell her they're going to divorce. She's expected this but doesn't want to hear it, believe it, or talk about it. She expresses her pain, anger, and fears as wishes to be animals; for example, to be as prickly as a porcupine so that nothing could hurt her. In spite of her intensity, her parents calmly show that they understand her feelings, reassuring her that they will always be her mom and dad, will always love and care for her, and will still do with her individually the things they've always enjoyed. Their comforting words give the girl safety to feel secure with both of them, which brings relief. A detailed note to parents discusses ways to help children cope with divorce. Providing empathy with the painful initial feelings about parents' divorce, this story gives soothing answers to children's most frightening questions.

Ages: 4–8   **Cultural context:** European-American

It's Not Your Fault, KoKo Bear **by Vicki Lansky.**
Illus. by Jane Prince. 32 pages Book Peddlers, 1998.
Divorce raises practical and emotional issues for children. When KoKo's parents divorce, KoKo expresses confusion, sadness, and anger—feelings that KoKo's parents accept. Dealing with practical realities, the story shows kids the logistics of living in MaMa and PaPa's separate houses, and addresses issues around telling KoKo's teacher about the divorce. There is lots of reassurance that KoKo is not to blame, that MaMa and PaPa are still part of KoKo's family, and that both parents love KoKo. Eventually KoKo's feelings are resolved, as KoKo realizes that KoKo, MaMa, and PaPa are still a family, despite the divorce. In addition to an introduction for parents, each page includes text for parents about ways to help children cope. This story provides reassurance about common concerns among young children whose parents are divorcing, offering hope that, like KoKo, they will eventually feel better.

Ages: 3–7   **Cultural context:** N/A

Loon Summer **by Barbara Santucci. Illus. by Andrea Shine.**
32 pages Eerdmans, 2001.
Family activities can evoke losses that kids have experienced when their parents divorced. Rainie visits the lake with Dad for the first time since her parents' divorce, and she misses Mom. She gradually learns to do new things, finding ways to enjoy the things she used to do with both parents in different ways, such as eating blueberries instead of Mom's blueberry jam. By the time they leave the lake, she's accepted that despite her wishes, things can't be the way they used to. She realizes that even though she's experienced an irrevocable loss, she can still depend on some things—just as the loons will always come back to the lake, so will she and Dad. Rainie's experience shows children a way to move through a grieving state to a more differentiated state in which they can acknowledge both the losses and still having much that they value.

Ages: 5–8   **Cultural context:** European-American

Mama and Daddy Bear's Divorce by **Cornelia Maude Spelman.**
Illus. by Kathy Parkinson. 24 pages Whitman, 1998.
Feelings of loss, confusion, and disruption arise for Dinah when she
learns that her parents are divorcing. She and her sister are to live
with Mama during the week and Daddy on most weekends. Although
she misses the parent who isn't with her, Dinah finds ways to keep
contact with that parent. Eventually her sadness and worry dissipate
as she comes to understand that her parents will always be her parents
and that they still love her. Including a note for grownups, this sweetly
told story conveys a sensitive understanding of children's needs for
continuity, providing hope that they'll feel better and reassurance that
both parents still love them. It acknowledges children's sense of loss,
while at the same time communicating that the loss is not total.

Ages: 2–6   **Cultural context:** N/A

Missing Rabbit by **Roni Schotter. Illus. by Cyd Moore.**
32 pages Clarion, 2002.
Feeling pulled apart is often part of divorce for children. Kara has special
times with each parent, and when she leaves one parent's house to go to
the other, she's both happy and sad. As if to say that a part of her wants
to stay, she always declares before leaving that her special toy, Rabbit,
wants to stay. Rabbit stays, but Kara inevitably misses Rabbit at the
other parent's house, forcing the first parent to bring Rabbit to Kara.
At each house, Rabbit asks Kara where he lives. In the beginning, she
doesn't know, but she eventually tells Rabbit that he lives with her. Then
Rabbit wants to know where Kara lives. Mama and Papa tell Rabbit
that Kara lives in each's house sometimes and is always in both parents'
hearts. Kara can make sense of this because it's similar to the way in
which Rabbit is always in *her* heart. This story shows children a way to
resolve the pulled-apart feeling they often have when parents divorce,
along with the security that both parents will always love them.

Ages: 3–7   **Cultural context:** European-American

On the Day His Daddy Left by **Eric J. Adams and Kathleen
Adams. Illus. by Layne Johnson. 24 pages Whitman, 2000.**
Guilt is an important part of divorce for many children. On the day
his daddy moves out, Danny writes down a secret question: "Is it my

fault?" He shares the question with his teacher, his friend, his dad, and his mom, who all reassure him that the answer is no. His mom writes "No" on the piece of paper, suggesting that he keep the answer with him and look at it whenever he asks the question. Danny does this until the question falls apart and blows away in the wind. Even then, he continues to ask whatever questions he needs to about his father's departure. An afterword for adults suggests ways to talk to children about divorce. A strength of this story is its acceptance of Danny's questions and his need for reassurance, no matter how often they occur. In addition, it addresses children's self-blame especially well, helping kids find a way to cope with it.

Ages: 4–8   **Cultural context:** Multicultural
Main character's cultural background: European-American

Priscilla Twice **by Judith Caseley. 32 pages Greenwillow, 1995.**
Like many children, when her parents divorce, Priscilla struggles with the meaning of family and her place in it, as well as with feelings of help-lessness, sadness, and anger. Each parent reassures Priscilla that they both will always love her and that their divorce had nothing to do with anything she did. When she expresses her distress by being messy, defi-ant, and insulting, each parent continues to love her no matter what. In the end, Priscilla feels secure in loving both parents. The illustrations have a quality that is both simple and at the same time full of color, tex-ture, and detail. This story shows a child who successfully resolves her feelings about her parents' divorce, demonstrating that parents will help contain kids' feelings even when they feel overwhelmed. It also gives chil-dren some good ideas about how to use drawing pictures and talking with a good friend to help them work through their feelings.

Ages: 4–8   **Cultural context:** Multicultural
Main character's cultural background: European-American

Saturday Is Pattyday **by Lesléa Newman.**
Illus. by Annette Hegel. 24 pages New Victoria, 1993.
When their parents divorce, kids feel sad, and may worry about losing the noncustodial parent. Frankie lives with one of his moms, Allie; his other mom, Patty, has recently moved out. Frankie says he's heard

them argue when they thought he was sleeping. Allie reassures him that although they're sad, it will ultimately be better this way. When Frankie argues with Patty, he worries that he and Patty might get divorced, just as Allie and Patty did. Patty explains that divorce is only for adults, and she assures Frankie that both will 'always, always, always, always' be his moms. Giving children the reassurances they need when their parents are divorcing, this story shows them that they can find a way to keep loving connections with both parents.

Ages: 3–7   **Cultural context:** Multicultural
Main character's cultural background: European-American

Two Places to Sleep **by Joan Schuchman.**
Illus. by Jim LaMarche. 32 pages Carolrhoda, 1979.
Divorce brings many sources of confusion, from questions about living arrangements, to guilt, to divided loyalties. After his parents' divorce, David lives with Dad and sees Mom on weekends. He notices that his friends who have divorced parents live with their mothers and asks Dad why he lives with him. Dad reminds David that Dad, Mom, and the judge had decided with David that it would be better for David not to have to move. David straightforwardly expresses his dislike of the divorce, and Dad acknowledges this. Mom reassures David that she isn't divorced from *him*, that both parents will always love him, and that the divorce wasn't his fault. He notices that she seems to listen better now. It's okay with both parents that David loves them both. By the end of the story, David is beginning to adjust to the divorce, conveying acceptance of children's dislike of parents' divorce and reassurance that they'll feel better eventually.

Ages: 4–8   **Cultural context:** European-American

PART 6

RELATIONSHIPS

Chapter 20

Friendship

Children initially learn about relationships from their parents and sometimes other family members. As kids grow, they develop relationships outside their family. Friendships can be a enormous source of support, companionship, and learning about oneself and the world. The picture books summarized in the first part of this chapter celebrate the joys of friendship and show children how to make and keep friends. Friends can also be a source of distress sometimes. The second part of this chapter summarizes picture books about one of the potential downsides of friendship: peer pressure. These stories are helpful in showing kids how and why to resist pressures to be untrue to themselves.

MAKING AND KEEPING CONNECTIONS

Learning how to create and sustain friendships is one of the important developmental tasks of childhood. This involves gradually moving from a normal self-centered perspective, in which the child sees things only from her or his own point of view, to a perspective that recognizes that others are the center of their own worlds and see things from *their* point of view. When friends care for each other and acknowledge each other's individuality, it's possible for them to work together constructively for the benefit of both. Because conflicts, separations, and divergent individual development can stress friendships, children need to learn how to facilitate the survival and growth of their friendships under these difficult conditions

See also Chapter 18 for stories about separations between friends when one of them moves to a new house.

39 Uses for a Friend **by Harriet Ziefert.**
Illus. by Rebecca Doughty. 34 pages Putnam, 2001.
Friends do many things for each other. Each of the whimsical drawings in this book illustrates one of these, from the emotional (for example, "audience", "listener", and "hand holder") to the more practical ("hairdresser", "bug remover," and "napkin"; that is, one child wiping hands on another's shirt). A rich, multifaceted picture of friendship emerges from this simple format.
Ages: 3–8   **Cultural context:** Multicultural

Be Quiet, Marina! **by Kirsten DeBear. Illus. by Laura Dwight.**
32 pages Star Bright, 2001.
Friends are similar in some ways and different in others, and part of friendship is finding a way to live with the differences. Marina and Moira are four-year-old classmates who both like to dance, play ball, and play with dolls and blocks. But Marina likes noise and expresses anger by screaming, whereas Moira likes quiet and feels frightened by noise. So when Marina screams, Moira leaves in search of a quiet place. One day, Moira responds to Marina's screaming by asking her politely but firmly not to scream. Marina settles down, and they play quietly. They become best friends. Moira isn't scared any more, and Marina controls her anger. Marina has cerebral palsy and Moira has Down's syndrome. In a very accessible way, this story makes clear the give-and-take required for friendship.
Ages: 3–6   **Cultural context:** European-American

Being Friends **by Karen Beaumont. Illus. by Joy Allen.**
32 pages Dial, 2002.
In this rhyming book, two girls celebrate a friendship that makes room for each one's individuality. For example, they can paint together, with each using her favorite colors. One prefers red, while the other prefers blue, but both like purple. Similarly, they both appreciate their uniqueness and their togetherness. Wearing very different kinds of costumes, they can trick-or-treat together. In spite of all their differences, what they have in common is their enjoyment of being friends. This story helps children understand that with cooperation there's room for both individuality and unity in a good friendship.
Ages: 4–8   **Cultural context:** Multicultural
Main character's cultural background: European-American

Best Friends **by Steven Kellogg. 32 pages Dial, 1985.**
Children may be disappointed when a friendship doesn't live up to idealized expectations. Kathy and Louise are best friends. Their imaginary play includes a wonderful horse called Golden Silverwind that lives between their houses. When Louise goes on a fun summer vacation, Kathy is lonely and resentful. She feels better anticipating a new puppy from their neighbor's dog's litter, but, to her bitter disappointment, there's only one puppy, and Louise gets it. But Louise decides that the puppy will belong to both children. They name the puppy Golden Silverwind, and it lives in a doghouse between their houses. Just as the puppy isn't as wonderful as the magical horse, the children's friendship isn't the idealized one that Kathy wishes for, but both the puppy and the friendship are real and special. Kids will learn how to put aside unrealistic expectations and to accept and value the caring that is part of genuine friendships.
Ages: 4–9   **Cultural context:** Multicultural
Main character's cultural background: European-American

Blue Horse **by Helen Stephens. 26 pages Scholastic, 2001.**
A make-believe friend can be a bridge to making friends with other children. When Tilly moves to a new town, she doesn't have any friends. Her Blue Horse becomes her best friend, and she has lots of adventures with him, imagining herself as a brave astronaut and a prize-winning cowhand. Upon seeing a girl in the park, when Tilly feels too shy to say hello,

Blue Horse encourages her, reminding her of her courage in their adventures. So Tilly invites the girl, Pip, to play —and it turns out that Pip has a special toy friend, too. After this, Tilly is able to make lots of friends. This colorfully illustrated story shows children how to use a "practice" friendship with a toy as a transition to friendships with other kids.

Ages: 2–6.   **Cultural context:** Multicultura
Main character's cultural background: unclear

Bravo, Mildred and Ed! **by Karen Wagner.**
Illus. by Janet Pedersen. 33 pages Walker & Company, 2000.
Sometimes being yourself means being apart from a friend, but friendship can support and survive this. Mildred and Ed are best friends and do everything together, but Mildred's violin recital conflicts with Ed's art show. They practice doing things separately so that they can get used to it, and they miss each other. On the night before the recital and show, they're sad and doubtful. But Mildred plays her violin for Ed, and Ed shows her a portrait of her that he's displaying at the art show. They know they'll be together in their hearts even when they're apart, and reminders of each one's presence cheer the other. Children will understand that friends support each other, even if it means having to be apart—and that this doesn't in any way diminish their joy in being together.

Ages: 4–8   **Cultural context:** N/A

Enemy Pie **by Derek Munson. Illus. by Tara Calahan King.**
34 pages Chronicle, 2000.
Friends can sometimes be found in unlikely places. A boy tells about his enemy, Jeremy Ross, who laughs at him when he strikes out in baseball and doesn't invite him to his party. The boy's dad understands about enemies and proposes that they use Enemy Pie to get rid of an enemy. Dad explains that Enemy Pie can only work if the boy spends a day with his enemy. So the boy reluctantly spends a day with Jeremy and finds that he has fun. By the end of the day, the boy is afraid that if Jeremy eats the Enemy Pie, he'll be poisoned. Jeremy has become his friend. This story shows children that even someone you don't like at first can end up as a friend.

Ages: 5–8   **Cultural context:** Multicultural
Main character's cultural background: European-American

Farfallina and Marcel **by Holly Keller. 32 pages**
Greenwillow, 2002.
An important part of friendship is its capacity to survive individual development. Farfallina, a caterpillar, and Marcel, a gosling, like each other immediately and become friends. Each is tenderly considerate of the other. One day, Farfallina feels strange and goes up into a tree to rest. She's getting ready to make her cocoon, but neither she nor Marcel knows that. While he waits for her, Marcel grows into an adult goose, and eventually gives up looking for Farfallina. Meanwhile, when Farfallina comes out of the cocoon, metamorphosed into a butterfly, she can't find Marcel. She goes to the pond where he is swimming, but he's changed so much that she doesn't recognize him. Unwittingly, Marcel, the grown goose, starts a conversation with her, and they discover that each is the other's long-lost friend. This resonant story emphasizes the enduring power of friendship and its ability to withstand even the most dramatic change.
Ages: 3–8   **Cultural context:** N/A

Friends **by Rob Lewis. 32 pages Holt, 1999.**
Give and take is an important part of friendship. Oscar (a rabbit) moves to a new house and hopes to make new friends. Unfortunately, he has a bit of a bossy streak and only wants friends who will want to do what *he* wants to do: go swimming. When he first meets the rabbits in his new neighborhood, he can't make friends because they don't want to swim and their activities don't appeal to him. His mother explains that he "will have to join in with what they like doing." He's skeptical, but when he sees others doing this, he realizes that having friends might be more important to him than swimming. Once he tries doing what the other rabbits want to do, his new friends join him for a swim. By showing that an important aspect of making friends is seeing things their way as well as your own way, this story helps children understand the role of mutuality in friendship.
Ages: 3–7   **Cultural context:** N/A

Henry and Amy (Right-Way-Round and Upside Down)
by Stephen Michael King. 32 pages Walker, 1999.
Even "perfect" people can learn from their friends. Henry can't seem to do anything "right", though it's clear that he has a unique and creative

perspective. He meets Amy, who seems to do everything right. He admires her enormously, and she teaches him how to do many things. But Amy wishes that she didn't do things so perfectly. So Henry teaches her how to select mismatched clothes and roll down a hill sideways. Henry and Amy pool their competence and creativity to create a wonderful tree house. This story imparts the important ideas that friends can always learn from each other, and even when one seems "better," the friendship enriches the perspectives of both.

Ages: 3–7   **Cultural context:** European-American

How to Be a Friend **by Laurie Krasny Brown and Marc Brown. 32 pages Little, Brown, 1998.**
In this kid-friendly guide to making friends, illustrated with charming drawings of human-like dinosaurs, the authors acknowledge the value of both solitude and togetherness. They define friendship and give clear examples of friendly and unfriendly behavior. Providing practical, accessible suggestions for joining in with other kids, coping with feeling shy, dealing with bullies, and overcoming arguments productively, this book offers kids helpful, constructive information about the process of friendships.

Ages: 3–8   **Cultural context:** N/A

I Like the Way You Are **by Eve Bunting. Illus. by John O'Brien. 48 pages Clarion, 2000.**
Great friendships include togetherness, individuality, support, and mutual problem solving. Turtle and Spottie are friends who exercise, plant a garden, go to movies and restaurants, and hike together. When one is better at something than the other, he doesn't brag—each supports the other's self-esteem, and they discover that their combined strengths benefit both. When they disagree about what they want, they compromise, or find ways for each to get what he wants. They express appreciation for each other's friendship and individuality, showing children many ways to be a good friend.

Ages: 5–9   **Cultural context:** N/A

Making Friends by Fred Rogers. Illus. by Jim Judkis.
32 pages Putnam, 1987.
In this gentle, kid-friendly guide, illustrated with color photographs, Mr. Rogers explains who a friend is and reminds children that they can have more than one friend. He discusses the difficulties of sharing and compromising with friends, but points out that when friends do this, they can learn from each other. He describes some of the kinds of things friends can do together, acknowledging that friends can make each other feel bad, and he encourages children to talk about any bad feelings like this with an adult they trust. Including a note for adults, this book will help young children understand what friendship is and how it works.
Ages: 2–6   **Cultural context:** Multicultural

Nothing Scares Us by Frieda Wishinsky. Illus. by Neal Layton.
27 pages Carolrhoda, 2000.
Friends work together to help both feel good about themselves. Lucy and Lenny are best friends who play brave make-believe games and enjoy thinking of themselves as fearless. Lucy is anxious and ashamed when she discovers she's afraid of a TV monster that doesn't frighten Lenny—until she finds out that he's afraid of spiders, which don't frighten her. In the end, they decide to stick to activities where both can feel brave. This story vividly illustrates the role of a genuinely caring friendship in managing fears and feeling good about yourself.
Ages: 3–8   **Cultural context:** European-American

Share and Take Turns by Cheri J. Meiners.
Illus. by Meredith Johnson. 40 pages Free Spirit, 2003.
Sharing is a necessary skill for friendship. This friendly, practical book explains that sharing helps people get along and tells about four ways to share: dividing things, using things together, trading, and taking turns. Sharing can be hard, and there are other things kids can do when they don't want to share, such as sharing something else. An afterword for adults suggests ways to use each page of the book with children, describing games intended to promote sharing. Accessible text and cheerful watercolor illustrations show children the importance of sharing and specific ways to share.
Ages: 2–6   **Cultural context:** Multicultural

***Sunshine and Storm* by Elisabeth Jones.**
Illus. by James Coplestone. 30 pages Ragged Bears, 2001.
An important idea for kids to understand is that sometimes friends make each other angry. Sunshine, a cat, and Storm, a dog, are best friends. After a walk in the rain, Storm forgets that Sunshine hates to get wet and shakes himself dry near her. She gets angry, and Storm is hurt by her anger. Soon, they're both sorry about having hurt each other. Storm licks Sunshine in apology, and she can't help licking him back. They realize that feelings like anger can change as fast as the weather, but their friendship is permanent, reminding children that friendship can survive anger.
Ages: 3–7   **Cultural context:** N/A

***Wallace's Lists* by Barbara Bottner and Gerald Kruglik.**
Illus. by Olof Landström. 40 pages Tegen/HarperCollins, 2004.
Being friends with someone whose personality is different from one's own can expand our sense of who we are. Wallace decides what to do on the basis of to-do lists, but his new neighbor, Albert, has some interesting ideas that aren't on Wallace's lists. Albert likes adventures, but Wallace doesn't. When Albert takes off on a spontaneous trip and a storm starts, Wallace rushes to warn Albert of the danger so he won't fly his plane—a process that turns out to be quite an adventure. Wallace finds his own capacity to do more spontaneous things, like telling jokes, and he treasures the new friend who has helped him learn this about himself. Through this story, kids will see that although making a new friend might involve changing your ideas in ways that seem scary, it can also be fun. They'll understand that through friendship, people can develop capacities they never thought they had.
Ages: 4–7   **Cultural context:** N/A

PEER PRESSURE

One struggle that children may have in their relationships with other kids is figuring out how to stay true to themselves and at the same time, connected to others when they disagree with other kids. The stories summarized below show ways in which children may experience this struggle and give children models for trusting themselves without giving up their relationships.

See also *Ira Sleeps Over* (Chapter 11) and *Hey, Little Ant* (Chapter 21) for additional relevant stories.

Arnie and the Skateboard Gang by Nancy L. Carlson. 32 pages Viking, 1995.

What if kids will only accept you if you do something that you think is a bad idea? Arnie, who skateboards, is happy to be accepted by the skateboard gang at the park, but then they tell him to ride down a very steep hill, where a more-experienced kid has already gotten hurt. Arnie realizes that if he does this, the gang will think he's really cool, but after imagining himself with multiple casts and crutches, he tells them that they're crazy to suggest it, and proposes going back to the park. Suddenly, he's become a leader, and everyone agrees with him. Although such a positive outcome seems less than likely, Arnie is a good model for thinking through consequences and acting on the basis of his good judgment, regardless of what other kids think.

Ages: 3–7 **Cultural context:** N/A

Hunter's Best Friend At School by Laura Malone Elliott. Illus. by Lynn Munsinger. 32 pages HarperCollins, 2002.

Peer pressure can grow out of the idea that being best friends is liking all the same things and doing everything together. When Stripe is feeling mischievous one day, he does goofy things that his best friend, Hunter, feels compelled to imitate—sticking out his tongue with his half-eaten snack on it, and cutting up his artwork into many pieces. The difference is they aren't fun for Hunter. His mother explains that friendship doesn't always mean doing what your friend wants, adding that sometimes friendship requires helping your friend to be the best he can be. The next day, Hunter finds he really doesn't want to do the disruptive things Stripe is doing. He gives Stripe a look and ignores Stripe's attempts to get him to act disruptive, inspiring Stripe to copy his positive behaviors and acknowledge Hunter's genuine friendship. This story shows children how to trust their own judgment, even when a friend disagrees. It also makes clear how this self-trust can actually benefit the friend and the friendship.

Ages: 3–7   **Cultural context:** N/A

Willie's Not the Hugging Kind by Joyce Durham Barrett. Illus. by Pat Cummings. 32 pages HarperCollins, 1989.

Sometimes peer pressure comes in the form of shaming. Willie's friend Jo-Jo tells him that hugs are silly, so he stops hugging his parents and his sister, Rose. It's obvious to Rose that it's Jo-Jo who's silly. She suggests that if Willie agrees with Jo-Jo, maybe he just isn't "the hugging kind." But Willie knows inside that hugs aren't silly and wants one more than anything. He hugs a tree and his bike, but he misses the safe, warm feeling of hugging a person. He finally hugs his mama, and his whole family welcomes his hugs back. After that, when Jo-Jo teases him, he can stand up to him, knowing inside that hugs are good. Kids will benefit from this example of trusting your own instincts and being true to yourself in spite of others' opinions.

Ages: 5–8   **Cultural context:** Multicultural
Main character's cultural background: African-American

[CHAPTER 21]

Bullying

Bullying has been receiving increasing attention as a problem among children. Bullying can include name-calling, hate speech, and other forms of contempt, threats or actual physical harm, sexual harassment or abuse, or isolation and exclusion. Signs that a child may have been bullied include bruises, physical symptoms that keep him/her home from school, missing belongings or money, sleeping problems, bedwetting, irritability, problems with concentration and/or schoolwork, and unexpected changes in routine. None of these means that the child has definitely been bullied, but they may prompt you to find out more. Consider both direct and open-ended questions; for example, about what happens during recess. Listening and offering to help can reduce the intimidation that comes with bullying. Kids also need to know that it isn't their fault if someone bullies them. They may also need support in making friends. A verbally assertive response can sometimes solve the problem of bullying. In some situations, friendliness or creativity may be better. Sometimes adult intervention is necessary and effective. If your child bullies others, it's important to communicate clearly that this behavior is not okay and to discuss why the child does it and ways to stop it. Consider asking this child whether something is bothering him/her and how he/she gets along with other kids. Praise appropriate behaviors directed toward other kids.

See also *How to Be a Friend* (Chapter 20) for more about coping with bullies.

Arthur's April Fool **by Marc Brown. 32 pages**
Little, Brown, 1983.
Creative problem solving can sometimes stop bullying. Arthur is worried because his classmate, Binky, has threatened to beat him up. When Arthur presents a magic show, Binky frightens him by volunteering to participate in a trick. He turns his fear around by announcing that he'll saw Binky in half. This throws Binky off balance, enabling Arthur to perform the most amazing trick of all: he makes Binky disappear. Sending the positive message that even very threatening bullies can be outwitted, this positive story shows kids how to overcome bullies by using the power of their brains.
Ages: 5–8   **Cultural context:** N/A

Bully **by Judith Caseley. 32 pages Greenwillow, 2001.**
When a friend becomes a bully, sometimes the friend just needs some extra caring. Jack, who used to be a friend, starts bullying Mickey— stepping on Mickey's hand at the park, stealing Mickey's cookies at school, threatening to beat him up, and getting him into trouble with their teacher. Mama advises Mickey to be nice to Jack. She realizes that Jack has a new baby in his family and may be upset about this. His sister, Jenna, advises him to give Jack cookies. He takes her advice, and Jack responds positively to his friendliness. He's able to make Jack laugh, which enables the boys to be friends again. This outcome may be more positive than is often realistic, but in some situations, kindness may be just what's needed.
Ages: 4–8   **Cultural context:** Multicultural
Main character's cultural background: European-American

Geez Louise! by Susan Middleton Elya. Illus. by Eric Brace.
32 pages Putnam, 2003.

Showing competence can be one way to stand up to a bully. Louise, a stinkbug, doesn't have many friends because she's so stinky. She considers entering a skating contest, but Kiki, a cockroach and a bully who teases Louise about her stinkiness, is also entering, and Louise hates the thought of losing to Kiki. Louise's one friend encourages her to enter on behalf of all the bugs that Kiki bullies. Although she's terrified, Louise gets courage from the thought that she could show the other bugs that there's more to her than stinkiness, and she skates flawlessly. Kiki plugs her nose as she skates past Louise and is so distracted by this that she's thrown off balance, giving Louise the victory. The other bugs like her even though she stinks, because she's stood up to Kiki. Written in witty rhyme and illustrated in a modern, almost retro, style, this story offers a positive message about standing up to a bully in a safe situation.

Ages: 4–8   **Cultural context:** N/A

Hazel's Amazing Mother by Rosemary Wells. **32 pages Dial, 1985.**

Sometimes the only solution to a bully problem is a parent's intervention. Three kids accuse Hazel of taking their ball, and they take her beloved doll, Eleanor, from her, ruining Eleanor. Hazel cries out for her mother, who, on the other side of town, knows instinctively that Hazel needs her. Mother is swept up by the wind and blown to the very tree where Hazel is sitting. Mother commands the children to fix Eleanor, punctuating her words with tossed tomatoes. The bullies fix Eleanor and go away. When asked how she did it, Hazel's mother replies, "It must have been the power of love." Children will feel safe knowing that their parents can protect them—and may even learn something from Mother's responses that they can use themselves when bullied.

Ages: 3–7   **Cultural context:** N/A

Hey, Little Ant by Phillip Hoose and Hannah Hoose.
Illus. by Debbie Tilley. 25 pages Tricycle, 1998.

Bullying can result when the one child doesn't see things from another's perspective. When a kid threatens to squish an ant, the ant pleads for its life. The kid responds that the ant is very small and couldn't even feel pain—a good metaphor for the dehumanizing aspects of both bullying and war—causing it to retort that it and the kid are actually quite similar. Adding the element of peer pressure, the kid disagrees, saying that his friends think he should squish the ant. Once again, this elicits an appeal from the ant, who tries to get the kid to see things from an ant's point of view. The story ends by asking the reader whether the ant should be squished. Encouraging kids to develop empathy, which is likely to reduce the risk of their becoming bullies, this story also shows kids who are bullied that they have the right to be safe.

Ages: 3–8   **Cultural context:** Multicultural

Main character's cultural background: European-American

Karate Girl **by Mary Leary. 32 pages**
Farrar, Straus and Giroux, 2003.
Martial arts can be useful for coping with bullying because it helps kids feel strong and teaches them *not* to fight. A girl is angry and scared when kids bully her younger brother, so she starts studying karate. The story describes the karate lessons in detail: the *gi* (uniform); different belt colors; use of breathing, relaxation, and warm-up exercises; *kata* (sequenced moves); and development of self-control, confidence, dedication, and concentration. When the bullies appear again, the girl shows them she isn't afraid, telling them that if she really has to fight, she can and will. In the end, they walk away, and she has learned her *sensei's* (teacher's) first lesson; she has become sure enough of herself to avoid fighting. Children can use this valuable nonviolent alternative as a way to cope with bullying, with or without karate instruction.

Ages: 5–9   **Cultural context:** Multicultural

Main character's cultural background: European-American

The King of the Playground **by Phyllis Reynolds Naylor.**
Illus. by Nola Langner Malone. 32 pages Atheneum, 1994.
When kids can evaluate bullies' threats realistically, they may be less afraid than they would otherwise be. Sammy says he's the king of the playground and threatens Kevin when he comes to play there. Kevin feels frightened, and his father helps him evaluate Sammy's threats. With a few examples, Kevin realizes that he doesn't need to be afraid

and is even able to engage Sammy first in imagination and later in cooperative play. This story will help kids find their strength when confronted with bullying.

Ages: 4–8   **Cultural context:** European-American

Mim, Gym, and June **by Denis Roche. 32 pages**
Houghton Mifflin, 2003.
Conflict can often be resolved when people focus on a goal that requires both their efforts to attain. When Mim and June disagree about who gets to walk at the front of the line, June becomes angry and threatening, and Mim is increasingly scared. She gives June a cupcake in an attempt to be friends, and June just squashes it. In gym class, June wins the wrestling event and Mim wins the 50-yard dash. As they both sulk, June acknowledges that Mim *is* faster than any of the other kids, and Mim responds by acknowledging June's strength. They realize that pooling these resources would make them a good team and decide to be partners for the last event, an obstacle course. When they win, they walk back to class at the front of the double line. The teamwork displayed here illustrates the hope of coping with bullying through mutual respect.

Ages: 5–8   **Cultural context:** N/A

Nobody Knew What to Do: A Story about Bullying
by Becky Ray McCain. Illus. by Todd Leonardo.
24 pages Whitman, 2001.
When there's nothing left to do to stop bullies, adult intervention can solve the problem, as it does at one school where bullies intimidate kids by threatening and hitting, so that everyone is afraid to resist and no one knows what to do. After helplessly watching them torment another boy, the narrator finally tells his teacher. The principal calls the parents of all the bullies, and the bullying stops. An afterword for adults discusses bullying prevention. With an empathic example of how to stop bullying, this story gives the clear messages that it's okay to seek adult help and that it's possible to stop bullying even when it feels as if there's no way out.

Ages: 4–8   **Cultural context:** Multicultural
Main character's cultural background: African-American

The Rat and the Tiger by Keiko Kasza. 32 pages Putnam, 1993.
Sometimes bullying can become a problem between friends, as it does
for Rat and Tiger. Tiger, who is big and tough, took all the good parts in
make-believe play and the biggest piece of doughnut, and expected Rat
to get flowers for him. Rat felt too small to object. When Tiger knocks
over Rat's block castle, Rat is angry and sad. He yells at Tiger, even
though this makes him scared. When Tiger finally treats Rat the way
he wants to be treated, they learn to take turns and share, becoming
friends again. Emphasizing the lack of empathy and mutuality involved
in bullying, this story encourages children to stand up to bullies.
Ages: 3–7   **Cultural context:** N/A

The Recess Queen by Alexis O'Neill.
Illus. by Laura Huliska-Beith. 32 pages Scholastic, 2002.
Sometimes kids bully when they don't know how to be friends. This
seems to be the case with Mean Jean, who rules the playground, at-
tacking kids who have the nerve to play with the equipment before
she does. When little Katie Sue joins the class, she doesn't know about
Jean's reputation and plays the way she wants to. Jean tells Katie
Sue that Jean always has to go first. Katie Sue calls Jean on her bossi-
ness and instead of turning over the ball Jean wants, she runs away
with it. She then invites Jean to jump rope with her, marking the first
time anyone has asked Jean to play. Jean eventually joins Katie Sue,
both have fun, and Jean never bullies again. With a potential solution
to bullying, this story tells kids how to make friends with a bully and
defuse the bully's aggressive tendencies.
Ages: 4–8   **Cultural context:** Multicultural
Main character's cultural background: European-American

Stand Tall, Molly Lou Melon by Patty Lovell.
Illus. by David Catrow. 32 pages Putnam, 2001.
Feeling good about yourself is a source of resilience to bullying, as
Molly Lou Melon shows in this story. She's short and clumsy, has
buck teeth, and speaks in a strange-sounding voice, but she also has
a grandma who teaches her to be self-confident anyway. When she
goes to a new school, a bully picks on her repeatedly. Each time, she

uses her supposedly negative attributes to succeed, and each time, the bully feels foolish. He finally decides to be friendly to her. The illustrations include strangely proportioned faces that suggest a nightmare. By valuing herself, Molly Lou shows kids how to find the strength to resist bullying.

Ages: 3–7   **Cultural context:** Multicultural

Main character's cultural background: European-American

A Weekend with Wendell by Kevin Henkes. 32 pages
Greenwillow, 1986.

By definition, bullying is one-sided, as Wendell shows when he spends the weekend with Sophie. He bullies her by making up all the rules when they play, taking all the important parts in make-believe games, scaring her, ruining her toys, and getting away with behavior that Sophie could never get away with. At the end of the weekend, Sophie finds a way to make the rules in a make-believe game and take the part she wants. Although Wendell is distressed at first, they're soon having fun together, and by creatively introducing mutuality into their play, Sophie has made bullying impossible.

Ages: 3–7   **Cultural context:** N/A

[CHAPTER 22]

Diversity and Prejudice

Prejudice can be based on many attributes, including cultural background (including issues around color, national origin, language, or customs), gender, and social class. Many children are hurt, and even traumatized, by others' prejudice against them, and some are limited by their own biased attitudes. The picture books summarized in this chapter can be useful for children in both of these situations. They celebrate diversity among people, demonstrate the harmful effects of intolerance, and inspire strength in coping with prejudice. Some stories use a generic kind of "differentness", different species, or multiple kinds of differences among people to show how arbitrary prejudice is.

See also *Happy to Be Nappy* (Chapter 2), *Sumi's First Day of School Ever* (Chapter 13), *Yoko's Paper Cranes* (Chapter 18), *Be Quiet, Marina!* (Chapter 20), and *The Color of Home* (Chapter 33) for related stories. Chapters 26 and 27 include stories that address prejudice related to medical conditions, and Chapter 33 summarizes stories showing the role of arbitrary hatred over differences between cultures in war.

Amazing Grace by Mary Hoffman. Illus. by Caroline Binch. 26 pages Dial, 1991.

Prejudice threatens kids' sense of what's possible for them, as it does for Grace, who loves to act out stories. When her teacher says that the class is going to perform *Peter Pan*, Grace wants to be Peter, but other children discourage her because Peter is a boy and isn't black. Her Ma and her Nana assure her that she can be whoever she wants to be. Her class unanimously elects her to play Peter, and Ma and Nana celebrate her amazing performance and her capacity for self-determination. Grace is a powerful role model for being the person you want to be, regardless of other people's attempts to impose restrictions based on gender and ethnic background.

Ages: 4–7   **Cultural context:** Multicultural
Main character's cultural background: African-American

Baseball Saved Us by Ken Mochizuki. Illus. by Dom Lee. 32 pages Lee & Low, 1993.

The "relocation" camps to which Japanese Americans were sent during World War II are an example of large-scale racism. The narrator of this story describes playing baseball in the camps, using the energy of his anger at the camp guard, and all he represents, to hit his first home run. When he returns home, he finds the community still racist, although his baseball teammates grudgingly acknowledge his skill and provide some encouragement. He again uses his anger at racism to hit a home run. Raising children's awareness of racism's pernicious effects, while helping them understand the historical context of prejudice against Japanese Americans, this story shows an example of constructive coping with prejudice.

Ages: 6–10   **Cultural context:** Multicultural
Main character's cultural background: Asian American

The Colors of Us by Karen Katz. 28 pages Holt, 1999.

Differences among people can be a cause for celebration. Seven-year-old Lena joyfully acknowledges the delicious colors of her friends', relatives', and acquaintances' skin, from cinnamon, to French toast, to peanut butter, to chocolate, to peachy. She happily paints pictures of everyone she knows, each one a unique and beautiful color. The mixed-media illustrations are full of color and activity, adding an eye-catching element to this beautiful book that appreciates diversity among people in a genuinely positive way.

Ages: 3–7 **Cultural context:** Multicultural

Main character's cultural background: Latina

Different Just Like Me by Lori Mitchell. 32 pages Charlesbridge, 1999.

Prejudice involves an oversimplification that emphasizes differences among people to the exclusion of similarities. In *Different Just Like Me*, April learns about both differences and similarities among people. For example, she sees a deaf girl on the bus, who, unlike April, communicates in sign language, but like April, waves goodbye. As April continues on her journey, she meets people of many different shapes, sizes, colors, and abilities. The variety of flowers in Grammie's garden, fruits at the farmer's market, and downtown shops become symbols of the human diversity that April appreciates. Resources include several "same and different" exercises that give children practice in identifying both what is the same and what is different about several pictures. In a positive, accepting tone, this book promotes a differentiated understanding of diversity among people.

Ages: 3–8 **Cultural context:** Multicultural

Main character's cultural background: European-American

Flowers From Mariko by Rick Noguchi and Deneen Jenks. Illus. by Michelle Reiko Kumata. 32 pages Lee & Low, 2001.

Hope and endurance are essential for surviving racism. This story follows a Japanese-American girl named Mariko as she and her family leave the "relocation" camps of World War II. Her father, a gardener, had left his truck with their landlord, who has sold it and left town.

She's worried and profoundly discouraged. Her father gives Mariko some seeds, and for the first time, she plants a garden entirely on her own. The process of waiting for the flowers to grow parallels the endurance the family needs to get through the resettlement process. When the flowers bloom, her father gets a job as a gardener, and she finally feels that things are going to be all right. Mariko's hope has contributed to her family's survival of the internment, which is described in an afterword. Helping children understand the racism that has been directed at Japanese Americans, this story emphasizes the roles of hope and endurance in surviving prejudice.

Ages: 6–9   **Cultural context:** Asian American

Goin' Someplace Special **by Patricia C. McKissack.**
Illus. by Jerry Pinkney. 34 pages Atheneum, 2001.
The arbitrariness and pain of racism and the sustaining quality of community support are clear in this autobiographical story. 'Tricia Ann, who is African-American and lives in the South under Jim Crow segregation, goes to her favorite place by herself for the first time. She has to sit in the back of the bus, hastily gets up from a "whites only" park bench, and attracts an angry crowd when she inadvertently wanders into a hotel where a family friend works at the door. The clear sense of support within the African-American community in the midst of this outrage is shown by a woman who tells 'Tricia Ann that her grandmother is with her in her heart to help her. The ending reveals that 'Tricia Ann's favorite place is the public library, where "all are welcome." Children will understand the pain and wrongfulness of racism from inside a person who is experiencing it, while understanding how a caring community strengthens its members against racism.

Ages: 4–8   **Cultural context:** Multicultural
Main character's cultural background: African-American

Hope **by Isabell Monk. Illus. by Janice Lee Porter. 32 pages**
Carolrhoda, 1999.
Prejudice may be directed at people of multicultural backgrounds. Such is the case for Hope, during a visit to her Aunt Poogee. Hope and her aunt run into an old friend of Aunt Poogee's who stares and asks

Aunt Poogee whether Hope is "mixed." Hope can't stop wondering about this question, which her aunt seems to push aside, but at bedtime, Aunt Poogee tells her the story of how she got her name—"what it truly took to make Hope." Affirming the worth of people from all cultural backgrounds, this story lovingly celebrates the rich heritage of Hope's African-American mother and European-American father, and their hope for a world in which all people are recognized as belonging to the *human* race.

Ages: 5–8   **Cultural context:** Multicultural

I Look Like a Girl **by Sheila Hamanaka. 32 pages Morrow, 1999.**

If girls' appearance suggests submissiveness or weakness, don't be fooled. In this poetic book, girls assert that although they look like ordinary girls, they have the fierceness of a tiger, the agility of a dolphin, the speed and strength of a mustang, and the freedom of a condor. They aren't waiting around for any princes—they have strong, independent identities, their own motivations and desires, and the intense energy to fulfill them. This powerful book affirms girls' right to be themselves and to be powerful, in spite of others' expectations that they conform to gender stereotypes.

Ages: 3–7   **Cultural context:** Multicultural

Marianthe's Story **by Aliki. 62 pages Greenwillow, 1998.**

Immigration can be painful and difficult, particularly in the face of narrow-minded attitudes. This book contains two stories, "Painted Words" and "Spoken Memories", which together tell the story of Marianthe's immigration to the United States. In "Painted Words," she begins school in the United States and unable to speak English, expresses herself through painting pictures with the assistance of an understanding teacher. Although most of the children are kind, some insult her because of her limited English skills. Her mother reassures her and her teacher supports her. "Spoken Memories" contains the story she tells her class verbally, when she has learned enough English. She describes being raised in a small, poor Greek village in a loving family and immigrating because of the availability of education in the United States. Children who have similar life stories will feel validated, and others will gain a greater understanding of the experience of immigration.

Ages: 4–8   **Cultural context:** Multicultural

Main character's cultural background: European-American

Metropolitan Cow **by Tim Egan. 32 pages Houghton Mifflin, 1996.**

An important problem with prejudice is that it limits connections between people. Bennett is a cow, and his urbane parents only grudgingly allow him to play with his new neighbor, Webster, a pig. Although they tell Bennett that he is "far too dignified" to play with a pig, Bennett and Webster become great friends. When Bennett's mother tries to end their friendship, Bennett disappears, and only Webster can find him. Bennett's parents apologize to Webster's and begin to recognize the similarities between the two families. This appealing story makes it very clear that an overemphasis on differences among people leads us to overlook similarities, and as a result, to lose potential friendships.

Ages: 3–7   **Cultural context:** N/A

The Name Jar **by Yangsook Choi. 33 pages Knopf, 2001.**

One difficult aspect of immigration is the sense of being "different" that it often brings. When Unhei moves from Korea to the United States, kids at school tease her about her name. Her name symbolizes herself, which she experiences as different, and she feels ashamed. At first, in spite of her mother's support, Unhei refuses to introduce herself to her class. Because she wants to choose an "American" name, her classmates offer her several to choose from. It's only when one of Unhei's classmates, Joey, learns her name and clearly accepts it, that she has the courage to introduce herself to her class using her real name. She then discovers that Joey has taken a Korean name that means *friend*. Children who immigrate can use Unhei to learn self-acceptance, while others can use Joey to learn how to join with someone from a different culture in a genuinely accepting way.

Ages: 4–8   **Cultural context:** Multicultural

Main character's cultural background: Asian American

The Other Side by Jacqueline Woodson. Illus. by E. B. Lewis.
32 pages Putnam, 2001.
When cultural difference appears to signal danger, people are unable to make connections that they would otherwise have. Clover, who is African-American, and Annie, who is European-American, overcome this limitation. Both girls' mamas have told them not to play on the other side of the fence that separates their homes and the two sides of town because it's dangerous. After Clover has watched Annie sit on the fence for some time, she feels brave enough to talk to Annie. They discover that neither one's mama has forbidden sitting *on* the fence, and they sit there together, becoming friends. In this way they transform the fence, which was intended to keep them apart, into a way to bring them together. Children will understand that it's possible to reach out to people who appear different from them—and that this can result in connections that might not have seemed possible before.
Ages: 4–8   **Cultural context:** Multicultural
Main character's cultural background: African-American

A Pig Is Moving In! by Claudia Fries. **26 pages Orchard, 2000.**
If people have expectations that affect their perceptions of others, they often end up with mistaken impressions which limit their possibilities. The animals hope their new neighbor will be quiet and tidy, so they're worried when they find out he's a pig. After all, they expect him to be a slob. Initially, their expectations seem to be confirmed, but not everything is as it seems. Although Theodore the pig makes a few messes, he cleans up after himself. The "mud" they saw him carrying was clay, for making pottery. Theodore offers his neighbors tea and homemade cookies, and when the animals get over their embarrassment, everyone is pleased. This story clearly conveys the message that prejudices can be inaccurate and that if we assume that they're correct, we'll miss out on good friends.
Ages: 4–7   **Cultural context:** N/A

Pugdog by Andrea U'Ren. **32 pages**
Farrar, Straus and Giroux, 2001.
Prejudice involves having arbitrary expectations for an individual based on group membership. Assuming that his puppy, Pugdog, is

male, Mike allows Pugdog to chase squirrels, dig holes, and roll in dirt. When he finds out that Pugdog is female, he immediately demands that she become "ladylike," like the poodle at the park, and "watch [her] figure." She's given a bubble bath and perfumed, and put in fussy, restrictive clothes. She isn't allowed to chase squirrels, dig holes, or roll in dirt. Miserable, she runs away to the park to do the things she enjoys. Mike learns that being who she is makes Pugdog happy and promises not to oppress her with his ideas of what's feminine. Showing kids that gender-role norms depend on arbitrary assumptions, this story promotes flexibility in acceptance of self and others for who they are.

Ages: 3–7   **Cultural context:** European-American

The Sneetches. In *Sneetches and Other Stories* by Dr. Seuss. **24 pages Random House, 1989.**

Not only can the bases for prejudice can be ephemeral, but also, prejudice works against both oppressor and oppressed. As this story opens, the star-belly sneetches (a kind of large bird) repeatedly snub the plain-belly ones—the star-belly sneetches think they're "better." Sylvester McMonkey McBean arrives on the scene and makes a lot of money because of the sneetches' wish to change their appearance to that of whatever group is dominant at the time (which is constantly changing in the interest of McBean's economic state). The optimistic ending reveals that the sneetches discover that a sneetch is a sneetch whether or not they have stars. This brilliant story clearly communicates that prejudice is arbitrary, that it can be exploited, and that people feel happier and more connected when they work together instead of forming in-groups that work against each other.

Ages: 3–8   **Cultural context:** N/A

We Are a Rainbow by Nancy María Grande Tabor. **32 pages Charlesbridge, 1995.**

When a child moves to a new country, things are different in many ways. This book, which is bilingual in English and Spanish, portrays immigrant and native people initially appearing different to each other and sometimes experiencing frustration when they try to communicate with one another. The frustration leads to hurt feelings and separateness. The immigrant child character responds to these feelings with an awareness of people's similarities across cultures and a celebration of the value of friendship. For children who immigrate, this story offers empathy and normalizes some of the difficulties involved with an upbeat outcome. For children who are not immigrants, it provides an understanding of the experience of immigration.

Ages: 3–6   **Cultural context:** Multicultural

Whoever You Are **by Mem Fox. Illus. by Leslie Staub. 32 pages Harcourt, 1997.**
The diversity and unity of children throughout the world are celebrated in this engaging book. Children around the world differ in skin colors, homes, schools, geography, language, and lifestyles, but they're alike in their capacity for emotion, their laughs, smiles, pain, and love. The author encourages children to remember these fundamental similarities when they've grown up. The folk art-inspired illustrations are bordered with hand-carved wood, plaster, and faux gem frames. While acknowledging and celebrating diversity, this book conveys the message of fundamental similarity of all people.

Ages: 2–6   **Cultural context:** Multicultural

William's Doll **by Charlotte Zolotow.**
Illus. by William Pène Du Bois. 32 pages HarperCollins, 1972.
Gender-related prejudice can be expressed in judgments about toy choices. William wants a doll more than anything else. His father brings him a basketball and an electric train, and although he enjoys these, he still wants a doll. Although kids tease him about being a "sissy" and a "creep," his grandmother understands and brings him a doll. When his father objects, she explains to him that William will learn about being a father from playing with the doll. While showing the constricting nature of stereotypes, this story expresses a powerful message about the value of nurturance for males.

Ages: 3–7   **Cultural context:** European-American

Part 7

HEALTH, HEALTH PROBLEMS, AND HEALTH CARE

[CHAPTER 23]

Health and Nutrition

When children are first born, adults take care of all of their health needs, but as they grow, children gradually take on more self-care tasks—even little ones like washing their hands before meals. One way to stay healthy is to eat nutritious foods, and choosing appropriate foods is easier when kids know which foods they need. Some children are unwilling to eat the foods their parents want them to. Each of these aspects of health is addressed by the picture books summarized in this chapter.

STAYING HEALTHY

Knowledge about how to keep themselves healthy empowers children to make positive health choices. Kids benefit from age-appropriate information about health-related issues such as self-care, ordinary health problems, disease transmission, first aid, exercise, adequate rest, and stress management. Understanding how the body works can help kids take care of their health.

Dinosaurs Alive and Well! by Laurie Krasny Brown and Marc Brown. 32 pages Little, Brown, 1990.

When children know how to keep themselves healthy, they feel safer in the world. This book explains why we should take care of ourselves, and includes simple, practical information about nutrition, cleanliness, exercise, common health problems (such as colds and flu), and first aid. It also addresses feelings, friendship, asking for help, and getting enough rest, and suggests ways to relax and visualize positive experiences. Presenting information in a positive, supportive, friendly tone, with humorous, down-to-earth dinosaur illustrations, this book gives kids confidence in their ability to care for themselves in age-appropriate ways.

Ages: 3–7   **Cultural context:** N/A

From Head to Toe by Barbara Seuling. Illus. by Edward Miller. 32 pages Holiday House, 2002.

When kids know how their body works, taking care of it makes more sense. This colorful book provides a good introduction to the major body systems: skin; bones; joints; muscles; and nervous, respiratory, cardiovascular, urinary, and digestive systems. There are kid-friendly explanations for body functions from breathing, perception, and joint movement, to peeing, pooping, and farting. The book starts with a description of the body as an effective machine and ends with a speculation about the possibility of replacing body parts in the future, which may strike some readers as a little odd. Regardless, this foundation of information about body mechanics will help children understand how to take care of themselves.

Ages: 6–11   **Cultural context:** Multicultural

Germs Make Me Sick by Melvin Berger.
Illus. by Marylin Hafner. 32 pages Crowell, 1985.

Understanding contagious disease can help children avoid illness. Beginning with a fairly detailed description of germs (bacteria and viruses), this book explains that although germs are ubiquitous, the body has various ways to keep them out or prevent illness. The author explains that if illness is persistent or severe, medical attention is necessary, and he describes some diagnostic and treatment procedures. He also includes a list of ways to keep healthy, such as staying away from people who have colds or flu, hand washing, eating well, and getting enough sleep and exercise. With an upbeat ending that emphasizes kids' ability to keep themselves healthy, this book will help children understand how bacteria and viruses cause illness, and how they can treat and prevent illness themselves.

Ages: 4–8 **Cultural context:** European-American

No Measles, No Mumps for Me by Paul Showers.
Illus. by Harriett Barton. 40 pages Crowell, 1980.
Immunization is an important strategy for maintaining health. In this book, a boy introduces the idea of immunization by describing the illnesses that his grandmother had: whooping cough, mumps, and measles. The boy is glad he won't ever get those diseases because he's been immunized. He explains how white cells destroy viruses and bacteria, including the "weak germs" in an immunization. Walking the reader through the experience of getting a shot, he says that it hurt "a little" for a very short time, but he didn't mind because he knew it would help him stay healthy, providing a valuable lesson for kids who are scared of shots.

Ages: 6–10 **Cultural context:** Multicultural
Main character's cultural background: European-American

NUTRITION

Parents can't make children eat, but when kids understand the basic concepts of nutrition, they're empowered to choose foods that support their health. Few picture books give explicit nutritional information, although one of the picture books summarized below is a non-fiction work on nutrition for children. More typically, these stories celebrate nutritious foods, especially fruits and vegetables, in ways that may add to their appeal for children, including humor, cleverness, and vegetable gardening. One story points out the negative side of fast food.

Eating the Alphabet: Fruits & Vegetables from A to Z by Lois Ehlert. 34 pages Harcourt Brace Jovanovich, 1989.

Although this vividly colorful book doesn't contain explicit nutritional information or principles, it makes fruits and vegetables look very interesting and appealing. Because it includes illustrations of fruits and vegetables whose names begin with each letter of the alphabet, it's also a good alphabet-learning tool. A postscript contains information about each fruit or vegetable in the book. Through its visual appeal, this book has the potential to stimulate children's interest in eating fruits and vegetables.

Ages: 1–5   **Cultural Content:** N/A

Fast Food! Gulp! Gulp! by Bernard Waber. 32 pages Lorraine/ Houghton Mifflin, 2001.

Fast food is thought to contribute to nutritional problems in the contemporary United States. This rhyming story starts with the frenetic activity of making, serving, and eating fast food. Fast-food restaurants make meals that can be eaten in thirty seconds—you don't even have to chew them. The illustrations mirror the busyness conveyed by both the content and the rhythm of the text. Overwhelmed by all the gulping, munching, crunching, chewing, chomping, slurping, and hurrying, the fast-food cook eventually quits. She goes to work at a health food restaurant, and suddenly the illustrations are dominated by a soothing green, and people have slowed down, creating an atmosphere in which vegetables have much more appeal than the fast food.

Ages: 3–7   **Cultural context:** N/A

Good Enough to Eat: A Kid's Guide to Food and Nutrition by Lizzy Rockwell. 33 pages HarperCollins, 1999.

A non-fiction guide to nutrition can be informative for kids who are interested in eating well. This book describes the functions of hunger, food, and nutrients such as protein and vitamins. The author describes digestion and the (now outdated) U.S. Department of Agriculture Food Guide

Pyramid, adding that food is fun to eat and to prepare. Five recipes are included. Because of material such as a statement that too much fatty food "can make you heavy," this book would probably not be suitable for children who have excessive concerns about nutrition; for example, normal-weight children who restrict their food intake and/or try to lose weight. Otherwise, it gives good basic information in a kid-friendly form.
Ages: 6–12   **Cultural context:** Multicultural

Growing Vegetable Soup **by Lois Ehlert. 26 pages**
Harcourt Brace, 1987.
Watching vegetables grow can make them seem special, as they do in this story. A father and child plant, tend, and harvest vegetables, and make them into soup. The vividly colored illustrations show the plants changing as they grow from seeds into full-grown plants; captions differentiate among types of plants, as well as identifying plant parts, garden and kitchen tools, and a worm. The child comments that the soup is the best ever—the recipe is included. Although there's no explicit nutritional information, the vegetables themselves and the process of growing them make them seem appealing.
Ages: 1-5   **Cultural context:** Multicultural

How Groundhog's Garden Grew **by Lynne Cherry. 34 pages**
Blue Sky/Scholastic, 2003.
The satisfaction of eating home-grown vegetables may help promote good nutrition, as it does for Little Groundhog. Squirrel scolds Little Groundhog for taking vegetables from others' gardens and shows him how to grow his own, helping him through all the garden's stages, which are described and illustrated in detail. At the end of the story, Little Groundhog prepares a delicious feast for his friends with his home-grown vegetables. Gardening resources for children are included. Although this book doesn't address nutrition directly (other than to describe the produce as nutritious), the groundhog's joy in eating home-grown vegetables, the illustrations, and the connection between vegetables and friendship might inspire some children.
Ages: 3–8   **Cultural context:** N/A

***Muncha! Muncha! Muncha!* by Candace Fleming. Illus. by
G. Brian Karas. 32 pages Anne Schwartz/Atheneum, 2002.**
A garden full of delicious vegetables can be hard to resist, as it is for three
mischievous bunnies in this story. Mr. McGreely plants a garden, happily
anticipating filling his tummy with lettuce, carrots, peas, and tomatoes,
but unfortunately for his stomach, the bunnies get into the garden and
eat the vegetables first. An angry Mr. McGreely builds one barrier after
another (resulting in some delightful repetition in the story) until he
finally creates one that keeps the bunnies out. However, he can't keep
them out of the basket that he brings into the garden to carry vegetables
in. In the end, he shares with the bunnies. Children will enjoy the humor
of this story, which encourages them to identify with the bunnies who
will stop at nothing to get those delicious vegetables.

Ages: 3–7   **Cultural context:** European-American

***Soup for Supper* by Phyllis Root. Illus. by Sue Truesdell.
32 pages Harper & Row, 1986.**
Eating nutritiously may be more appealing when it's connected with
humor, music, and friendship. A giant digs up all the vegetables from
a woman's garden, but she assertively and cleverly gets them back.
When she discovers that he didn't know they were hers, and only
wanted a pot of soup, she allows him to make the soup with her, and
they become friends. The book includes lyrics (by the author) and music (by Linda Sanders) for "The Soup Song" sung by the giant in the
story. While no explicit nutritional information is given, the vegetable
soup serves as a humorous context for friendship.

Ages: 3–8   **Cultural context:** European-American

FUSSINESS ABOUT EATING

Many parents would like their children to eat a wider variety of foods.
The picture books summarized in this section address ways in which a
character overcomes reluctance to eat specific foods—with an emphasis on vegetables—or to taste foods other than their limited repertoire
of favorites. The characters find that eating more foods allows them
to discover more foods that they enjoy and to be part of more social

situations. Humor is often used effectively in these stories. While encouragement to eat a variety of nutritious foods may be helpful to children, it's also important not to pressure them about food. Many kids who have sensitive temperaments find it difficult to tolerate foods that are even a little strong-flavored, and often, maturation is all that's needed. In the meantime, most children do fine as long as their basic nutritional needs are met.

Bread and Jam for Frances by Russell Hoban.
Illus. by Lillian Hoban. 31 pages Harper & Row, 1964.
Fussy eating may satisfy a child's need for predictability, as it does for Frances. She won't eat anything but bread and jam, causing her to make up funny little songs about her food preferences. But when her mother gives her nothing but bread and jam, she gets bored, decides to try other foods, and finds that she likes them. Fussy eaters will understand that not only is a change of pace pleasant, but also that even a fellow fussy eater likes some variety at times.
Ages: 3–7   **Cultural context:** N/A

Green Eggs and Ham by Dr. Seuss. 62 pages Beginner, 1960.
It's common for children to be reluctant to try foods that seem strange. In this exuberant, rhyming classic, a creature repeatedly expresses a strong dislike for green eggs and ham, and refuses to eat them under any conditions. Ultimately, the creature tries them just to quiet another creature who persistently offers them—and is surprised to discover a liking for them. This clever tale teaches kids that you don't really know whether you like a food (even one that seems as weird as green eggs and ham) until you taste it.
Ages: 2–7   **Cultural context:** N/A

Oliver's Vegetables by Vivian French. Illus. by Alison Bartlett.
26 pages Orchard, 1995.
Sometimes it takes a special situation to get kids to try new foods. When Oliver stays with his grandparents, who grow their own vegetables, he says he doesn't eat vegetables, except French fries. Grandpa responds with a deal: Oliver can have French fries if he finds the potatoes in the garden, but if he finds something else, he

has to eat it with no complaints. Each day Oliver finds a vegetable and eats it with no complaints—in fact, with increasing enjoyment. At the end of a week's visit, he finally finds the potatoes, and they eat homemade French fries. Oliver is a good role model because even though he doesn't like vegetables (or so he thinks at the beginning of the story), he's willing to try new things and to acknowledge when he's found something good.

Ages: 3–6 **Cultural context:** European-American

Picky Mrs. Pickle **by Christine M. Schneider. 32 pages**
Walker and Co., 1999.
At times, a disinclination to try new foods may represent a more general fear of novelty, as it does for Mrs. Pickle. Mrs. Pickle's favorite color is green, and she only eats pickle-flavored foods. She likes what she already knows she likes, so she sees no need to try anything new, be it foods or anything else. Her niece, Sophie, realizes that Mrs. Pickle is afraid of trying new things and stubbornly bribes her to try a new food. Having tried eggplant ice cream, Mrs. Pickle realizes that she likes it even better than pickle ice cream, acknowledging that she very much wants to try new things. This funny story helps children see that the next food they might like is a food that they haven't tried yet.

Ages: 2–6 **Cultural context:** Multicultural
Main character's cultural background: European-American

CHAPTER 24

Minor or Acute Illness

Virtually all children will experience a minor illness at some time, and many preschoolers and early school-age children do so frequently. Minor illnesses involve feeling physically different from the way the child usually feels, often in uncomfortable ways, having to behave differently, and having emotional reactions to these changes. The picture books summarized in this chapter address common childhood health problems, including colds, flu, stomachaches, allergies, injuries, and head lice, or are more generically about being sick in a way that is clearly not too serious. Stories about acute, but more serious, health problems, such as chicken pox, are also included in this chapter. Like real-life children, characters often feel frustrated, bored, and lonely when they're sick, requiring extra caring attention from adults. They cope with being sick by resting, playing quietly, reading, listening to stories, using their imagination or their dreams, watching TV, eating special foods, receiving care from adults, and spending time with pets. Sometimes it's necessary to take medicine or visit a doctor. Some kids are initially pleased to have to stay home from school, but may become bored later or disappointed about missing all the fun that's going on at school.

Aaron's Awful Allergies by Troon Harrison.
Illus. by Eugenie Fernandes. 32 pages Kids Can, 1996.

Allergies can be a problem when they mean giving up pets, as happens for Aaron, who loves animals more than anything else. One summer, Aaron begins to have allergy symptoms: a headache, itchy eyes, coughing, sneezing, fatigue, and malaise. After testing, his doctor finds he is allergic to animals. In a funny moment, she says he shouldn't play with cats, dogs, guinea pigs, skunks, orangutans, or leopards. Aaron is resentful and angry that his pets have to move away. He grieves, comforting himself with listening to the sounds of wild animals in his yard. His mother gives him a pet fish, which doesn't interest him at first. Eventually, though, he names the fish Flash and finds lots of ways to have fun with it, and learns to can enjoy butterflies, frogs, snakes, and turtles, too. Through Aaron's experience, children will be able to acknowledge their sadness about giving up furry pets and understand that they can enjoy other kinds of animals.

Ages: 3–7   **Cultural context:** N/A
Main character's cultural background: European-American

The Chalk Doll by Charlotte Pomerantz.
Illus. by Frané Lessac. 31 pages Lippincott, 1989.

Sometimes a story from a parent can help children tolerate being sick. Rose copes with a cold by listening to her mother's stories about her own childhood. When Mother describes her favorite rag doll, Rose decides to make one of her own. Rose's emotional need for care for is depicted sensitively, and this story shows kids how to use imagination and a personal connection to cope with being sick.

Ages: 3–8   **Cultural context:** Afro-Caribbean

The Cow Buzzed by Andrea Zimmerman and David Clemesha.
Illus. by Paul Meisel. 32 pages HarperCollins, 1993.

Having a sense of humor about the annoyances of a cold can help children cope. In this funny story, a bee visits a farm and transmits a strange cold to the cow. Not only does the cow cough, sniffle, and sneeze, but also, she catches the bee's buzz. When she sneezes, the pig catches the cold—and the cow's moo. The cold is passed to all the animals by sneezing, and each catches another animal's voice. The sensible rabbit covers his mouth when he sneezes and stops the spread of the cold. In the meantime, the farmer is confused by their strange voices and gives them food that matches their voice, not their true identity, making the animals feel grumpy. Eventually, everyone recovers, and they all get their own voices back, vowing to keep their sneezes to themselves. Using humor to help children tolerate having a cold, this story also slips in good advice about prevention.

Ages: 3–6   Cultural context: European-American

Henry and Mudge Get the Cold Shivers by Cynthia Rylant.
Illus. by Suçie Stevenson. 48 pages Bradbury, 1989.

Even dogs can catch colds. When Henry is sick with a sore throat, fever, or cough, his parents bring him Popsicles, comic books, and crackers for his dog, Mudge. Then Mudge gets sick, and Henry and his mother take him to the vet, who diagnoses Mudge with a cold and prescribes rest and medicine. Henry cares for Mudge in many of the same ways that his parents cared for him. Showing children that everyone gets colds, this story reassures them that colds don't last very long.

Ages: 4–8   **Cultural context:** European-American

I Have a Cold by Grace Maccarone. Illus. by Betsy Lewin.
32 pages Cartwheel Books/Scholastic, 1998.

A description of what a cold is like can help young children make sense of the experience. In this book, a boy describes the symptoms of a cold. He reads, watches TV, plays in bed, and rests. The boy's mother brings soup, toast, and tea, while Dad gives him bad-tasting medicine that he tolerates by holding his nose. The boy feels frustrated about being sick, prays that the cold will go away, and looks forward to playing again. Knowing that others have colds and feel frustrated by them, too, will give kids the empathy they need when they're under the weather.

Ages: 2–6   **Cultural context:** Multicultural
Main character's cultural background: European-American

Itchy, Itchy Chicken Pox by Grace Maccarone. Illus. by Betsy
Lewin. 31 pages Cartwheel Books/Scholastic, 1992.
Though less common than it once was, chicken pox still affects many
children. In this rhyming story, a child (probably intended as male)
comes down with chicken pox and itches all over. Treatment includes
lotion, an oatmeal bath, and rest. The child eats, reads, and plays inside while ill. Soon the child is all better and happily returns to school.
With language that's a soothing antidote for children's itching, this
story reassures them that it won't last forever.
Ages: 2–6   **Cultural context:** European-American

Nora's Roses by Satomi Ichikawa. 32 pages Philomel, 1993.
Imagination is an important resource for coping with the frustration
and boredom of being sick, as Nora discovers when she's stuck in bed
with a stuffy nose. She watches people pick the roses in front of her
window, resentful that the roses are going to fun places where she
can't go. Lying in bed, Nora dreams of (or imagines) a magical party
in the roses. When there's only one rose left, she wants to keep it and
decides to make a picture of it—as it looked in her dream—so that she
can keep it forever. With a subtle power, this story illustrates the importance of imagination for alleviating the frustration of being sick.
Ages: 3–7   **Cultural context:** Multicultural

Peter's Patchwork Dream by Willemien Min. 27 pages
Barefoot Books, 1999.
When kids are sick in bed, an ordinary object can spark their imagination and help them manage. Peter is sick in bed and bored, but as
he lies in bed, his eyes wander over his patchwork quilt, inspiring an
imaginary adventure. He picks berries and apples, meets birds and
bunnies, sails in his basket, and waters flowers. At the end of the story,
his friends have come to visit, bringing many of the things he'd imag-
ined, and he feels better. With Peter, children will see that imagination
can help them feel better when they're sick.
Ages: 3–7   **Cultural context:** Multicultural
Main character's cultural background: unclear

***Solomon Sneezes* by Marilyn Singer. Illus. by Brian Floca. 20 pages HarperFestival, 1999.**

The symptoms of a cold may seem overwhelming when kids don't have the perspective they need. In a style reminiscent of Dr. Seuss, this funny story celebrates the strength of Solomon Snorkel's sneezes, which blow leaves off trees and even make the Martians cold. Reducing the relative size of a real child's sneezes, this story makes them seem tolerable by comparison.

Ages: 3–7   **Cultural context:** Multicultural
Main character's cultural background: European-American

***"Stand Back," Said the Elephant, "I'm Going to Sneeze!"* by Patricia Thomas. Illus. by Wallace Tripp. 32 pages Lothrop, Lee & Shepard, 1990.**

A sense of humor can be helpful in coping with colds, as it is in this rhyming book that takes a humorous approach to sneezing. An elephant warns the other animals that he's about to sneeze, because this is always very disruptive to them. He wishes he could keep from sneezing—and at the last moment, a mouse scares the elephant, distracting him so that he forgets to sneeze. When the mouse points this out to the elephant, he finds it very funny, and his laughter causes all the same disruptions that a sneeze would have. Children can use this story to see the funny side of the sneezing that comes with their colds.

Ages: 3–8   **Cultural context:** N/A

***There's a Louse in My House* by Cheri Hayes. Illus. by Tom Dineen. 24 pages Jay-Jo, 2001.**

Head lice are a common problem among children, and this rhyming story describes their treatment and prevention. It includes a quiz for kids and an afterword for parents. After a girl is treated for lice by combing her hair with a special lice comb, and her mom has washed and dried all the sheets on the hottest setting, vacuumed the carpet and the girl's bed, and sealed her stuffed animals in a bag for two weeks, the school nurse finds that there are no lice on the girl. With useful information on lice prevention, this story clarifies the mysteries of head lice for kids, giving them concrete facts about the condition.

Ages: 3–7   **Cultural context:** Multicultural
Main character's cultural background: European-American

A Visit from Dr. Katz by Ursula LeGuin. Illus. by Ann Barrow.
32 pages Atheneum, 1988.
Even when kids can't do much because they're sick, they can still enjoy
pets. When Marianne has the flu and has to stay in bed, she is comforted by her two "doctor" cats. One cat purrs and lies on Marianne's
stomach, administering the Stomach Cure. The other cat plays all
over Marianne's room and pounces on her feet, chewing them through
her blanket to administer the Toe Cure. Sprawled on Marianne's lap
and each other, the two orange tabbies wash their paws, each other,
and Marianne's hands. When she falls asleep at the end of the story,
Marianne has moved from sadness and frustration to comfort and con-
tentment. This story celebrates the curative powers of connection with
animals.

Ages: 3–7   **Cultural context:** European-American

When Francie Was Sick by Holly Keller. **24 pages
Greenwillow, 1985.**
When you're sick, it's hard to miss the fun of everyday life, as Francie
finds when she wakes up with a sore throat, stomachache, and no ap-
petite. She stays in bed, listening to the sounds of her parents in the
house, and napping with her cat. Later in the day, her mama brings
her soup, and her aunt brings her a book of jokes. The soup and the
jokes help Francie feel better, although in an anachronistic moment,
Mama gives Francie an aspirin. Helping children understand that getting sick is an ordinary part of life, this story shows them the brevity
of illness and the healing power of humor.

Ages: 3–7   **Cultural context:** European-American

CHAPTER 25

Medical Care

All children will need medical care at some time in their lives, even if it's just well-child care. Medical care can raise concerns for them about whether they'll be hurt or embarrassed, and on a deeper level, whether their body is okay. This chapter summarizes picture books about visiting the doctor and about being treated in a hospital.

VISITING THE DOCTOR

Although children ideally begin regular well-child visits to their primary health care professional from birth, they may develop fearfulness or confusion about medical visits. Understanding what happens at a visit to the doctor and seeing doctors as kind and caring will help allay fears.

See also *No Measles, No Mumps for Me* (Chapter 23) for children whose concerns about well-child visits relate primarily to getting immunizations.

Barney and Baby Bop Go to the Doctor **by Margie Larsen.**
Illus. by Dennis Full. 24 pages Lyrick, 1996.
When kids are scared of a well-child checkup, they may need reassurance and information. Baby Bop gets both of these in this story. At Baby Bop's physician visit, Barney and Nurse Julie explain that a checkup is when a doctor checks the child all over to be sure the child is healthy and strong. Nurse Julie and Dr. Russell weigh and measure Baby Bop, and Dr. Russell listens to her lungs and heart, looks at her ears and eyes, and tests her reflexes. Baby Bop concludes that a visit to the doctor isn't so scary after all and that doctors help kids to stay healthy. Offering empathy for children's worries about a checkup, this story provides useful information and a role model that can help allay their fears.

Ages: 1–3   **Cultural context:** Multicultural
Main character's cultural background: N/A

Going to the Doctor **by Fred Rogers. Illus. by Jim Judkis.**
32 pages Putnam, 1986.
Information, explanations, and reassurance can make doctor visits easier for kids. Mr. Rogers' gentle, straightforward description starts by explaining the visit's purpose: taking kids to the doctor is one way that parents take care of them, whether to help them to stay healthy or to help them recover from illness. With information that orients kids to the presence of staff and use of the waiting room, he explains why you have to take your clothes off and describes some of the procedures that occur at a checkup; for example, weighing and measuring, looking in the child's ears, nose, and throat, listening to the heart and lungs, and administering injections (which, he acknowledges, can hurt briefly). Telling children that many doctors are also parents, he encourages kids to discuss their feelings about going to the doctor and ask their doctor questions. Like Mr. Rogers' other books, this book has a calm, soothing tone that provides reassurance to even the most hesitant kids.

Ages: 2–6   **Cultural context:** Multicultural

Shanna's Doctor Show **by Jean Marzollo. Illus. by Shane W.**
Evans. 20 pages Jump At The Sun/Hyperion, 2001.
Make-believe play can help children feel ready for a doctor visit, as it does for Shanna and her brother, Shane, who get ready for their

checkups by playing doctor and nurse, respectively, to their toy animals. Shanna explains that doctors wear a lab coat and name tag, use a stethoscope to listen to patients' hearts, keep everything very clean, give booster shots, and advise children to stay healthy, eat well, and play safely. Giving children a basic understanding of what happens during a doctor visit, this story shows them how playing about it can help them to feel prepared.

Ages: 2–5   **Cultural context:** African-American

When I See My Doctor **by Susan Kuklin. 32 pages**
Bradbury, 1988.
With this book, kids watch four-year-old Thomas, accompanied by his mommy, visit Dr. Mitchell for a checkup, helping them feel more prepared for their own. Thomas explains everything that happens, as Dr. Mitchell listens to his heart and lungs, looks in his ears, eyes, and mouth, and checks his neck, belly, joints, and reflexes. Kathy, a nurse, checks his blood for iron content (which hurts a little), assesses his blood pressure, administers polio vaccine, and measures Thomas's height and weight. Dr. Mitchell comes across as kind, and the emphasis is on the role of physician visits in keeping children healthy, creating positive expectations for children who read this story before their checkups.

Ages: 2–6   **Cultural context:** N/A
Main character's cultural background: Asian-American

HOSPITAL STAY

Occasionally, a child may need inpatient treatment, which can be frightening and confusing. They're in a strange environment with unfamiliar routines, often in pain or otherwise not feeling well, sometimes subjected to painful procedures, possibly worried about whether their body will be okay, encountering many new people, and sometimes separated from parents. This chapter summarizes stories about going to the hospital for ear tubes, a tonsillectomy, eye surgery, or treatment for injuries. In one case a child stays overnight, and others go home the same day as their surgery. Two nonfiction books discuss going to the hospital in more general terms. All of these books include information about things that may happen during a hospital stay, including use of X rays, masks, wheelchairs, patient ID bracelets, IVs, and monitoring equipment.

***Blueberry Eyes* by Monica Driscoll Beatty.**
Illus. by Peg Michel. 34 pages Health, 1996.
Sharing another's experience of surgery can make a child's own experience less frightening. Meaghan, who has big blue eyes that her family calls "blueberry eyes," has had problems with her eyesight since birth and has corrective surgery at age six. Her main worries are that the operation will change the way she feels and will change the appearance of her "blueberry eyes." Her mother and surgeon reassure her that she'll be asleep and won't feel anything. Meaghan's experience of the trip to the hospital is described in detail, and she's given lots of appropriate choices, such as walking to the surgical suite or riding on a gurney. She's honest about feeling awful right after the procedure, but she receives cards and presents, and happily returns to school a week later. Almost as if Meaghan is a friend who has been through something similar, her real-life character will allow kids to have realistic expectations about surgery.

Ages: 6–9   **Cultural context:** European-American

Chris Gets Ear Tubes by Betty Pace. Illus. by Kathryn Hutton.
48 pages Gallaudet University Press, 1987.
Chris has the scary problem of poor hearing, and his doctor explains that he has fluid in the ears that requires tubes. Chris expresses his concerns straightforwardly, and Dr. Lowe answers his questions, explains what will happen at the hospital, and acknowledges his fear. Although Chris feels better after talking with Dr. Lowe, he still worries about the surgery and uses play to cope. Chris meets the hospital admissions clerk, gets an identification bracelet, has health checks by a nurse, and visits the hospital playroom before the procedure. The nurse brings him into the operating room on a gurney and general anesthesia is administered. Later, Chris wakes up thirsty, drinks some juice, and is glad to see his parents. He goes home the same day, feeling happy that he can hear better. In a calm, reassuring tone, this

story offers helpful information about hospital treatment in general and ear tubes in particular.

Ages: 3–7 **Cultural context:** Multicultural
Main character's cultural background: European-American

Franklin Goes to the Hospital **by Paulette Bourgeois.**
Illus. by Brenda Clark. 32 pages Kids Can, 2000.
Fears can be a difficult aspect of hospitalization, as they are for Franklin when he needs inpatient surgery because of an injury sustained during a soccer game. His friend, his father, and a nurse tell him that he's brave, but he's afraid of X rays because he worries that they'll show that inside, he's scared. His doctor's reassurance and understanding of his fears allow him to feel ready to have the surgery. Many aspects of surgery are depicted (for example, the use of masks and wheelchairs, patient ID bracelets, anesthetic cream for IV insertion, monitoring of vital signs). In addition to being well informed about staying at the hospital, kids will understand that it's OK to be scared, and that they can still be brave even when they're frightened.

Ages: 3–8 **Cultural context:** N/A

Going to the Hospital **by Fred Rogers. Illus. by Jim Judkis.**
32 pages Putnam, 1988.
Reassuring explanations can go a long way in allaying kids' fears about hospitalization. With obvious sensitivity to children's needs, Mr. Rogers gently but straightforwardly describes why kids may need to go to the hospital and what might happen there. He encourages asking questions, playing about concerns, and expressing feelings, while reassuring children that they will be well cared for. The book, which is illustrated with color photographs, ends on an upbeat note, as children go home from the hospital and their parents feel proud of them. A foreword for adults suggests ways to be helpful to children when they have to go to the hospital, and overall, this comforting book offers children helpful information, understanding, and encouragement for coping with a hospital experience.

Ages: 2–7 **Cultural context:** Multicultural

The Hospital Book by James Howe. Illus. by Mal Warshaw.
95 pages Morrow, 1981.

Here's a book for kids who find information especially reassuring. It explains hospital procedures and introduces staff in detail, acknowledging the scared, upset, angry, and sad feelings that may accompany hospital treatment and honestly stating that some of the procedures will hurt. The author offers reassurance and coping strategies for specific fears such as the need for a surgical incision, the sometimes scary appearance of hospital staff wearing masks, and the possibility that kids might wet their bed. He encourages children to express feelings appropriately, to ask questions, and to discover sources of strength inside themselves. Some of the information is a bit dated; for example, the use of analogue oral or rectal thermometers, but not digital or ear thermometers. In spite of this, this book informs children, validates their emotional experience, and encourages positive coping.

Ages: 7–12   **Cultural context:** Multicultural

Tubes in My Ears: My Trip to the Hospital by Virginia Dooley.
Illus. by Miriam Katin. 24 pages Mondo, 1996.

Children who anticipate surgery will feel better knowing that other kids have had similar experiences, both in terms of the medical procedures and their feelings. Luke provides this as he narrates the story of his outpatient surgery to get ear tubes. Several medical terms are defined, and the difference between ear tubes and bicycle tubes is explained. Luke straightforwardly expresses his fear of the procedure, embarrassment about wearing hospital clothes, and hunger from not being allowed to eat beforehand. At the same time, he seems able to contain his concerns, and his parents are a constant source of support. Children who anticipate surgery—especially those who are to have similar procedures—will be well informed in an age-appropriate way. They will feel a sense of empathy from Luke, who shows them how to use parents' support and acknowledge feelings without being overwhelmed.

Ages: 3–7   **Cultural context:** Multicultural
Main character's cultural background: African-American

**A *Visit to the Sesame Street Hospital* by Deborah Hautzig.
Illus. by Joe Mathieu. 32 pages Random House, 1985.**
Visiting the hospital can help kids understand what happens there.
When Grover needs to have his tonsils removed, he's worried about going to the hospital, so Dr. Keats arranges a hospital tour. Grover sees
many places in the hospital and has an opportunity to ask questions
that many children will have. Nurse Spinner takes Grover, Ernie, and
Bert to visit a patient room, where they see how the beds and nurses'
call button work, as well as the nurses' station, the playroom, the radiology department, the surgical suite, the medical library, the nursery, and the gift shop. Grover meets a child who has had her tonsils
removed, which helps him relax. A limitation of this book is that the
actual hospital stay is not depicted; however, it will give children a
clear idea of what a hospital environment is like.

Ages: 2–5   **Cultural context:** Multicultural
Main character's cultural background: N/A

CHAPTER 26

Serious or
Chronic Illness

In addition to the issues raised by minor or acute illnesses (Chapter 24), children who have serious or chronic illnesses may have to face fears of death, the emotional reactions of people close to them, permanent changes in their lives, and a sense of being different because of chronic disease. The picture books summarized in this chapter address these issues. Characters are described as having a specific disease—asthma, cancer, diabetes, epilepsy, HIV/AIDS, rheumatic fever, or rheumatoid arthritis—or are described more generically as seriously ill. Some books specifically acknowledge that children may have feelings about their illness and that it's okay to talk about those feelings. Characters cope with serious or chronic illness by using creativity and imagination, receiving love and support from their families, affirming both their strength and the fact that the disease does not define who they are, and making connections with animals. They sometimes manage feelings of difference by being open with, and educating, those around them about their illness. However, some children (specifically, many who are HIV-positive) feel that they have to keep their status secret. Stories acknowledge both the despair and the hope of seriously ill children.

Although these books are probably intended for children who are themselves seriously ill, many (if not all) will also be helpful to children who are working toward understanding the illness of someone close to them (see Chapter 27).

An Alphabet about Kids with Cancer by Rita Berglund. Illus. by Katy Tartakoff and Laurie Shields. 62 pages Children's Legacy, 1994.

Childhood cancer has profound emotional implications. In this alphabet, each two-page spread contains a letter that stands for a word related to cancer, from *C* for *cancer*, to *D* for *dying*, to *F* for *feelings*, *J* for *joy*, and *U* for *understanding*. One page has a brief discussion of the word, and the facing page has a black-and-white photograph of a child or children who have cancer. Realities are acknowledged in a caring, straightforward way. The author encourages kids to talk about their feelings and supports them in seeing cancer as part, but not all, of their identity. Many pages invite children to think about the concept of that page as it applies to the child's own life. At the end, pages are provided to make your own alphabet. This book offers understanding and support.

Ages: 6–12   **Cultural context:** Multicultural

Becky the Brave by Laurie Lears. Illus. by Gail Piazza. 32 pages Whitman, 2002.

One component of chronic illness may be shame, as it is for Becky. According to her younger sister, Sarah, the big difference between her and Becky is that Becky is brave, even about her epilepsy. Sarah knows that seizures won't hurt Becky, but they're still scary. Sarah is surprised to learn that Becky has a fear—she's afraid her classmates will find out about her epilepsy. Inevitably, she has a seizure at school and initially refuses to go back. By chance, Sarah teaches Becky's class about epilepsy, and they send notes to Becky about how much they miss her. Becky compliments Sarah on her courage in talking to the class about epilepsy, and Sarah responds by acknowledging Becky as her role model for bravery. A note to adults explains what epilepsy is and what children with epilepsy need, while children who have epilepsy will find empathy, encouragement, and support in this story.

Ages: 5–9   **Cultural context:** Multicultural

Main character's cultural background: European-American

Carousel **by Brian Wildsmith. 32 pages Knopf, 1988.**

A child who's sick for a long time can feel profoundly discouraged, as happens to Rosie when she has a fever that lasts several months. Her brother, Tom, and her friends work together to find ways to give Rosie hope. Her friends make her pictures of her favorite things to ride on the carousel she loves, and Tom gives her a toy carousel. Inspired by this, she has a magical dream, which is the turning point in her illness, allowing her to get stronger until she's completely well and giving readers hope for recovery.

Ages: 4–9   **Cultural context:** European-American

Even Little Kids Get Diabetes **by Connie White Pirner.**
Illus. by Nadine Bernard Westcott. 24 pages Whitman, 1991.

Information, a supportive family, and a role model for self-acceptance and openness about feelings all help kids cope with chronic disease. In this charmingly illustrated story, a girl describes her experiences of being diagnosed with diabetes at age two and the adjustments she must make in her daily life. Emphasizing that she's a "regular kid," the narrator openly discusses her own and family members' feelings. The fact that she knows her family loves her is clearly a comfort. An afterword for parents is included in this accessible story that offers both information and acceptance of feelings.

Ages: 2–7   **Cultural context:** European-American

Fat Chance **by Lady Borton. Illus. by Deborah Kogan Ray.**
32 pages Philomel, 1993.

Being sick for a long time requires endurance, as it does for first-grader Marty Louise when she has rheumatic fever. Although her mother encourages her to work on learning letters, which is particularly difficult for her, she prefers to build a make-believe circus. During this time, she befriends a sick stray cat, whom she names Chancy—who is not only a great comfort to her but also inspires her to learn to write. Although some children may be distressed by the descriptions of Chancy's health conditions, this story offers hope, along with encouragement for persistence.

Ages: 5–8   **Cultural context:** European-American

Henry and the White Wolf **by Tyler Karu and Tim Karu.**
31 pages Workman, 2000.
Empathy and encouragement are important in helping children cope with cancer. In this moving story, a hedgehog named Henry becomes very ill. His mother is advised to seek help from the White Wolf, even though an important rule of the woods is to avoid the wolf's den. The White Wolf tells Henry that healing is painful, and that he'll lose his quills and fur, while simultaneously encouraging his courage and persistence, saying that hope will support his physical recovery. Empathizing with Henry's fear, the White Wolf gives him a stone to keep with him to remind him that he's strong and brave. Every day, he drinks an awful potion that the White Wolf gives him. He's tired and sick and loses his quills and fur. But he recovers, goes home, and celebrates with his friends, all the while holding the stone. Packaged with a stone, this book includes a section for the reader to record times of bravery and strength as a reminder to him- or herself. Conveying a strong sense of empathy and acknowledgement, this story provides powerful images of healing.

Ages: 3–9   **Cultural context:** N/A

I'm Tougher Than Asthma! **by Alden R. Carter and Siri M.**
Carter. Illus. by Dan Young. 32 pages Whitman, 1996.
Information and a positive role model can help kids cope with a chronic disease. Siri explains that in addition to being a regular kid, she has asthma. She explains what asthma is, how she, her parents, and health care professionals care for her asthma, and what may trigger attacks. She acknowledges that an asthma attack is scary, while also expressing positive expectations. Illustrated with color photographs, this book includes questions and answers for adults. Children will benefit from the information provided as well as Siri's confidence that she can do anything if she takes good care of her lungs.

Ages: 4–8   **Cultural context:** European-American

I'm Tougher Than Diabetes! **by Alden R. Carter.**
Illus. by Carol Shadis Carter. 32 pages Whitman, 2001.
A realistic, positive approach is helpful to children with a chronic disease. Natalie demonstrates this as she explains what diabetes is and how she cares for herself with insulin injections, blood sugar monitoring, careful eating, and exercise. She describes her classmates' positive reaction when she tells them about her diabetes and its treatment. Natalie briefly describes the onset of her diabetes at age six and her experience of the symptoms of low and high blood sugar. This book is illustrated with photographs and includes an introduction by a health psychologist, answers to adults' frequently asked questions, and a resource list. Along with a positive role model for a confident, upbeat attitude, this book offers useful information about what diabetes is and how to care for it.

Ages: 5–10   **Cultural context:** European-American

Kathy's Hats: A Story of Hope **by Trudy Krisher.**
Illus. by Nadine Bernard Westcott. 32 pages Whitman, 1992.
Serious illness brings changes in the meanings of everyday things, and in Kathy's case, this ultimately helps her cope with cancer. In her life, hats symbolize special times (a hair ribbon just after birth, the swim cap she wore when she first learned to swim), then embarrassment about being "different" because of having cancer, then a "thinking cap," and finally, her hopes for the future (a mortarboard and wedding veil). When Kathy complains about having to wear hats because she's lost her hair during chemotherapy, her mother suggests that she put on a "thinking cap" because thinking differently about things helps people manage challenges. She finds that when she puts pins on her hat, she starts to like it. By the end of the story, Kathy announces the end of her chemotherapy and her remission, and her classmates join her in wearing hats. Based on the author's experience of her daughter's childhood cancer, this story provides empathy, a model of positive coping, and hope.

Ages: 4–9   **Cultural context:** Multicultural
Main character's cultural background: European-American

The Lion Who Had Asthma by Jonathan London.
Illus. by Nadine Bernard Westcott. 32 pages Whitman, 1992.
Imagination can help kids manage chronic illness, as it does Sean, an imaginative child whose make-believe play is interrupted by an asthma attack. His parents treat it using a nebulizer, along with lots of imagination. Sean's physical and emotional experiences of the attack are described straightforwardly. The illustrations show a realistic picture of Sean on one page (for example, making believe he's a lion, surrounded by his toy animals) and a picture of what he's imagining (a lion in the jungle) on the facing page. When he uses the nebulizer, he pretends he's a jet pilot. A foreword for adults describes the author's experiences with his own child's asthma. This positive, empathic story encourages the use of imagination as a way to cope with asthma.

Ages: 3–7   **Cultural context:** European-American

Little Tree: A Story for Children With Serious Medical Problems by Joyce C. Mills. Illus. by Michael Chesworth.
32 pages Magination, 1992.
When they're seriously ill, children may experience self-blame, loss, and worry, as Little Tree does in this gentle story. When the little tree has several branches blown off in a storm, a tree wizard fixes some of the tree's branches and removes the ones that can't be fixed. Another tree wizard encourages Little Tree's friend, a squirrel, to stay with her and teaches Little Tree a visualization and relaxation exercise. Little Tree worries that she might have caused the problem with her branches, and the tree wizard assures her that it was not her fault. Little Tree learns that although the branches she has lost will not grow back, the ones that remain are strong and will grow beautiful flowers and leaves. The book also includes an introduction for parents and instructions for the Magic Happy Breath relaxation/visualization exercise. In addition to learning relaxation and visualization, children will uncover the hope and strength inside themselves when facing serious illness or injury.

Ages: 3–8   Cultural context: N/A

You Can Call Me Willy: A Story for Children About AIDS
by Joan C. Verniero. Illus. by Verdon Flory. 32 pages
Magination, 1995.
Severe illness can be stressful in itself, and discrimination by others makes it worse, as it does for eight-year-old Willy, who has been HIV-positive since birth. Willy describes the sense of care and security she has with her grandmother, who is raising her, as well as her love of baseball, her strong friendship with her neighbor Dexter, and the differences and stresses she experiences because of her HIV-positive status. These include discrimination by other children and their parents, throughtout which her grandmother and Dexter support her. Willy says that she would rather not think about AIDS and death, preferring to think about "happy things." She has to take medicine, see her doctor, eat special foods to gain weight, and stay home not only when she's sick, but sometimes when she's feeling well, to avoid catching ordinary viruses and infections. This book includes an introduction for parents and a resource list on AIDS and HIV, and gives kids the support and strength they need to fight discrimination based on HIV/AIDS.

Ages: 4–8   **Cultural context:** Multicultural

Main character's cultural background: African-American

CHAPTER 27

Illness of
Another Person

The illness of someone close affects children in many ways, depending on that person's role in their life, the seriousness and other attributes of the illness, and the child's other life circumstances. Kids have a range of emotional reactions, including worry, sadness, helplessness, guilt, anger, and frustration. This chapter summarizes picture books that address children's experiences of the illness of another person (usually a serious illness). In many of these stories, someone older becomes ill, most often a parent, but sometimes an uncle, a teacher, or an older friend. These adults suffer from arthritis, stroke, cancer, dementia, AIDS, and unnamed illnesses. Stories address what happens when an adult is ill; for example, by showing the adult's fatigue and malaise, and hair loss of parents undergoing chemotherapy for cancer. Children in these stories cope creatively with adults' limitations, particularly those that threaten to disrupt their connection to the child, and are empowered by playing a helpful, but age-appropriate, role in the adult's care. A well parent is an important source of support to the child.

Other stories describe the experience of having a peer who is ill. The ill child is HIV-positive or has leukemia, an unnamed severe illness, chicken pox, or an unspecified minor illness. The sick child is a classmate, friend, or sibling. Having a seriously ill brother or sister disrupts the child's life and may evoke feelings of loss and/or jealousy around the parents' attention and care (even if the illness isn't severe), guilt about the possibility of having caused the sibling's illness, or worries about their own health. Children may cope with the illness of a peer by receiving support from adults, making art to express their feelings, and giving gifts; in one story, a brother courageously participates in a bone marrow transplant.

See also Chapter 26 for more stories about serious illness. Illness is followed by death in *Flamingo Dream, A Quilt for Elizabeth,* and *Rudi's Pond* (Chapter 31).

Come Sit by Me by Margaret Merrifield, M.D.
Illus. by Heather Collins. 32 pages Women's Press, Ltd. 1990.

When a classmate is HIV-positive, children may be confused about HIV transmission, as occurs with Karen. Some of her preschool classmates aren't allowed to play with her friend, Nicholas, because he "has AIDS" (more specifically, he is HIV-positive). Karen's mother, a physician, explains that when she gets sick, "fighter cells" in her blood help her get well, but when a person has AIDS, the fighter cells can't do this. After other parents won't let their children play with Karen because she plays with Nicholas, her parents arrange a meeting at school to educate parents about HIV/AIDS transmission, and the children begin to accept Nicholas. An afterword explains to children how HIV is *not* transmitted (for example, sharing dishes or toys, or swimming, playing, eating, or drinking with someone), and a section for adults provides information about HIV/AIDS and suggests ways to talk with children about it. In the context of a child-friendly story, this book provides straightforward, age-appropriate information about HIV and its transmission.

Ages: 3–8   **Cultural context:** Multicultural
Main character's cultural background: European-American

Dear Daisy, Get Well Soon by Maggie Smith. 34 pages
Crown, 2000.
When your best friend is sick, it's hard to wait for her to get better so
she can play with you again. Peter's friend Daisy comes down with
chicken pox, and he sends her gifts each day. Finally, at the end of a
week, she's well enough to play with him. This is also a counting book
(Peter sends one note, two bouquets, three coloring books, etc.). The
colorful illustrations include jungle animals (who bear a remarkable
resemblance to Peter's toys) who deliver the gifts to Daisy; Peter is
clearly using his imagination in a positive way to cope with having to
wait for her. Demonstrating positive ways to deal with a friend's illness,
this story encourages them to be patient by showing a happy outcome.
Ages: 2–5   **Cultural context:** European-American

Good Luck, Mrs. K.! by Louise Borden. Illus. by Adam
Gustavson. 32 pages McElderry/Simon & Schuster, 1999.
The illness of a teacher can lead to feelings of loss and helplessness.
The students in Mrs. Kempczinski's third grade class love their teacher. When she is absent for two weeks, they discover that she is in the
hospital with cancer. The students write to her about what they liked
best in third grade. When she makes a special visit to the class just
after school ends in June, all the students wish her good luck—and she
returns to school the next fall. Children in similar situations will find
empathy in this story, which shows how to handle an important adult's
illness by expressing care, keeping her in their hearts, and going on
being kids.
Ages: 6–10   **Cultural context:** Multicultural
Main character's cultural background: European-American

I Wish I Was Sick, Too! by Franz Brandenberg.
Illus. by Aliki. 32 pages Greenwillow, 1976.
Like many children, Elizabeth is jealous and resentful when her
brother, Edward, receives special attention from their parents, grandmother, aunt, and uncle when he is sick for a few days. She has to take
care of herself and do homework and chores. When she becomes sick,
their parents and relatives look after her in the same ways they'd done

for Edward. Then *he* has to take care of himself and do homework and chores. Elizabeth finds herself wishing she could do these things. After she gets getter, she and Edward find ways to enjoy time with their aunt, uncle, grandmother, and parents even though they're well, showing that it's inevitably more fun to be healthy than sick.

Ages: 3–7   **Cultural context:** N/A

I'll See You in My Dreams **by Mavis Jukes.**
Illus. by Stacey Schuett. 32 pages Knopf, 2002.
The anticipatory grief that comes with terminal illness is difficult to bear. On a commercial jet flight to see her uncle, a pilot who is terminally ill, a girl imagines skywriting a loving farewell to him. Her mother gives her permission not to see her uncle if that would be too upsetting, but she decides to go. Acknowledging to herself that he might not know she's there, she feels that what's important to her is that she'll know it. It is clear that she will always have him with her, in part by imagining herself as a pilot, like him. In the painful situation of terminal illness, this story will promote children's courage to say good-bye.

Ages: 5–9   **Cultural context:** Multicultural

Miss Tizzy **by Libba Moore Gray. Illus. by Jada Rowland.**
33 pages Simon & Schuster, 1993.
When an adult is ill, children can cope with their sadness and worry by using the inner resources that the adult has helped them develop. Miss Tizzy brings the neighborhood children joy in many ways, such as baking cookies, roller skating, dressing up, singing, and making music. When Miss Tizzy becomes ill and has to stay in bed, the children keep doing the things they'd done with her, finding ways to share them with her, which brings her joy. This story shows kids that they're capable of making a difference when an adult they love is ill, which both helps the sick person feel better and reduces their own sense of helplessness.

Ages: 4–8   **Cultural context:** Multicultural

The Music in Derrick's Heart **by Gwendolyn Battle-Lavert.**
Illus. by Colin Bootman. 32 pages Holiday House, 2000.
One way to cope with the illness of someone close is to do what that person can no longer do. Derrick learns to play the harmonica from his Uncle Booker T. He's passionate about learning, practicing for hours and sleeping with the harmonica every night. His uncle tells him that music is something that needs to be felt in his heart, which, in spite of Derrick's eagerness, takes time and patience. When Uncle Booker T. is unable to play because of arthritis, he passes along his harmonica to Derrick, who learns through this experience to make music from his heart, a unique gift for his uncle. From this story, children will see how to cope with a loved one's illness by carrying with them the person's special qualities and using them in a healing way.
Ages: 4-8   **Cultural context:** African-American

Now One Foot, Now the Other **by Tomie dePaola.**
48 pages Putnam, 1981.
Although children may feel helpless when an adult they love is sick, they can also have a meaningful role in the adult's healing. Bobby's grandfather, Bob, teaches him how to walk and tells him stories. They have many special times together. When Bobby is five years old, Bob has a stroke that leaves him unable to talk, walk, or recognize family members. Bob is in the hospital for months, and Bobby misses him. His parents are helpful and realistic about Bob's condition. Now Bobby tells Bob stories, and he teaches Bob to walk again just as Bob had taught him, carrying a powerful message about children's capacity to help heal adults using the nurturance that adults have given them.
Ages: 3–7   Cultural context: European-American

Promises **by Elizabeth Winthrop. Illus. by Betsy Lewin.**
32 pages Clarion, 2000.
When an important adult is seriously ill, children worry about whether they can count on her or him, as Sarah does when her mommy has cancer. Sarah experiences a range of feelings: loving, protective, overwhelmed, angry, sad, and frightened. She visits Mommy in the hospital, where Mommy, who has lost her hair, matter-of-factly acknowledges that she *does* look funny this way. In a sweet moment, Sarah gives

Mommy her baseball cap. At the end of the story, Mommy has gotten better, is running again, and her hair has grown back, though she still likes to wear Sarah's baseball cap. Sarah asks her to promise that she won't be sick anymore. Mommy honestly says that she can't promise that, but she can promise to get her ice cream, read to her today, and make more promises tomorrow. Children will find validation for their feelings in this story, along with hope that it's possible to cope even when the promises they want aren't possible.

Ages: 4–8　　　**Cultural context:** Multicultural
Main character's cultural background: European-American

The Rainbow Feelings of Cancer **by Carrie Martin and Chia Martin. Illus. by Carrie Martin. 32 pages Hohm, 2001.**
The serious illness of someone close brings complex feelings, as ten-year-old Carrie shows in her words and drawings about her experience of her mom's cancer. Carrie feels helpless, angry, and scared at times. She also learns what will help her mom, uses her mom's reassurance to feel strong and safe, has a reliable confidant in her dad, and realizes that she has a lot to love. She also acknowledges complex feelings straightforwardly; for example, she likes mom's doctors because they help mom get better, but she envies them because they get a lot of time with her mom. Conveying a strong sense of empathy and strength, this story acknowledges the complexity of watching someone struggle with a disease.

Ages: 6–12　　　**Cultural context:** unclear

Raymond's Perfect Present **by Therese On Louie.**
Illus. by Suling Wang. 32 pages Lee & Low, 2002.
In spite of the unpredictability of illness, children's caring for someone they love really matters, as Raymond discovers in this story. His mother has been in the hospital and is convalescing at home. He wants to give her a gift that would really bring her joy. He thinks she'd like flowers, because she's talked about missing flowers and birds, so he plants flower seeds in pots on their apartment's windowsill, but before they can bloom, his mother has to return to the hospital. They bloom while she's at the hospital, and when he visits, he promises her a surprise for her return home. Unfortunately, by the time she comes

home, they've wilted. Raymond feels terrible, but the birds that come to the windowsill to get the flowers' seeds delight his mother. And, for the first time, she's well enough to walk to the park with Raymond. With Raymond, children will learn that even if someone they love is seriously ill, they can still bring joy to that person.

Ages: 4–8   **Cultural context:** Multicultural
Main character's cultural background: Asian American

Sammy and the Robots **by Ian Whybrow.**
Illus. by Adrian Reynolds. 22 pages Orchard, 2001.
Children can use their creativity to express caring for someone who is seriously ill, as Sammy does in this story. When his robot has to go to the "robot hospital," he decides to make another one to play with in the meantime. His gran offers to help, but before they can do this, she goes to the hospital because she has a cough. Sammy builds a robot that blasts coughs and brings it to Gran. He builds more robots for her, and she recovers quickly, with the robots' help. Soon, Sammy's first robot comes home, too, good as new. Children can make use of Sammy's wonderful experience of feeling that his caring not only matters, but helps.

Ages: 3–7   **Cultural context:** Multicultural
Main character's cultural background: European-American

Singing With Momma Lou **by Linda Jacobs Altman.**
Illus. by Larry Johnson. 32 pages Lee & Low, 2002.
Avoidance is a common response to a loved one's dementia, and Tamika experiences this in her relationship with her grandmother, Momma Lou, who lives in a nursing home and has Alzheimer's disease. Momma Lou used to be Tamika's best friend, but now she remembers very little. Tamika's father shows her a scrapbook with pictures of Momma Lou singing and participating in civil rights protests. Tamika uses the scrapbook to give Momma Lou's memories back to her, telling Momma Lou the stories that go with the mementoes. Remembering one demonstration inspires Momma Lou to laugh, and Tamika and her family laugh, too. Then Momma Lou begins to sing, and everyone nearby sings with her. Tamika promises that she'll keep Momma Lou's

memories with her, even when Momma Lou can't. Her own memories of these times with Momma Lou are a great comfort. An afterword describes Alzheimer's disease and includes resources. Through this moving story, kids will find hope that a special bond can persist in spite of the disconnection that comes with Alzheimer's disease.

Ages: 7–12   Cultural context: Multicultural
Main character's cultural background: African-American

Too Far Away to Touch **by Lesléa Newman.**
Illus. by Catherine Stock. 32 pages Clarion, 1995.
Terminal illness of someone close is painful and frightening for children. Zoe's Uncle Leonard, who has AIDS, takes her to a planetarium and tells her the stars are "too far away to touch, but close enough to see." Zoe loves the stars, and Uncle Leonard puts glow-in-the-dark stars on the ceiling of her room, and later, with his partner, takes her to the beach to look at real stars. Zoe and Uncle Leonard talk about his illness, and Zoe expresses her fear of his death. He says that when he dies, like the stars, he'll be "too far away to touch, but close enough to see." She realizes she will always be able to see him in her memories. This metaphor will help children face the terminal illness of someone they love, knowing that they will always have their memories of the person.

Ages: 5–9   **Cultural context:** European-American

When Eric's Mom Fought Cancer **by Judith Vigna.**
32 pages Whitman, 1993.
A parent's cancer often feels overwhelming to a child. When Eric's mommy has breast cancer, he's scared, sad, worried, and frustrated. Sometimes Mommy is too tired or sick to play with him, or even to enjoy the things he does to try to cheer her up. Mommy has frequent hospital treatments and loses her hair. Eric expresses concerns that are common for children in this situation; for example, that he caused, or could catch, the cancer. Eric and his daddy go skiing as a way to have some time off. After many bumps and tumbles, and some fear, Eric learns that he can pick himself up and go on—an important lesson for coping with Mommy's cancer, also. The story ends with hope for Mommy's eventual recovery. A "note for grownups" identifies common

concerns among children in this situation and suggests helpful ways to manage them, including expression of feelings. Conveying acceptance of children's feelings, even the difficult ones, this story offers both education and the possibility of hope.

Ages: 5–10   **Cultural context:** Multicultural

Main character's cultural background: European-American

When Molly Was in the Hospital: A Book for Brothers and Sisters of Hospitalized Children **by Debbie Duncan.**
Illus. by Nina Ollikainen. 40 pages Rayve Productions, 1994.
The hospitalization of a sibling presents special challenges, and here, Anna tells about her younger sister's illness, surgery, and hospitalization. Anna misses her mother when Mom is at the hospital with Molly, while she also worries that Molly might not recover from the surgery, that she caused Molly's illness, and that when she gets an ear infection, she'll need surgery, too. Grandma reassures her, and Anna visits Molly at the hospital, where she goes with her sister to physical therapy and does special art projects for siblings. When Molly recovers, the family rejoices, providing a sense of validation and hope to children in similar situations.

Ages: 3–8   **Cultural context:** European-American

Wilfrid Gordon McDonald Partridge **by Mem Fox.**
Illus. by Julie Vivas. 32 pages Kane/Miller, 1985.
A childlike perspective on "finding" lost memories can be surprisingly helpful. Wilfred lives next door to what is described as an old people's home. He is friendly with all of the residents, especially 96-year-old Miss Nancy. When his parents tell him that Miss Nancy has lost her memory, he looks for memories for her. He finds shells, a puppet, his grandfather's medal, his football, and an egg. Remarkably, when he gives Miss Nancy these things, they evoke her own memories, teaching children that their generosity can make a real difference when someone is ill.

Ages: 5–7   **Cultural context:** European-American

CHAPTER 28

Dental Care

Taking care of one's teeth is an important part of health care, and includes both daily hygiene and regular visits to the dentist. Children sometimes dislike tooth brushing or may be fearful of visiting the dentist. This chapter summarizes picture books related to both of these topics.

DENTAL HEALTH

Daily hygiene is important in maintaining dental health, and tooth brushing can be a difficult habit for kids to establish. They may have difficulty tolerating the feel of a toothbrush in their mouth or the taste of toothpaste. Because of their normal level of cognitive development, it may be difficult for young children to comprehend that brushing now improves health later. And of course, kids may find other things more fun to do. The picture books summarized below may help make tooth brushing more appealing, as well as giving good information about everyday dental hygiene.

See also Chapter 14 for stories about losing a tooth.

Bill and Pete by Tomie dePaola. 32 pages Putnam, 1978.

Some kids may be more willing to brush their teeth if they see their toothbrush as a friend. William Everett, a crocodile, picks out a new toothbrush—a bird named Pete. Pete becomes William Everett's best friend. When William Everett struggles with learning how to write his name, Pete shows him how to write *Bill*, making that his name from then on. Soon after, he and Pete have an adventure together, as a Bad Guy, who captures crocodiles to make them into suitcases, catches Bill. Pete picks the lock on Bill's cage, and Bill escapes into the Bad Guy's bath, frightening the Bad Guy into running away. This story takes a unique approach to showing children that their toothbrush can be their best friend, even in difficult situations.

Ages: 3–6   **Cultural context:** N/A

Clarabella's Teeth by An Vrombaut. 26 pages Clarion, 2003.

When kids feel as if tooth brushing takes too long, they need the perspective of a story like *Clarabella's Teeth*. All the animals brush their teeth in the morning, but Clarabella, a crocodile, has so many teeth that brushing takes her all day. Her friends play, eat lunch, and tumble. Finally, when they're brushing their teeth at bedtime, Clarabella is ready to play and disappointed. Her friends surprise her with a huge crocodile-sized toothbrush that will make her brushing quicker and promise to play with her tomorrow, which makes her happy. This story can help children realize that tooth brushing is part of every day—and luckily, just a *part*.

Ages: 1–5   **Cultural context:** N/A

Does a Lion Brush? by Fred Ehrlich. Illus. by Emily Bolam. 24 pages Blue Apple, 2002.

Some kids may wonder why they have to brush their teeth, if animals don't. This simple, upbeat book explains that animals don't brush their teeth because chewing and gnawing keeps them clean. But human teeth work differently, so people of all ages need to brush their teeth to keep them clean. Ending with an explanation of how to brush, this book shows children that brushing their teeth is a normal part of everyday life for humans.

Ages: 1–5   **Cultural context:** Multicultural

Dragon Teeth and Parrot Beaks: Even Creatures Brush Their Teeth by Almute Grohmann. Translated by Patricia Bereck Weikersheimer. 26 pages Quintessence, 1998.

Using animal characters, this book conveys information about ways to care for your teeth. On each page, an animal tells about taking care of its teeth: brushing (using fluoride-containing tusk paste), flossing, and eating sweets in moderation. Instructions for brushing teeth are given at the end. Overall, this book gives upbeat, kid-friendly information about everyday dental care.

Ages: 3–6   **Cultural context:** N/A

Sam's Science: I Know Why I Brush My Teeth by Kate Rowan. Illus. by Katharine McEwen. 26 pages Candlewick, 1999.

Sometimes having a loose tooth leads to curiosity about teeth. Sam, who has a loose tooth, has a bathtime conversation with his mother that includes information on dental hygiene, tooth anatomy, the names and functions of teeth, and the distinctions between baby teeth and adult teeth. This accessible story delivers child-appropriate information with a sense of humor.

Ages: 4–8   **Cultural context:** Multicultural
Main character's cultural background: European-American

VISITING THE DENTIST

Children are sometimes fearful about visiting the dentist and may not have a clear idea of what will happen to them there. The books summarized below tell about dental health care from different perspectives, including straightforward non-fiction accounts of a child's visit to a dentist and funny stories that include dentists and dental treatment.

The Crocodile and the Dentist by Taro Gomi. 32 pages Millbrook, 1994.

Kids who think they're the only ones scared of a dental visit will get an alternative perspective from this amusing book, in which a crocodile and a dentist have identical worries about their visit together. During the visit, both get hurt and tell themselves that it won't help to be angry about this, so they just endure till the visit is over, thanking each other politely. They're both relieved, and both acknowledge the need for regular brushing to minimize these difficult visits. Children who feel scared about visiting the dentist will enjoy the humor and might pretend to be a crocodile to help cope with their fears.

Ages: 4–7   **Cultural context:** unclear
Main character's cultural background: N/A

Doctor DeSoto **by William Steig. 30 pages**
Farrar, Straus and Giroux, 1982.
Introducing some humor may make dental visits less scary for kids. Dr. DeSoto is a mouse dentist who reluctantly takes on a fox as a patient. The fox has a rotten tooth that needs to be extracted. Although he's miserable, he realizes that Dr. DeSoto would make a nice snack. Dr. DeSoto and his wife/assistant realize that the fox is thinking of eating him, and together they cook up a clever scheme that makes this impossible. The fox's exiting line, "Frank oo berry mush," makes a delightful and long-lasting family joke. Helping children see the dentist as human, this story also promotes connecting a dental visit with humor.

Ages: 4–8   **Cultural context:** N/A

What to Expect When You Go to the Dentist **by Heidi E. Murkoff.**
Illus. by Laura Rader. 26 pages Harper Festival, 2002.
Here's a good choice for kids who like lots of details. Narrated in a cheerful, chatty, matter-of-fact tone, this non-fiction book contains an enormous amount of information about what happens at the dentist; for example, tooth cleanings, X rays, and fillings. There are point-by-point descriptions of the dentist's equipment as well as the sounds and tactile sensations involved in a dental checkup. Reasons are given for taking care of teeth, and kids are encouraged to ask the dentist questions. Some parents may find some of the dental hygiene recommendations less than realistic; for example, "always brushing or swishing and swallowing" after fruit snacks, but a useful foreword for parents suggests ways to help prepare children for dental visits. Kids who like to know all the details will be well informed before their first dental visit.

Ages: 2–6   **Cultural context:** Multicultural

When I See My Dentist by Susan Kuklin. **32 pages**
Bradbury, 1988.

Seeing another child go through a dental visit can make it seem more familiar and tolerable. Illustrated with photographs, this book shows a real visit to Dr. Steve by four-year-old Erica, accompanied by her mother. Photographs of dentists' equipment and instruments allow readers to get a close look at them. Dr. Steve and dental hygienist Marcia explain procedures to Erica before performing them. Marcia cleans and scales Erica's teeth and administers fluoride treatment, and Dr. Steve examines her mouth and takes X rays. Both professionals educate and encourage her about regular brushing and limiting sugar in her diet. Children will become knowledgeable about dental visits, and they'll see that Erica does fine with hers and that her dentist and dental hygienist are kind and informative.

Ages: 2–5   **Cultural context:** European-American

[CHAPTER 29]

Vision Problems

Children may have a range of emotional reactions to wearing glasses for the first time, from joy in being able to see, to relief in being able to function better, to worries about how they'll look or whether kids will tease them about their glasses. Some kids are pleased to get glasses, whereas others are reluctant. The picture books summarized in this chapter address a range of possibilities.

See also *Blueberry Eyes* (Chapter 25) for a story about a child who has surgery at age six to correct weakness in her eye muscles.

All the Better to See You With! by Margaret Wild.
Illus. by Pat Reynolds. 33 pages Whitman, 1992.

Sometimes nearsightedness isn't obvious until something unusual happens. Kate is quieter than her four brothers and sisters, so no one notices that she's nearsighted until one day she has trouble finding her family at the beach. Her mother takes her to the eye doctor, who prescribes glasses. She looks forward to them with excitement and is glad to be able to see well. Her uncorrected vision is depicted with indistinct watercolors, but when she has her glasses, the same scenes are shown more clearly in watercolor and ink. This story presents a positive perspective on wearing glasses.

Ages: 3–7   **Cultural context:** European-American

Arthur's Eyes by Marc Brown. 27 pages Little, Brown, 1979.
Kids have mixed feelings about wearing glasses if they lead to teasing, even if they help the child function better. Arthur has difficulty seeing, and his friends don't want to play with him because of this; for example, they don't want to play basketball with him because he misses. His optometrist prescribes glasses, but his friends call him "four-eyes" and "sissy" when he wears them. Since none of his friends or family members wears glasses, he feels alone wearing them and so avoids wearing them, causing him more problems than ever because of his nearsightedness. When he discovers that his teacher has glasses like his, he wears his own. He can suddenly do the things that his nearsightedness impeded, bringing admiration from his friends. Offering a positive resolution to children's mixed feelings about their glasses, this story addresses many of the difficulties involved with first glasses.

Ages: 4–7   **Cultural context:** N/A

Bumposaurus by Penny McKinlay. Illus. by Britta Teckentrup. 26 pages Fogelman/Penguin Putnam, 2003.
When you need glasses, not wearing them causes all kinds of mishaps, as shown in the story of a baby dinosaur who is named Bumposaurus because he's so nearsighted that he bumps against his shell trying to hatch. He thinks he's bumped into his father, but it's really a tree. Thinking that the tree's nonresponse to him indicates his father's anger, he decides to leave home. He stumbles across a hungry tyrannosaurus and is rescued by his parents and others, leading to an encounter with Grandma, who wears glasses. When he tries on Grandma's glasses, he's delighted to see smiling faces all around him. Children who need glasses will enjoy the humor of Bumposaurus's adventures, and they will appreciate both the disadvantages of not having glasses and the joys of being able to see.

Ages: 3–7   **Cultural context:** N/A

Fenton's Leap by Libba Moore Gray. Illus. by Jo-Ellen Bosson. 34 pages Simon & Schuster, 1994.

Poor vision causes problems, and as a nearsighted frog named Fenton learns in this story, seeing again is a great relief. Not only does he think of himself as clumsy, but he also ends up in dangerous places as a result of not seeing where he's going. Finally, when he bumps into a fishing line, releasing a catfish, the catfish offers him a favor in return. He asks to be able to see, and the catfish brings him a pair of glasses from the bottom of the swamp. Fenton is delighted to be able to see, and the world looks beautiful to him. Fenton has an unusual sensitivity to sounds, which is used delightfully in the text, and when he's able to see, he still has it. Using language in a charming way, this story clearly conveys the idea that vision is a genuine gift.

Ages: 3–8   **Cultural context:** N/A

Glasses: Who Needs 'Em? by Lane Smith. 32 pages Viking, 1991.

Sometimes kids are more concerned about how they look than how they see, as is the boy in this story, who needs glasses but doesn't want them because he worries that he'll look like a dork. His doctor responds that the boy's parents and sister wear glasses, as do various increasingly outlandish creatures. The boy retorts that the doctor needs glasses because he is "seeing things"—but when the doctor puts glasses on the boy, he suddenly sees things he'd never seen before and decides to wear his glasses after all. In a playful way, this story shows children that sight is more important than personal appearance.

Ages: 6–8   **Cultural context:** European-American

Spectacles by Ellen Raskin. 49 pages Atheneum, 1978.

Some children may be reluctant to wear glasses because they fear giving up a unique perspective. However, according to Iris, things looked strange before she got her glasses. For example, Great-Aunt Fanny looked like a fire-breathing dragon. She objects to getting glasses with cries and screams, and refuses all the frame styles offered by the optician—until he offers her the choice of looking like a movie star. She finds that having glasses solves a lot of problems, and when she chooses to, she's still able to use her imagination about what things look like.

Clearly showing the value of seeing things as they are, this story also gives kids permission to see in a fanciful way when they want to.

Ages: 3–7   **Cultural context:** Multicultural
Main character's cultural background: European-American

Winnie Flies Again **by Valerie Thomas. Illus. by Korky Paul. 26 pages Kane/Miller, 1999.**
Difficulty seeing causes problems even for a witch. Winnie is a witch who likes to fly on her broomstick with her cat, Wilbur. But lately she's been bumping into things—helicopters, hang gliders, tall buildings. She turns her broomstick into a bicycle, a skateboard, and finally, a horse, but she continues to have accidents. After these adventures, she goes into a shop looking for a cup of tea and leaves with a new pair of glasses that allow her to fly happily again. Children will enjoy the humor and understand the importance of being able to see.

Ages: 3–8   **Cultural context:** European-American

PART 8

LOSS AND GRIEF

[CHAPTER 30]

Death of a Pet

The death of a pet is a painful experience in a child's life. This is many children's first experience with death, and the death of a pet may loom especially large if the pet has been a part of the child's entire life. Also, because of their developmental stage, young children may struggle with developing a cognitive understanding of what it means to be dead, as well as with finding ways to resolve their feelings of loss. When a pet dies, kids need extra love and support. It's important to listen to children's feelings and to let them know that their sadness is normal. Kids need to mourn their pet in their own way.

See also *Lifetimes* and *When Dinosaurs Die* (Chapter 31) for books about death in general. *The Boy Who Didn't Want to Be Sad* (Chapter 7) shows children why it's important to accept all their feelings, even sadness and loss. *The Family Book* (Chapter 15) acknowledges the sadness families feel when someone they love dies. In *Grandmother Bryant's Pocket* (Chapter 32), a girl grieves her dog's death when her family's barn burns down.

The Black Dog Who Went into the Woods by **Edith Thacher Hurd. Illus. by Emily Arnold McCully. 32 pages Harper & Row, 1980.**

When a pet has died, it's helpful for children to know that there are many ways to grieve. A farm family's old, disabled dog, Black Dog, is missing, and Benjamin knows that she has gone off into the woods to die. After a discussion, the family finally concludes that Benjamin is right, and each one has a dream in which she or he remembers and says good-bye to Black Dog in a unique way, helping children understand that each of us grieves in our own way.

Ages: 5–9   **Cultural context:** European-American

A Dog Like Jack by **DyAnne DiSalvo-Ryan. 32 pages Holiday House, 1999.**

A pet's death brings a complex set of emotions. Mike remembers his family's adoption of Jack from an animal shelter, their good times with Jack, and finally, Jack's aging and his death at home. Sensitively portraying Mike's feelings of sadness and unreality, the story makes a subtle link to the greater worry that the loss of a dog might mean the loss of a person, too. Mike acknowledges the variety of feelings evoked by seeing other dogs, as well as the possibility of having another dog someday when he and his parents are ready. An afterword for adults discusses ways to help children cope with a pet's death. With a finely tuned balance between gentleness and a straightforward acknowledgement of this painful experience, the story offers empathy to children whose pet has been an important part of their life.

Ages: 3–8   **Cultural context:** Multicultural

Main character's cultural background: European-American

Goodbye Mousie by **Robie H. Harris. Illus. by Jan Ormerod. 26 pages McElderry/Simon & Schuster, 2001.**

When a pet has died, it's important for kids to understand what death means, to acknowledge their feelings, and to say good-bye, even if the pet is a mouse. When a boy wakes up to find his pet, Mousie, dead, he reacts with disbelief, anger, and sadness. His father explains the difference between sleep and death, adding that although they can't be sure exactly why Mousie died, he was very old for a mouse. The boy's parents are supportive and caring, and they help him bury Mousie in the yard. The boy has creative ideas about what to put in the box with Mousie, and his parents accept them all. After a simple, child-appropriate funeral, the boy has accepted Mousie's death. Showing both the feelings that accompany a pet's death and the helpfulness of saying goodbye from their heart, this poignant story will resonate with kids, especially those who have lost a pet mouse.

Ages: 2–6   **Cultural context:** European-American

Goodbye, Max by Holly Keller. 32 pages Greenwillow, 1987.

When a child is grieving, sometimes the need to go on with life brings the child into contact with sources of support. This happens to Ben after his dog, Max, dies. Ben experiences anger, sadness, and disbelief. His gentle, nonintrusive Papa brings home a puppy, but Ben has no interest in it. He doesn't even want to play with his friend, Zach, but when the two boys recall some of their times with Max, Ben is able to grieve, and Zach cries with him. After this, Ben is able to accept the puppy. This sensitively told story offers empathy with children's feelings of loss, acceptance of the need to cry, and respect for the process of mourning. It also shows the helpfulness of talking with someone who cares about you.

Ages: 4–8   **Cultural context:** European-American

Goodbye, Mitch by Ruth Wallace-Brodeur.
Illus. by Kathryn Mitter. 32 pages Whitman, 1995.

A complex set of feelings comes with a pet's illness and death. Michael's cat, Mitch, has always been part of his life, and there's a strong, deep bond between them. When Mitch becomes terminally ill, Michael shows a real sensitivity to his needs. He cries with anticipatory grief. Mitch finally dies peacefully in Michael's arms, and the family buries him in their garden, giving Michael the opportunity to express deep sadness over the loss, gladness for the time he had with Mitch, and love for Mitch. Children will feel an authentic sense of empathy with their own sadness.

Ages: 5–10   **Cultural context:** European-American

I'll Always Love You **by Hans Wilhelm. 31 pages Crown, 1985.**
Kids can use their memories of a loving relationship with a pet to help
cope with the pet's death. A boy has known his dog, Elfie, all his life,
and every day, he tells Elfie that he'll always love her. When she grows
old and becomes too disabled to climb stairs, he carries her up to his
room to sleep every night. One morning, he wakes up to find that Elfie
has died overnight. With his parents, brother, and sister, the boy buries
Elfie, using the memory of having told her he loved her to ease his sadness. He imagines he'll have another pet someday and will tell it that
he loves it every day, affirming the capacity to love in spite of loss.
Ages: 4–8   **Cultural context:** European-American

Jasper's Day **by Marjorie Blain Parker.**
Illus. by Janet Wilson. 32 pages Kids Can, 2002.
Saying good-bye to a family pet can be very painful. Riley's dog, Jasper,
who is older than Riley, is in pain from cancer. Riley and his parents have
decided to take a day off to celebrate Jasper's Day, the last day of his life.
They give Jasper his favorite breakfast of people food and take him to
visit his favorite places. At each place, the family and those with them
share their memories of Jasper. Finally, Dad takes Jasper to the clinic
to be euthanized. In the midst of Riley's sadness, he recognizes Jasper's
pain and has a moment of realizing that Jasper may be ready to die. The
family buries Jasper in the yard with some of his favorite things, laughing and crying as they recall his life. Riley goes to sleep acknowledging
that the day has been both sad and good, and he plans to make a memory
book about Jasper's life. This story offers children empathy with the experience of loss and the possibility of a good good-bye.
Ages: 4–10   **Cultural context:** Multicultural
Main character's cultural background: European-American

Jim's Dog Muffins **by Miriam Cohen. Illus. by Lillian Hoban.**
32 pages Greenwillow, 1984.
A genuine connection with another person is an important in healing
from grief. Jim has this experience when his dog, Muffins, dies. He
doesn't come to school at first, and when he does, he's preoccupied.
Other children say well-intentioned but unhelpful things, such as

suggesting that he might forget Muffins. Jim rejects these comments, and his teacher explains that he needs time to be sad. His best friend, Paul, connects with him through their humorous ritual of a pizza snack and their acknowledgement of Muffins' role in it. Although this story may be more helpful for friends of a bereaved child than for the child him- or herself, it shows children that they have a right to be sad, to reject unhelpful comments, and to grieve in their own time when a pet has died.

Ages: 4–7   **Cultural context:** Multicultural
Main character's cultural background: European-American

Not Just a Fish **by Kathleen Maresh Hemery.**
Illus. by Ron Boldt. 10 pages Centering, 2000.
The death of small pets such as fish may be trivialized by others, only adding to the child's grief. Marybeth loves her fish, Puffer, who was a gift from her beloved Aunt Lizzie. She remembers how she enjoyed and could be comforted by him, and describes Puffer's illness and death. Her attachment to Puffer is poignantly contrasted with the reactions of many people around her, who tell her that Puffer was "just a fish." With the help of an understanding friend, she decides to bury Puffer— but it's too late; Dad has flushed him down the toilet. Aunt Lizzie suggests a memorial service, at which Marybeth reads a eulogy she has written. This book has an unusual format, with a great deal of text on each of only four pages. Validating children's feelings of grief for a pet who has died, this story shows them a way to say good-bye.

Ages: 4–8   **Cultural context:** unclear

Petey **by Tobi Tobias. Illus. by Symeon Shimin. 32 pages**
Putnam, 1978.
At first, loss may mean a wish for things to be just as they were, but when children are ready to accept other possibilities, they can move through their grief. When Emily comes home to find her gerbil, Petey, shivering in the corner of his cage, uninterested in treats, she feels frightened, sad, and angry. With Daddy's help, she cares for Petey and comforts him as well as she can, but after a night of disrupted sleep, she awakes to find him dead. Together, the family remembers

his life, and many everyday situations remind Emily of Petey. After a while, friends offer her two baby gerbils. At first, it doesn't feel right because it wouldn't be the same. Mommy wisely acknowledges that it won't be the same but that it might be good in another way, allowing Emily to consider the possibility of a new gerbil. Children will identify with Emily's helplessness when Petey is sick and her sadness when he dies, and ultimately they'll understand that it's possible to move through grief.

Ages: 4–9 **Cultural context:** European-American

Saying Goodbye to Lulu **by Corinne Demas.**
Illus. by Ard Hoyt. 32 pages Little, Brown, 2004.
It can be difficult to say goodbye to a loved pet. A girl's elderly dog, Lulu, has been in her family since before the girl was born. As Lulu ages, the girl cares for her tenderly, carrying her outside when she can't walk anymore. One day, when the girl comes home from school, Mommy tells her Lulu is dead. She offers the girl a chance to say goodbye, but the girl can't; she just cries. The family buries Lulu in the yard, and still the girl can't say goodbye. It's only the next spring, when they plant a tree at Lulu's grave, that the girl can finally say goodbye. The family plans to get a new puppy, and although the girl knows he isn't Lulu, she can still love him, and looks forward to playing with him under Lulu's tree. This story patiently shows children that it's okay to wait till you're really ready to say goodbye, and after that, it's possible to experience joy again.

Ages: 3–8 **Cultural context:** Multicultural
Main character's cultural background: European-American

The Tenth Good Thing About Barney **by Judith Viorst.**
Illus. by Erik Blegvad. 28 pages Atheneum, 1971.
Remembering a lost pet can help children grieve. When a child's cat dies, the child's mother suggests thinking of ten good things about Barney to say at his funeral. At first, the child thinks of only nine; the tenth is that now that he's in the ground, Barney is helping the plants grow. The child's feelings of grief are addressed straightforwardly. The child and a friend discuss whether Barney is in heaven (on the "is,"

"is not" level). A limitation of this story is that the child is encouraged to think only about Barney's positive attributes; a greater sense of wholeness would have been possible if both his endearing and annoying characteristics had been acknowledged. But in spite of this limitation, this story movingly portrays the transition from raw grief to the beginning of a resolution.

Ages: 3–7   **Cultural context:** European-American

Tough Boris **by Mem Fox. Illus. by Kathryn Brown.**
32 pages Harcourt Brace Jovanovich, 1994.
Here's a particularly helpful story for children who feel that they have to be tough and that it's not okay to cry, even when they're grieving. The text tells the story of Boris, who is as tough, massive, scruffy, and scary as any other pirate. But when his parrot dies, he cries—and all pirates cry. Meanwhile, the pictures tell another story: Boris finds a violin in a treasure chest, and a boy steals it. Boris makes the boy play for the pirates, and his music engages Boris's tender side. When the parrot dies, Boris buries it overboard in the violin case, and the boy grieves with him. There's another loss as the boy is put ashore with the violin. The message comes across clearly that no matter how tough you are, it's okay to cry when you've experienced a loss.

Ages: 3–7   **Cultural context:** Multicultural
Main character's cultural background: European-American

When a Pet Dies **by Fred Rogers. Illus. by Jim Judkis.**
32 pages Putnam, 1988.
When a pet dies, children may struggle with both the meaning of death and the feelings it evokes. This nonfiction book addresses both. Mr. Rogers explains that sometimes a pet is too old, sick, or badly hurt for anyone to be able to keep it alive. He acknowledges the feelings of sadness, anger, guilt, and wishing to be alone that may occur when a pet dies, adding that the feelings are temporary, even if they don't always feel that way. He emphasizes the importance of talking to people you love about your feelings. The book includes a simple explanation of what death is and discusses the possibility of having a new pet when the child is ready. With kindness and empathy, this gentle, straight-

forward book offers useful information and reassurance that children's pain won't last forever.

Ages: 2–7 **Cultural context:** Multicultural

[CHAPTER 31]

Death of an Important Person

The death of someone close to a child involves painful emotions, including sadness, loneliness, anger, guilt, shock, and numbness or disbelief. Their behavior may change, with kids sometimes behaving in ways that are immature for them (for example, having difficulty separating from parents, or returning to thumb sucking) or in angry, explosive ways. Sharing grief is an important coping strategy that promotes both individual healing and a sense of connection with other survivors. Children need to know that it's okay to talk about the death and about their feelings. As difficult as it can be to support your child while you're grieving yourself, you can let them know this by listening, encouraging them to ask questions, exposing your own feelings, and showing how you cope. Kids also have the additional task of dealing with the distress of adults around them, who, in some cases, were closer to the person who died. This is particularly difficult in developmental stages when children simply aren't able to see things from others' points of view. In addition, young children may not understand what it means that someone is dead. They need to learn that death is permanent and inevitable for all living things, and that all life functions stop when someone dies. They also need to know the real reasons that people die, in age-appropriate terms.

When children understand that all living things die, they may worry that they, or a surviving parent, will die soon, too. They need reassurance that most children grow up to become very old adults, and that you are doing all you can to stay healthy and expect to live long into the child's adulthood. As you talk with young children about death, it's important to use words like "dead" and "died," rather than euphemisms that can confuse the child. No matter how good your explanations are, it's important to clarify what the child is thinking so that you can clear up any misunderstandings. Finally, be sure to allow children's grief to take its natural course over time.

See also *The Boy Who Didn't Want to Be Sad* (Chapter 7) for a story about the importance of embracing life even though it includes sadness. *The Family Book* (Chapter 15) acknowledges that part of family life is to be sad when a loved one dies. For other stories in which children anticipate or cope with someone's death, see *Grandmother's Song* (Chapter 1), *The Summer My Father Was Ten* (Chapter 7), *The Memory String* (Chapter 15), *I'll See You in My Dreams and Too Far Away To Touch* (Chapter 27), *The Color of Home, Sami and the Time of the Troubles*, and *Sweet Dried Apples* (Chapter 33).

DEATH IN GENERAL

Grandpa's Soup **by Eiko Kadono. Illus. by Satomi Ichikawa.**
33 pages Eerdmans, 1999.
Sometimes a connection with others can help kids keep a connection with someone who has died. In this story, Grandma has died, and Grandpa, who is sad and lonely, tries to make Grandma's meatball soup. Three mice come to share it with him, but it doesn't taste quite right. Each day he tries making the soup again, each time remembering an ingredient he's forgotten and making a little more soup than the day before, and each day more animals come to share the soup.

When he makes a big pot of soup, all the animals and the neighborhood children come to eat with him, and it tastes just right. Skillfully illustrating grief that recedes bit by bit, this story acknowledges the role of connection to other people in healing from grief.

Ages: 2–7   **Cultural context:** Multicultural

Main character's cultural background: European-American

Lifetimes: The Beautiful Way to Explain Death to Children
by Bryan Mellonie. Illus. by Robert Ingpen. 40 pages
Bantam, 1983.
When someone dies, children need to know what it means to be dead. This book calmly explains that death is an intrinsic part of life. It gives examples of the "lifetimes," or life spans, of many different living things (plants, animals, people). It explains that living things usually recover from illnesses or injuries, but sometimes that isn't possible. Addressing feelings about death only in the most minimal way, this book would be helpful for children who struggle with understanding the nature of death.

Ages: 4–7   **Cultural context:** European-American

A Story for Hippo: A Book About Loss **by Simon Puttock.**
Illus. by Alison Bartlett. 26 pages Scholastic, 2001.
Finding ways to keep with us someone who has died helps to heal grief, as Monkey does when Hippo dies. The old, wise hippo is Monkey's dearest friend and tells him wonderful stories. When she warns Monkey that she'll die, he feels scared, angry, and sad. After her death, his sadness deepens. Little Chameleon finally convinces him to tell her a story, reminding him that he has all the stories that Hippo told. When Monkey tells Little Chameleon a story, they grieve together and look forward together to new stories that incorporate their unique qualities. Children will understand that they'll always have the stories of the person whom they've lost, learning to integrate their past with someone they've loved into their future.

Ages: 3–8   **Cultural context:** N/A

We Remember Philip by Norma Simon.
Illus. by Ruth Sanderson. 32 pages Whitman, 1979.

This book would be a good choice for a child who isn't directly affected by a death, but is close to someone who is. In this story, Sam copes with the accidental death of his teacher's adult son, Philip. His discusses his worries about the possibility of his own death, the sadness of adults around him, and his wish to help Mr. Hall, and reexperiences sadness about the death of his dog. With help from his mother, the principal, and his classmates, Sam finds ways to help Mr. Hall: writing him a letter, talking to him when he returns to school, asking to see pictures of Philip, and planting a tree in Philip's memory. Mr. Hall seems less burdened by grief over time and clearly accepts the children's caring. An afterword addresses talking with children about death. Children will understand how mourning occurs over a period of time and how to empathize with another person's grief.

Ages: 7–10   **Cultural context:** Multicultural
Main character's cultural background: European-American

When Dinosaurs Die: A Guide to Understanding Death
by Laurie Krasny Brown and Marc Brown. 32 pages
Little, Brown, 1996.

Here's a nonfiction book that addresses the meaning of death, the emotions kids experience, and ways to cope. It briefly explains what death means and some of the ways people die (including suicide). Addressing concerns children may have when someone dies, the authors encourage children to talk about them and to cope in other ways such as being alone when you need to, drawing, and exercising. They discuss ways to say good-bye, including funerals for pets and people, and briefly review diverse cultures' customs related to death. A glossary is included. One limitation of the book is that a child who is putting food into a hamster's coffin is told, "dead hamsters don't get hungry," which addresses the literal aspects of the situation appropriately but misses a symbolic aspect that may be important to children. In addition to lots of helpful information, this book, which is illustrated with charming humanoid dinosaurs, provides a strong sense of acceptance for children's feelings and practical ideas for coping.

Ages: 4–8   **Cultural context:** N/A

DEATH OF A GRANDPARENT

Most children will experience the death of a grandparent at some time in their life. A grandparent may be the first important person in a child's life to die. The death of a grandparent may also prompt children's awareness that growing old leads to death.

The Blue Roses **by Linda Boyden. Illus. by Amy Córdova.**
32 pages Lee & Low, 2002.
Rosalie lives with her momma and grandfather, whom she has named Papa and with whom she has a special closeness. Papa plants a red rose-bush when Rosalie is born, adding pink and yellow ones, but despite Rosalie's request he can't plant blue roses because they don't exist. Later, when one of her plants dies, he explains that the dead plants will help other plants grow, and so nothing is ever completely gone from the garden. The next winter, Papa dies. Rosalie dreams of Papa in a garden of blue roses, telling her that they'll be together as each one tends his or her own roses. Eventually, her grief fades, though it doesn't go away, and one day, she discovers that the roses she's planted at Papa's grave have bloomed blue. Illustrated in intense colors, this beautiful story shows children that they can keep a loved one with them in their hearts and lives, and that mourning transforms grief into hope.
Ages: 6–12   **Cultural context:** Multicultural
Main character's cultural background: Native-American

The Cat Next Door **by Betty Ren Wright.**
Illus. by Gail Owens. 32 pages Holiday House, 1991.
This story uses two visits to a girl's grandparents to show the changes that come with death. The girl is especially close to her grandma, who assures her that the cat next door—that also has a special relationship with the girl—will always love her. Grandma tells her that each of these joyful days will last forever because they'll remember each day forever. The following year's visit is sad because Grandma has died, and the girl misses her terribly, but when the cat next door comes to visit, she brings kittens. In the kittens, the girl finds her capacity to experience joy again, using Grandma's favorite word to tell the cat that Grandma would have loved the kittens. Honestly acknowledging the sadness and

change that come with death, this story shows children that change also brings birth, and that connection and happiness are still possible.

Ages: 5–9 **Cultural context:** European-American

Grandma's Purple Flowers **by Adjoa J. Burrowes. 32 pages Lee & Low, 2000.**

Although the process of grieving can be long, it moves in its own natural rhythm. In this story, which is illustrated using wonderfully textured cut-paper collages, a girl loves visiting her grandma. She brings Grandma's favorite purple flowers, and they garden together. One winter day, Grandma is very tired. The girl embraces Grandma, who rubs her back and braids her hair. Grandma dies that night, and the winter reflects the girl's sadness. When spring finally comes, the girl sees tiny purple flowers in Grandma's garden and feels a mixture of joy and sorrow. Eventually, the purple flowers come to mean the warmth of Grandma's presence. Acknowledging the depth of loss, this story will help children to be patient with the gradual process of grief and to find their own personal ways to remember the person they've lost.

Ages: 3–8 **Cultural context:** Multicultural
Main character's cultural background: African-American

The Hickory Chair **by Lisa Rowe Fraustino. Illus. by Benny Andrews. 32 pages Arthur A. Levine/Scholastic, 2001.**

Mourning involves finding new ways to feel the presence of the person who has died. When Louis's Gran dies suddenly, his sadness and loss are palpable, although they're expressed in few words. Her will says that she's hidden a note for each of her favorite people in the thing she's leaving to that person. The family hunts for notes, and Louis finds lots, but none for him. His father invites him to pick out whatever he'd like. He picks Gran's chair, where he can feel her with him. When he's an adult, Louis's grandchild finds Gran's note for him in the chair. The fact that Louis has been blind from birth is addressed in a matter-of-fact way, and it's clear that this is just one of the many characteristics that makes him unique. Children will understand that we can trust our heart to feel the presence of someone we love who has died.

Ages: 4–8 **Cultural context:** African-American

Marianne's Grandmother **by Bettina Egger.**
Illus. by Sita Jucker. 26 pages Dutton, 1987.
Making art, remembering the person who has died, and getting support from people who care about you can transform raw grief, as it does for Marianne after her grandmother's death. As this story begins, Grandmother has died some time ago. Marianne sadly remembers her last visit with Grandmother, and her confusion, sadness, anger, and worry when Grandmother died the next day. She recalls how her parents listened to her, answered her questions when they could, and shared her sadness. Marianne attends the funeral, and afterward, she talks to her doll about Grandmother. Later, painting a picture of Grandmother transforms Marianne's grief. The murky, dreamlike watercolor illustrations give the impression of memories. Like Marianne, children can use these ways to process grief and learn that their memories are permanent and they can still love the person who has died.

Ages: 4–7   **Cultural context:** European-American

Nana Upstairs & Nana Downstairs **by Tomie dePaola.**
31 pages Putnam, 1973.
With help from parents, children can use symbols to cope with loss. Tommy learns this at age four, grieving the death of his great-grandmother (Nana Upstairs), and he elaborates on this knowledge in adulthood, grieving the death of his grandmother (Nana Downstairs). When Nana Upstairs dies, he doesn't understand what this means, and his mother explains that Nana Upstairs won't come back, except in his memories of her. During Tommy's childhood, his mother interprets a falling star as a kiss from Nana Upstairs. After Nana Downstairs' death, he sees another falling star and reflects that now both grandmothers are "Nana Upstairs." The tenderness of Tommy's memories shows children a resolution of grief.

Ages: 3–7   **Cultural context:** European-American

Pearl's Marigolds for Grandpa **by Jane Breskin Zalben.**
24 pages Simon & Schuster, 1997.
Carrying on the traditions of someone who has died is a way to keep that person with you. When Pearl's grandpa dies, she doesn't feel like doing anything and has difficulty concentrating. Her parents and

friends are gentle and supportive. Grandpa used to send her marigold seeds. Papa provides the seeds now, and in growing flowers, Pearl learns that Grandpa lives through her. Although Pearl decides not to go to Grandpa's funeral, a postscript describes the funeral traditions of several religions. The small, framed illustrations give the impression of being treasures, much like the treasured memories of someone we've lost. Because this gentle story takes a child's point of view in a genuine way, children will identify easily with Pearl. With her, they will understand that when someone they love has died, they can keep that person with them by continuing that person's traditions.

Ages: 3–8   **Cultural context:** N/A

Thank You, Grandpa **by Lynn Plourde.**
Illus. by Jason Cockcroft. 32 pages Dutton, 2003.
Mourning involves saying good-bye and at the same time, keeping the person who has died with you always. A girl takes her first walks with Grandpa, who answers all of her questions about what she sees. When they find a dead grasshopper, and she asks what they can do, he responds that they can say "thank you and good-bye." As they bury it, he thanks the grasshopper for its hops, and she thanks it for surprising her. They find many small animals to thank together. When the girl must finally walk alone, she thanks Grandpa for their walks and for teaching her the words that she needs to say. She will always remember him. This quietly powerful story shows children how to say goodbye by speaking simply from their hearts, and how to keep what they've learned from someone with them always.

Ages: 3–9   **Cultural context:** European-American

When Grandpa Came to Stay **by Judith Caseley. 32 pages**
Greenwillow, 1986.
Sometimes it can be difficult for children to cope with adults' grief, as it is for Benny when Grandpa comes to visit for the first time since Grandma died. One evening, Grandpa cries because he misses Grandma. Benny shouts that he doesn't like a grandpa who cries, and he runs to his room. His mother explains that even grown-ups feel sad and cry. Benny acknowledges to Grandpa that he's been "mean," and

Grandpa accepts Benny's imperfections and helps Benny understand that they can be friends again. The next day, Grandpa takes Benny to visit Grandma's grave, where they plant flowers. They drink tea and eat cookies, both of which Grandma loved. This story promotes children's acceptance of talking about grief, even when it isn't primarily their own.

Ages: 3–7   **Cultural context:** European-American

DEATH OF A PARENT

When a parent dies, a child's whole world changes irrevocably. In addition to the wide variety of reactions that death evokes, children often worry about who will take care of them. If there is a surviving parent, the child needs to cope with that parent's grief as well as their own.

After Charlotte's Mom Died **by Cornelia Maude Spelman.**
Illus. by Judith Friedman. 24 pages Whitman, 1996.
When a child's grief is blocked, it's important to find ways to work through the feelings of loss. Six-year-old Charlotte's mom had died in a traffic accident about six months before the beginning of this story. She feels sad, angry, and frightened, and has some misconceptions about death, while her father is preoccupied with his own grief. When Charlotte acts out her anger, he realizes that they both need help with their feelings, and they see a therapist. In family therapy, Charlotte expresses her feelings and misconceptions through play, finds reassurance, and reaches resolution. Once she can express her grief more fully, she begins to feel that things will be right somehow again, even though Mom is gone forever. A foreword for adults encourages acceptance of children's sadness and finding ways to bring children hope. This story addresses the misconception that death is related to sleep and the worry that the surviving parent might die, while tenderly showing Charlotte's transition from raw pain to hopefulness.

Ages: 4–8   **Cultural context:** European-American

Everett Anderson's Goodbye **by Lucille Clifton.**
Illus. by Ann Grifalconi. 25 pages Holt, 1983.
Each page of this poetic story illustrates one of the stages of grief identified by Elisabeth Kübler-Ross as they appear in the life of a boy whose father has died: denial, anger, bargaining, depression, and acceptance. In the *denial* stage, Everett dreams constantly about Daddy. Experiencing *anger*, he declares that he doesn't love anyone, even his mama. In the *bargaining* stage, Everett promises to learn his math facts and improve his table manners if only Daddy will walk and talk again. When he enters the stage of *depression*, Everett can't sleep and sees no point in eating. Finally, with gentle support from his mama, Everett reaches the stage of *acceptance*, in which he understands that he can always carry his daddy's love with him. Helping children understand that grief can be expressed in many ways, this story shows that acceptance is possible.

Ages: 4–8   **Cultural context:** African-American

Flamingo Dream **by Donna Jo Napoli.**
Illus. by Cathie Felstead. 32 pages Greenwillow, 2002.
A girl lovingly recalls her last trip with Daddy to Florida, where they saw flamingos. When they return, she starts school and does regular kid things: making friends, listening to stories, playing marbles. Then, in beautifully crafted language, she tells us that Daddy is dying of cancer. She and her parents cry together. With Mamma, she visits Daddy in the hospital, where he dies the next day. Daddy's friends bring her flamingos, which she puts in her yard. A dream of flamingos helps her process her loss. Just as Daddy had made her a book of photographs each year, she now makes a book about the events of the year of Daddy's death which turns out to be this book and is illustrated with collages that include childlike drawings. Showing children how to keep someone they've lost with them in their memories by continuing their traditions, this story demonstrates the usefulness of words and art to resolve the pain of loss.

Ages: 5–10   **Cultural context:** Multicultural
Main character's cultural background: European-American

Geranium Morning by E. Sandy Powell.
Illus. by Renée Graef. 40 pages Carolrhoda, 1990.
It's important to share feelings when working through grief. Timothy recalls how his dad died in a traffic accident, after Timothy had declined to come with him to buy geraniums. Timothy has nightmares about this last morning with Dad and struggles with sadness, guilt, mood swings, troubles at school, and especially, loneliness. His mom is depressed and irritable. Then Timothy becomes friends with Frannie, whose mother is dying. Through this friendship, he transforms his pain to empathy and works through his grief, and finally, he goes to get Dad's geraniums. Offering empathy for the range of feelings children might experience when a parent dies, this story shows how much it helps to talk about feelings of loss.
Ages: 7–12   **Cultural context:** Multicultural
Main character's cultural background: European-American

A Quilt for Elizabeth by Benette W. Tiffault.
Illus. by Mary McConnell. 32 pages Centering, 1992.
Sharing feelings about loss and memories of the person who has died contribute to the resolution of mourning. Eight-year-old Elizabeth's father becomes ill and is hospitalized. Elizabeth's feelings about her father's illness—a combination of intense frustration, anger, guilt, sadness, and love—are met with loving acceptance. When he dies, she reacts with disbelief, outrage, and sadness; her mother stands by her, committed to help. She begins to heal when Mommy explains that Daddy is "'way down deep in our hearts.'" Elizabeth spends evenings with her paternal grandmother, who encourages her to make a quilt. The two laugh and cry together as each piece of fabric evokes memories of Daddy. Through this process, she comes to realize that she will always have these memories, offering kids an empathic, accepting, and hopeful image of healing.
Ages: 6-10   **Cultural context:** European-American

DEATH OF A CHILD

When another child dies, in addition to the experiences that accompany any loss, children will often have special concerns about their own mortality. If a child their own age can die, can they die, too? They also lose the special companionship of a friend or sibling and if a sibling dies, the child's role in the family changes.

I Had a Friend Named Peter: Talking to Children About the Death of a Friend by Janice Cohn. Illus. by Gail Owens. 32 pages Morrow, 1987.

A friend's death evokes a need to make sense of death and resolve difficult feelings. When Betsy's friend, Peter, dies in a traffic accident, she feels confused, curious, angry, worried, sad, and empathic toward Peter's parents. Her parents reassure her that children usually grow up to be old and explain that her anger toward Peter didn't cause his death. Betsy spontaneously thinks of ways to comfort Peter's parents and to commemorate his life by making pictures in his memory. Her class shares memories of Peter, and their teacher assures them that Peter will remain with them in their memories. A detailed introduction discusses ways to talk with children about their concerns about death. In a story they can easily relate to, this book offers young children helpful information and empathy.

Ages: 3–6   **Cultural context:** Multicultural
Main character's cultural background: European-American

A Little Bit of Rob by Barbara J. Turner. Illus. by Marni Backer. 32 pages Whitman, 1996.

When a sibling dies, the whole family grieves. As Lena and her parents go crabbing for the first time since her brother, Rob, died a month earlier, she realizes that they're all trying to suppress their grief; no one can even mention Rob's name. She begins to find a connection to Rob when she wears his sweatshirt. This connection continues when she catches five crabs—something no one but Rob has ever done before. To share this experience with her parents, she spreads out Rob's sweatshirt over the family, which allows them to acknowledge Rob verbally and to cry together. Portraying how genuine connections can facilitate moving through a process of mourning, this story assures children that someone who has died can stay with them in their memories, both individual and shared.

Ages 5–9   **Cultural context:** European-American

Rudi's Pond **by Eve Bunting. Illus. by Ronald Himler.**
32 pages Clarion, 1999.
Children may struggle with how to remember a friend who has died. A girl's friend, Rudi, is sick a lot and is eventually hospitalized. The girl's mom explains that he was born with a heart problem. Prohibited from visiting him, the girl realizes that she may never see him again—and she doesn't. Her parents are loving and supportive during Rudi's hospitalization and after his death. At school, the girl and her classmates write poems about Rudi, and, at the girl's suggestion, a pond is installed in his memory. The girl brings to the pond a hummingbird feeder that she and Rudi had made. One hummingbird seems to recognize her; the watercolor illustrations show the bird superimposed on a pale image of Rudi. The girl's connection with this bird becomes symbolic of her enduring connection with Rudi. Offering positive images of healing, this story shows an authentic sensitivity to the pain of a friend's death.

Ages: 4–10   **Cultural context:** Multicultural
Main character's cultural background: European-American

Stacy Had a Little Sister **by Wendie C. Old.**
Illus. by Judith Friedman. 32 pages Whitman, 1995.
An infant sibling's death evokes a unique kind of turmoil. Stacy expresses many of the feelings children often have when her sister, Ashley, is born: love, resentment, impatience for Ashley to be old enough to play with her. She wakes up one morning to her parents' and grandmother's distress. Ashley has died of Sudden Infant Death Syndrome. Stacy feels confused, and her parents are at times sad, irritable, and silent in their grief. She wonders whether she caused Ashley's death or could get SIDS herself, but once Mommy reassures her, Stacy begins to grieve with her family. Daddy gives Stacy a picture of her holding the baby sister whom she'll always remember. A foreword for adults summarizes children's reactions to a sibling's death from SIDS and gives contact information for the

SIDS Alliance. This story offers empathy and reassurance that even when a child's world seems to have turned upside down, there's hope for feeling better.

Ages: 3–6   **Cultural context:** European-American

Where's Jess? **by Joy Johnson, Marv Johnson, and Ray Goldstein with Heather Goldstein and Jody Goldstein. Illus. by Shari Barum. 24 pages Centering, 1992.**

When a young child's baby sibling dies, the child is faced with birth and death in close succession. In this story, the narrator's baby brother or sister, Jess, has died. Their parents explain death to the child. who acknowledges his/her capacity to remember Jess. The parents cry sometimes when they remember Jess, and Mommy reassures the child that it's okay to talk about Jess, even if she cries. She explains grief as emotional pain and acknowledges the healing role of crying. The parents comfort the child, saying that he/she is not to blame for Jess's death. Ending with the child's understanding that his/her parents love him/her, and he/she is okay, this calming story offers acceptance and information to young children whose sibling has died.

Ages: 2–4   **Cultural context:** European-American

PART 9

TRAUMA

CHAPTER 32

Natural Disaster

Natural disasters, including fires, floods, tornados, and hurricanes, are not only terrifying as they occur, but can carry with them a profound and ongoing threat to children's sense of the world as a safe place that includes a home that will always be there. Paradoxically, this threat contains within it the possibility of discovering a sense of oneself as someone who, with help from family and community, has the strength to survive great adversity. Children may respond to disasters with fear, difficulty with separation, nightmares, regression to younger behaviors such as thumb sucking, worsened school performance, tantrums, or withdrawal. They often need extra time and support from parents, including reassurance, honest acknowledgement of their feelings, and permission to cling. Talking about feelings and concerns, make-believe play, and drawing often help to resolve children's stress. As long as it's possible, kids benefit from keeping their regular schedules since it gives them a much-needed sense of security. While watching the disaster on the news repeatedly can be retraumatizing and should be avoided, positive actions such as helping to restore the community or working with classmates to make a book about the disaster can promote resilience.

See also *A Terrible Thing Happened* and *The Tin Forest* (Chapter 33) for stories that are helpful in traumatic situations without specifying a particular kind of traumatic event. For a story about a fire that breaks out in connection with riots, see *Smoky Night* (Chapter 33).

Aunt Minnie and the Twister by Mary Skillings Prigger. Illus. by Betsy Lewin. 37 pages Clarion, 2002.

A tornado can change kids' lives in unexpected ways. Fearless Aunt Minnie, a farmer, has adopted her nine nieces and nephews, and as they grow, the house gets crowded. Aunt Minnie reminds them that having each other is more important than having lots of room. When a tornado comes, she gathers the children in the root cellar, and everyone is safe. Upon reemerging, they discover that the tornado has picked up the farmhouse and turned it around. Aunt Minnie builds an addition onto the new back of the house with the help of a carpenter and the kids. Now there's more room, and the youngsters are secure in knowing that they have a home and each other. This spunky story conveys the message that parents' care is even stronger than tornadoes.

Ages: 4–7   **Cultural context:** European-American

A Chair for My Mother by Vera B. Williams. 32 pages Greenwillow, 1982.

Full recovery from disaster is a long, daily process, and a girl, her mother, and her grandma experience this while recovering from a house fire. Although the girl's feelings about the fire are not verbalized directly, the illustrations of her memories of the fire and what was left of the house are evocative. Friends and relatives support the family as they move into a new apartment, but they're still without soft chairs, and the girl's mother, who works at a diner, especially needs a comfortable place to sit after working hard on her feet all day. She saves her tips, and the girl saves half the money she gets from occasionally helping at the diner. Grandma contributes the money she saves when she buys food on sale. When they finally have enough money for the chair of their dreams, it makes the apartment truly feel like home to all of them. This process of saving coins shows how, after the initial emergency is taken care of, recovery from disaster happens gradually and everyone can contribute to it.

Ages: 4–8   **Cultural context:** Multicultural

Main character's cultural background: European-American

Come a Tide **by George Ella Lyon. Illus. by Stephen Gammell. 32 pages Orchard, 1990.**

Recovery from a disaster requires the participation of the entire community, and this is the case when a Kentucky town floods. Although neighbors delay evacuating, the narrator's family leaves immediately, going to Grandma's house on a hill, where she provides warm food. The next day, when the rain has stopped, the neighbors work together to dig things out of the mud. Offering children hope for getting through a flood, this book emphasizes the communal nature of disaster recovery.

Ages: 3–7   **Cultural context:** Multicultural

Main character's cultural background: European-American

Fat Chance Thanksgiving **by Patricia Lakin. Illus. by Stacey Schuett. 32 pages Whitman, 2001.**

Making connections can be an important part of coping with disaster. When a fire destroys Carla and Mama's apartment building, all Carla has left is a book about the pilgrims' Thanksgiving, which becomes a source of hope as she waits for a new home. After nearly a year in a hotel, they get a new apartment two weeks before Thanksgiving. She wants to plan a feast, but all Mama says is "Fat chance." Carla enlists the help of a new friend to hold a potluck in the apartment lobby, and by the end of the story, many new friends share a feast. Children will see how imagination, problem solving, and persistence promote healing from the losses of a fire.

Ages: 4–8   **Cultural context:** Multicultural

Main character's cultural background: Latina

Fire Diary **by Lily Rosenblatt. Illus. by Judith Friedman. 32 pages Whitman, 1994.**

A house fire has wide-ranging effects on a child's life, and April uses a diary given by her school psychologist to describe them. She has trouble sleeping because memories of the fire return, and sirens terrify her. At school, April doesn't feel safe and alienates herself from her classmates. With the school psychologist, April draws a picture of a cowgirl lassoing a fire monster, and she learns to cope with painful memories by "chang[ing] the pictures." She reconnects with her best friend, gets through a school field trip to the fire station with her friend's support, and with the help of relaxation techniques, sleeps well again. April helps Mama—who at first seems invulnerable—to draw pictures about her experience of the fire and make an escape plan for the new house, which is completed by the end of the story. This empowering story shows kids that they can feel safe again.

Ages: 8–12   **Cultural context:** Multicultural

Main character's cultural background: European-American

Grandmother Bryant's Pocket **by Jacqueline Briggs Martin. Illus. by Petra Mathers. 48 pages Houghton Mifflin, 1996.**
This is the story of a girl's healing from the trauma of a frightening fire and the loss of her beloved dog. In 1787, when the family's barn burns down, Sarah's dog dies and she has recurring nightmares. Staying with her patient, caring grandparents, Sarah takes in their love and concern. She finds strength as she overcomes her fear of their neighbor's mean geese. Sarah goes home with a new cat—not a replacement for her lost dog, but one who, like her, has been damaged and has accompanied her in her healing process. The patience shown toward Sarah in this story may help traumatized children to be patient with their own recovery. They'll learn that after a traumatic experience, things will never be the same, but they do get better and there are new beginnings.

Ages: 6–10   **Cultural context:** European-American

River Friendly, River Wild **by Jane Kurtz. Illus. by Neil Brennan. 40 pages Simon & Schuster, 2000.**
Based on the author's experience of the 1997 Red River flood in Grand Forks, North Dakota, this book uses poems to tell the story of a flood. The story vividly conveys the details of both the external experience—sand bagging, siren sounds, TV pictures of fires—and the narrator's internal experience—loss, fear, uncertainty, anger, sadness, gratitude,

and, finally, hope. The narrator leaves her cat when the family evacuates for "a few days," and when they return three weeks later, the cat is gone and the girl misses her. It's another two weeks before the cat reappears, having been cared for by a neighbor. A decision is made to build a dike in the neighborhood, but the narrator's house will be destroyed to make room for it. Though they survived the flood, they'll still lose their house and neighborhood; however, the story ends with an affirmation of the survivors' strength and the hope of making new memories, in spite of the ones that are lost.

Ages: 6–12   **Cultural context:** European-American

Sergio and the Hurricane **by Alexandra Wallner. 26 pages Holt, 2000.**

Children may think a hurricane is exciting until they experience one, as is the case for Sergio, who lives in Puerto Rico. Sergio helps Mama buy groceries and helps Papa put the outdoor furniture in the garage. But when he wakes up in the middle of the night during the hurricane, he's scared. Papa comforts him with a story about his grandmother's courage during a hurricane when she was young. In the morning, the hurricane is over, and Sergio understands the extent of the damage it did. Recovery is hard work, and it's some time before there's water and electricity again. Sergio tells Papa he'll never wish for a hurricane again. An afterword gives factual information about hurricanes, while the text and pictures give an honest look at the effects of hurricanes, as Sergio shows that kids can get through one, even if they're scared.

Ages: 4–8   **Cultural context:** Latino

The Strongest Man This Side of Cremona **by Georgia Graham. 32 pages Northern Lights, 1998.**

For children, the force of a disaster raises questions about their safety, as it does for Matthew. Matthew is very aware of Dad's strength, especially when Dad lifts him over fences and scares away cows that wander toward them, but when a tornado appears, Dad tries to outrun it, carrying Matthew. Finding shelter in a culvert, they're reunited with Ma after it's over. Though they're safe, the farm and other nearby farms are devastated. As neighbors work together to repair the damage, Matthew realizes that although Dad isn't stronger than a tornado, he's strong enough to keep Matthew safe, which provides the security he needs to return to a normal life.

Ages: 4–8   **Cultural context:** European-American

Time of Wonder **by Robert McCloskey. 63 pages Viking, 1957.**
A disaster can sometimes be an occasion for discovery. A hurricane (referred to by adults as "weather", though the word *hurricane* is used later) comes to an idyllic island in Maine. Two girls who spend summers there are comforted when their mother reads them a familiar story and by singing with their parents. When the storm is over in the morning, although familiar paths are blocked, there are new ones on top of fallen trees and new discoveries to be made. The children fertilize their garden with seaweed brought in by the storm. Demonstrating ways to feel safe in a scary situation, this story suggests ways to see something positive in it.

Ages: 6–9   **Cultural context:** European-American

Twister **by Darlene Bailey Beard. Illus. by Nancy Carpenter. 32 pages Farrar, Straus and Giroux, 1999.**
It's necessary to use whatever resources you have to tolerate a disaster, as Lucille and her younger brother Natt must do when a tornado strikes outside their trailer home. Mama sends them into a cellar shelter, and they wait out the storm there while she tends to their neighbor's safety. They wish Mama were with them, but manage their distress by playing and talking, and Lucille reassures Natt. After the tornado, there's an emotional reunion with Mama, who's safe under the porch with the neighbor. The four examine the damage, and Lucille finds she still feels that it's home. This story shows children that they can survive even a tornado with their sense of home intact.

Ages: 4–8   **Cultural context:** Multicultural
Main character's cultural background: European-American

[CHAPTER 33]

War and Violence

Many adults find it difficult to talk with children about war and community violence. The stories summarized in this chapter may help to provide a starting place. Children may react to war and violence with fear, difficulty around separation, nightmares and other sleep problems, regression to younger behaviors such as thumb sucking, physical complaints, worsened school performance, withdrawal, aggressive play, or other aggressive behavior. Children who have had other recent stressful experiences, who are fearful to begin with, or who are directly affected or close to someone who is (see *Pilot Mom*, Chapter 9) are at elevated risk. Kids often need extra time and support from parents, including calm reassurance, honest acknowledgement of their feelings, and permission to cling. Talking about their feelings and concerns, make-believe play, and drawing often help to resolve children's stress. Kids may need you to encourage them to express anger appropriately or to move from aggressive make-believe to playing the roles of doctors, firefighters, and others who save lives.

Let children take the lead in showing you what they need to talk about. Just talking with them, even if it isn't about war or violence, increases their connection with you and will help them feel safer. Kids also benefit from keeping their normal routines. It's important to limit exposure to TV news coverage, especially for younger children, and to watch with them so that you know what they're experiencing and can discuss what they've seen. If children respond with stereotyping or prejudice, this should be counteracted. Taking positive action, such as taking care of themselves, listening to others around them, and working with others to help people directly affected by the violence, can help maintain kids' sense of control.

See also *Hey, Little Ant* (Chapter 21) for another relevant story.

Boxes for Katje **by Candace Fleming.**
Illus. by Stacey Dressen-McQueen. 35 pages
Farrar, Straus and Giroux/Melanie Kroupa, 2003.
Many children experience an overwhelming sense of helplessness about war, and this story addresses the feeling in an inspiring way. In the Netherlands after World War II, people are desperately poor. Katje is surprised to receive a package from the Children's Aid Society in the United States. A girl named Rosie has sent her soap, wool socks, and chocolate. Katje generously shares these gifts and writes to Rosie. Rosie sends larger and larger packages, as more and more of her community becomes involved in sending things to Katje. As she shares the contents with larger and larger numbers of people in *her* community, Katje writes regularly to Rosie, and along with her mama and neighbors, sends Rosie tulip bulbs. Based on events that happened in the author's family, this story will decrease children's sense of helplessness about war by showing them a way that they can make a difference in a world affected by war.

Ages: 4–8   **Cultural context:** Multicultural
Main character's cultural background: European

The Bracelet **by Yoshiko Uchida. Illus. by Joanna Yardley.**
32 pages Philomel, 1993.
Loss and separation are difficult aspects of war. Emi, her mother, and sister are relocated to an internment camp for Japanese Americans during World War II. (Emi's father, who works for a Japanese company, has

already been sent to a prisoner of war camp). Emi's best friend, Laurie, who is European-American, brings her a bracelet as a going-away present, but soon after Emi arrives at the camp, she discovers she's lost the bracelet, seemingly her one connection to Laurie. The next day, as Emi finds other reminders of Laurie, she realizes that her memories of Laurie will always sustain her, regardless of physical objects like the bracelet. Showing kids that attachment to people lies within, this story will help them cope with the losses of war by trusting in themselves.

Ages: 6–11   **Cultural context:** Multicultural

Main character's cultural background: Asian American

The Butter Battle Book **by Dr. Seuss. 46 pages Random House, 1984.**

This story introduces the arbitrariness of war in a land where the Yooks and the Zooks are different because the Yooks eat their bread with the buttered side up, whereas the Zooks eat theirs with the buttered side down. Their hate over this difference leads to war. However, whenever a Yook has a new weapon, it turns out that the Zooks have one that's just as dangerous. When this happens, the Chief Yookeroo simply promotes the weapon's user and issues him a fancier uniform and a more complex, deadlier weapon. The story ends with a Yook and a Zook each dangling a bomb over the other's country, while the other Yooks are in underground bomb shelters. Clearly conveying hostility, fighting, and danger, but excluding explicit injury or death, this story effectively introduces children to the ideas of an arms race and war.

Ages: 6–9   **Cultural context:** European-American

The Butterfly **by Patricia Polacco. 50 pages Philomel, 2000.**

In this true story, a French girl named Monique meets Sevrine, a Jewish girl her own age whom her mother is hiding from the Nazis. Monique and Sevrine become close friends, and Monique feels a deep sense of empathy and generosity toward Sevrine. Monique sees a Nazi soldier crush a beautiful butterfly in an attempt to disturb her (and sees soldiers brutally drag away the town's beloved candy store owner). She brings a butterfly to Sevrine during the night, and when Sevrine misses her home, promises her that she will be as free as a butterfly someday. That night, a neighbor sees Sevrine, and she and her family must leave. Monique wishes for a sign that Sevrine is safe, and a flock of butterflies in their garden provides that sign. Monique's and her mother's courage are inspiring, and Monique's sense that Sevrine is safe illustrates the use of metaphor to cope with the unthinkable.

Ages: 8–12   **Cultural context:** European

The Cello of Mr. O **by Jane Cutler. Illus. by Greg Crouch. 32 pages Dutton, 1999.**
Despite extreme deprivation, courage and creativity are sometimes still possible. During wartime, a girl and her mother are living without her father (who is off fighting), heating fuel, adequate food, or school. After an attack stops a relief truck's weekly food deliveries, their neighbor, Mr. O, courageously plays his cello in the square at the time that the truck used to come—a cello that required international cooperation to make. When shells destroy the cello, he plays Bach on a harmonica in the square. The nurturing experience of the music inspires the girl to a creative—and grateful—act of her own, which allows her to recover her humanity against great odds.

Ages: 6–11   **Cultural context:** European

The Color of Home **by Mary Hoffman. Illus. by Karin Littlewood. 26 pages Fogelman/Penguin Putnam, 2002.**
The traumatic experiences of war include migration to a country with a new culture and language. When Hassan, who is from Somalia, starts school in the United States, he feels alone and confused even though people are friendly. He paints his first picture, which shows his home in Somalia, its destruction, and his uncle's murder by soldiers. An interpreter helps his teacher understand the picture, along with Hassan's experience of immigration. Having communicated this, he's able to make a happier picture of his home in Somalia, showing the animals he misses. His mother uses this picture to link the family's old and new homes. After this, although his environment in the United States had seemed colorless to him, he begins to notice colors and to feel that he can be at home there. While telling about some ways that war affects children directly, this story shows

how talking and drawing about those experiences helps kids cope with them.

Ages: 6–9   **Cultural context:** Multicultural

Main character's cultural background: African-American

Feathers and Fools **by Mem Fox. Illus. by Nicholas Wilton.**
36 pages Harcourt, 1996.

Emphasis on differences among people can lead to war, as it does in this story is about a flock of peacocks and a nearby flock of swans. As a peacock considers the differences between the two kinds of birds, he becomes afraid of the swans. He shares his fears with the other peacocks, who prepare a huge store of weapons. Realizing the situation, the swans amass their own weapons, and so both groups live in terror. When a swan flies by with what looks to the peacocks like a weapon—although it isn't—a bloodbath ensues from which there are no survivors. Then, a swan egg and a peacock egg hatch. The chicks approach each other, commenting on their similarities, and become friends. There are wonderful messages not only about the consequences of emphasizing difference over similarity, but also about children's potential to foster peace.

Ages: 5–8   **Cultural context:** N/A

Gleam and Glow **by Eve Bunting. Illus. by Peter Sylvada.**
32 pages Harcourt, 2001.

Even in dire conditions of war, hope is possible. Viktor's papa leaves his family to fight with the underground forces, but Viktor, his mama, and his sister, Marina, know that soon they'll also have to leave the country because of enemy attacks. Strangers stop at the family's house as they leave the country, and one stranger gives the family two pet fish, which he can't take with him. Marina names them Gleam and Glow. When Mama, Viktor, and Marina leave the country, Viktor releases Gleam and Glow into their pond. The family walks for many days until they finally reach a refugee camp across the border, where they're miraculously reunited with Papa. After many months, the family returns home, and though very little is left of their house, the pond is full of generations of Gleam and Glow's children, survivors like Viktor and his family. The symbol of the fish provides a powerful message of hope and a clear message about the resilience of humanity.

Ages: 6–10   Cultural context: European

Jenny Is Scared! When Sad Things Happen in the World by **Carol Shuman. Illus. by Cary Pillo. 32 pages Magination, 2003.** When bad things happen, it's important to talk about your feelings, make connections with people you love, and continue normal routines. Jenny is scared because "something bad happened." She's knows it's important because everyone's plans are canceled, even school and regular TV shows. Her parents explain that people usually do good things, but there are times when they do bad things. They encourage Jenny and her brother to talk about their feelings, and the children express fear, confusion, anger, difficulty concentrating, and wishes to control the situation or make it go away. Their parents reassure them that these feelings are normal and temporary and that they'll feel better if they talk to one another. Jenny learns that love helps everyone through difficult times. An afterword suggests ways to help children cope with traumatic events. This story reassures kids that they aren't alone in their emotional reactions to scary news, suggesting that continuation of normal routines and open expressions of love will reduce their feelings of helplessness.

Ages: 4–8   Cultural context: Multicultural
Main character's cultural background: European-American

Mole Music by **David McPhail. 32 pages Holt, 1999.** Being your own best self can contribute to making the world a better place. When Mole feels that something is missing in his life, he decides to learn to play the violin. It's more difficult than he'd thought, and he has to work hard for a long time before he can play well. But his music makes him happy. Under the ground, he imagines wishfully that his music could dissolve people's sadness and anger, and change the world. Meanwhile, unknown to him, opposing armies above ground hear his music, stop fighting, and make friends with each other. This story shows ingeniously how one small person's hard work can make a difference in promoting peace.

Ages: 4–8   Cultural context: N/A

On That Day: A Book of Hope for Children by Andrea Patel.
16 pages Tricycle, 2001.
This book, which is illustrated with vibrant tissue paper collages, is about the events of September 11, 2001, although it refers only to "that day." It acknowledges that bad things can happen, sometimes because people are mean to each other. It reassures children that they can contribute to healing from these kinds of trauma; for example, by sharing, playing, laughing, and being kind. This reassurance can work toward decreasing the helplessness that children feel in these kinds of situations.
Ages: 3–6   **Cultural context:** Multicultural

Sami and the Time of the Troubles by Florence Parry Heide and Judith Heide Gilliland. Illus. by Ted Lewin. 33 pages Clarion, 1992.
Even where there's chronic violence, there are ways for children to maintain hope and speak out against war. Sami lives with his sister, mother, grandfather, and uncle in his uncle's basement in Beirut during a violent time that has existed all his life. His father has died in a bombing. Occasionally it's safe for them to go out, but most of the time the family stays in the basement, telling stories, listening to the radio, and keeping nice things from Sami's house to remind them of better times. Sami tells about a day when children marched in the streets to protest the fighting and expresses his determination to march in another demonstration with children. Showing children ways to keep positive experience in their hearts even during extremely difficult times, this story acknowledges their voices in speaking out against war.
Ages: 8–11   **Cultural context:** Middle Eastern

Smoky Night by Eve Bunting. Illus. by David Diaz. 34 pages Harcourt, 1994.
Groups who traditionally see each other as outsiders can work together to make everyone safer. Daniel, who is African-American, lives with his cat, Jasmine, and his mama in Los Angeles. Mrs. Kim, a Korean-American grocer, has a cat that fights with Jasmine. Mama doesn't shop at Mrs. Kim's store because she prefers doing business with "our own people." At the beginning of this story, Daniel and Mama watch rioting and loot-

ing in the street below their window. Mama explains that rioting is an expression of anger. As the rioting spreads, the building catches fire, and in the chaos of the evacuation, Daniel can't find Jasmine. When Daniel, Mama, and Mrs. Kim are at a shelter, a firefighter finds Jasmine and Mrs. Kim's cat together. When the two cats share a bowl of milk, Mama and Mrs. Kim begin to come together. Vividly illustrated with acrylic paintings and intensely textured photographs, this book acknowledges the reality of urban violence in an age-appropriate way, while offering hope for cooperation and friendship.

Ages: 5–9 **Cultural context:** Multicultural

Main character's cultural background: African-American

Stars in the Darkness **by Barbara M. Joosse. Illus. by R. Gregory Christie. 30 pages Chronicle, 2002.**
A sense of community helps protect against the threat of community violence. A boy's older brother, Richard, who is an important source of safety for the boy, becomes involved in a street gang. Although Richard tries to hide this, both the boy and his mother know. The boy, who was already terrified of the violence in the streets, feels a palpable sense of loss. He and Mama initiate neighborhood peace walks, in which families walk through the streets with flashlights to reduce their isolation and promote an end to the fighting. As the boy's sense of helplessness is decreased by his actions, this story will help to decrease the powerlessness that children feel about urban violence. A resource list for gang prevention is included.

Ages: 6–10 **Cultural context:** African-American

Sweet Dried Apples: A Vietnamese Wartime Childhood **by Rosemary Breckler. Illus. by Deborah Kogan Ray. 32 pages Houghton Mifflin, 1996.**
Although war leads to painful separations, death, and forced emigration, there are ways for kids to keep the people they love in their hearts. When a Vietnamese girl's father goes to war, far from their village, her grandfather, Ong Noi, comes to live with her, her mother, and her brother. The girl and her brother become very close to Ong Noi, an herb doctor, and can't resist swiping the delicious dried apples

that he uses to sweeten the medicines he makes. As the war comes closer, Ong Noi travels for several weeks. While he's away, the children surprise him by collecting herbs for him and drying guavas to sweeten the medicines he'll make. Ong Noi is ill when he returns. After a devastating attack, he helps people who seek him and dies, exhausted. The girl, her mother, and brother flee across the ocean with their neighbors, and the girl remembers Ong Noi lovingly. This story shows children a way to carry the people they love in their hearts, even in a time of despair.

Ages: 8–11   **Cultural context:** Asian

A Terrible Thing Happened by Margaret M. Holmes.
Illus. by Cary Pillo. 32 pages Magination, 2000.
When children are exposed to war or other forms of violence, they may witness profoundly disturbing scenes. In this story, Sherman sees a terrible thing, which is not specified. At first he tries not to think about it, but this becomes harder and harder. He experiences physical discomforts, difficulty with sleeping and eating, nightmares, sadness, nervousness, and anger. When his anger gets him into trouble, he meets Ms. Maple, a child therapist. She helps Sherman express his feelings through drawings and words, and finally to draw and talk about the terrible thing that happened, helping him feel stronger and not so mean. An afterword for adults discusses ways to help kids cope with witnessing traumatic events. This book also includes a list of resources for (mostly older) children and adults. Offering empathy with the experience of trauma, this story promotes a sense of safety in expressing feelings about it and encourages hope for healing.

Ages: 4–8   **Cultural context:** N/A

The Tin Forest by Helen Ward. **Illus. by Wayne Anderson.**
31 pages Dutton, 2001.
This remarkable story depicts recovery from trauma—whether war, violence, or other traumatic events—through metaphor. An old man lives in a gloomy place full of other people's garbage, and dreams of a vibrant forest. When he wakes up to the same dreary world around him, he has an idea: he makes a forest out of the garbage. While not the forest he'd dreamed of, it's still a forest. A bird comes to the

man's tin tree, eventually bringing more and more life to his forest. Subtly and eloquently, this story communicates that there's hope for emerging from the bad things that have happened—"other people's garbage"—into a wonderful place that feels as if it's yours—a living, vibrant forest—if you hold onto your dreams and use imagination to bring them to reality.

Ages: 3–8   **Cultural context:** European-American

Why Did It Happen? Helping Children Cope in a Violent World by Janice Cohn. Illus. by Gail Owens. 32 pages Morrow, 1994.

When children are distressed by community violence, they need validation and reassurance by parents and teachers. Daniel's friend, the neighborhood grocer, is injured during a robbery. Daniel's parents talk with him about why people steal, explain that the offender will go to jail, and describe what they do to keep Daniel safe. Daniel has a nightmare and relives the robbery in make-believe play and drawing. He's angry; when he discusses the event with his classmates, they express sadness and fear about similar incidents. The class devises a list of ways they can feel better, which the grocer adds to when he and Daniel see each other again. A foreword for adults discusses the effects of violence on children and ways of coping with them. While acknowledging the reality of danger, this story offers a sense of warmth, safety, and rootedness in connections between people.

Ages: 5–10   **Cultural context:** Multicultural
Main character's cultural background: unclear

CHAPTER 34

Abuse and Abuse Prevention

Unfortunately, child abuse is relatively common. By conservative estimates, in North America between one in ten and one in five children is physically abused at some time, one in six girls and one in twenty boys is sexually abused, and about one in eight witnesses violence between their parents. The picture books summarized in this chapter address abuse prevention, experiences of physical and sexual abuse, and witnessing violence between parents.

CHILD ABUSE PREVENTION

While child abuse is never a child's fault and kids can't be held responsible for adults' behavior, children can be empowered by knowing what they can do to protect themselves against child abuse. Kids need to know what to do when approached by a stranger. It's vital that they're taught that their body is private, some touches are okay, and some are not. Children have good instincts about this, and they need to learn that it's appropriate to refuse unwanted touch, and they shouldn't keep any kind of abuse a secret, even if they're told to. It's crucial for kids to be aware of the importance of telling a trusted adult if they are abused, and should continue telling until someone believes them and helps them stay safe. Children should understand that although most people are nice, some aren't, and they should be prepared for this situation just as they'd be prepared for other dangerous situations, such as a fire.

See also *Just Because I Am* (Chapter 2) for an affirmation that it's okay to refuse uncomfortable touches.

It's MY Body by Lory Freeman. Illus. by Carol Deach.
30 pages Parenting, 1993.

Asserting their right to choose or reject physical contact may help kids avoid abusive situations. A child (who can be seen as male or female) tells readers that his/her body is something very special that belongs to him/her. Sometimes the child wants to share his/her body (for example, by hugging or sitting in someone's lap), but sometimes he/she doesn't; for example, if someone tickles too hard or holds him/her too tightly. In situations like this, the child encourages readers to express clear refusal of the touch. The child comments that it feels "warm inside" to share your body when you want to, but you shouldn't share your body if you feel "uncomfortable inside." There are no explicit references to sexual behavior or body parts. This book communicates a positive message of empowerment to children.

Ages: 3–6   **Cultural context:** European-American

Not Everyone Is Nice: Helping Children Learn Caution With Strangers by Frederick Alimonti and Ann Tedesco. Illus. by Erik DePrince and Jessica Volinski. 48 pages New Horizon, 2003.

Although stranger abduction is relatively uncommon, children need to know how to protect themselves. Kathy knows that she should only ride home from school with the person her parents specify that morning, but one day, she's waiting for her mom when a man drives up, asks her personal questions, and offers her candy and a ride. She declines the ride, but when he speculates that her mommy might be sick or hurt, she wavers. Just in time, her mom arrives and the man speeds off. Kathy's parents explain that although the man seemed nice, he wasn't. They use analogies to underwater animals whose pretty or plantlike appearance belies their dangerousness, adding that if it happens again, she should leave and tell an adult she knows. Kathy is sad that not everyone is nice, but she's happy that most people are. Afterwords give tips about strangers for kids and parents. By reading about Kathy's experience, kids can gain useful knowledge about handling risky situations.

Ages: 5–8   **Cultural context:** Multicultural
Main character's cultural background: European-American

Peanut's Emergency **by Cristina Salat. Illus. by Tammie Lyon. 32 pages Charlesbridge, 2002.**

Staying safe sometimes requires problem solving and persistence. When no one comes to pick Peanut up after school, she wonders whether this is an emergency. Because she's spent all her emergency phone money, she goes to a pay phone and calls "Operator," but she can't remember any phone numbers. Meanwhile, a man asks her to help find his puppy; she responds loudly, "'I DO NOT TALK TO STRANGERS!'" Peanut goes into a store that she often visits with Mommy, and the storekeeper, whom she knows, finds her parents' phone number, and Mommy comes to get Peanut. Peanut thinks she's been "bad" (a limitation of this book for families that don't use this kind of terminology) because she'd spent the emergency money and forgotten the phone numbers. But the adults remind her that she didn't go anywhere with a stranger, got home safely, and used problem-solving strategies until she found one that worked, making Peanut a good role model for how to stay safe in this kind of situation.

Ages: 3–6   **Cultural context:** Multicultural
Main character's cultural background: African-American

The Right Touch **by Sandy Kleven. Illus. by Jody Bergsma. 32 pages Illumination Arts, 1997.**

Children need to know that their bodies are private, and they should trust their instincts about touch. Jimmy's mother teaches this by talking to him about good touches and touching problems; for example, when you tell someone to stop tickling and they won't stop. She warns him about touching problems that can happen when adults or older kids try to trick children. One girl's neighbor tricked her into coming into his house and tried to put his hand into her panties. The girl's uncomfortable feeling in the neighbor's house is a warning signal, and Jimmy's mother encourages him to pay attention if he ever feels like this. His mother explains that his body is private, and some parts are extra private. The author suggests discussing the unlabeled illustration of boys' and girls' bodies using terms you're comfortable with. Jimmy's mother encourages him to tell her if anyone tricks him, even if the person asks him to keep it secret. A foreword for adults is included. With Jimmy, kids will learn ways to avoid sexual abuse.

Ages: 4–7   **Cultural context:** Multicultural
Main character's cultural background: European-American

Sometimes It's OK to Tell Secrets **by Amy C. Bahr. Illus. by Frederick Bennett Green 28 pages Grosset & Dunlap, 1986.**
This book takes an instructional approach to discussing the kinds of secrets to keep and the kinds to tell. It acknowledges secrets that are fun to keep, such as a birthday present or a surprise party. It encourages children not to keep some kinds of secrets; for example, when they've done something wrong (the illustration suggests a child who has stolen money from her mom's purse), or are ashamed of something (the illustration suggests a child who has wet his bed), or, finally, are sexually abused. The author explains to children that adults will ask children to keep the adults' wrongdoing secret, but children don't have to. She encourages them to share secrets that frighten them and to persist until someone listens. A foreword for adults encourages them to discuss the ideas in this book with their child. This book can help defuse the secrecy around sexual abuse by putting it in a broader context of the kinds of things that children should tell about.

Ages: 3–6   **Cultural context:** Multicultural

Uncle Willy's Tickles **by Marcie Aboff. Illus. by Kathleen Gartner. 31 pages Magination, 1996.**
In some situations, asserting the right to reject unwanted touches can help prevent sexual abuse. A boy's Uncle Willy takes him for ice cream, lets him sit in the driver's seat of his pickup truck, and wiggles his

ears. But Uncle Willy tickles the boy until it hurts, even when the boy tells him to stop. The boy begins to avoid his uncle, and his mom notices. Though he hesitates to tell her why, when he finally does, Mom compliments him for telling and affirms his right to decide when to accept a touch. The boy is able to tell Uncle Willy that he doesn't like his tickles, and Uncle Willy agrees not to do it any more, expressing approval of the boy's having told him. Uncle Willy is still fun, and the child still likes him. An introduction for adults is included. Giving kids the confidence to reject unwanted touches, this story provides a good model for communication.

Ages: 3–7   **Cultural context:** European-American

Your Body Belongs to You **by Cornelia Maude Spelman.**
Illus. by Teri Weidner. 24 pages Whitman, 1997.
This is an informational book about the distinction between wanted and unwanted touches. The author states that most touches, hugs, and kisses feel good. She also tells readers that it's okay to decline any touch that they don't want. She explains that the parts of a child's body that are covered by a swimsuit are "private parts" and should never be touched by another person, except to help with toileting or dressing, or if necessary for a medical examination. Children are urged to tell a trusted adult if someone tries to touch their private parts. An introduction for adults is included. In a very simple and positive way, this book explains a child's right to choose about being touched.

Ages: 2–5   **Cultural context:** Multicultural

PHYSICAL ABUSE

Signs of possible physical abuse include unexplained bruises or other injuries; avoidance of a particular person; general shrinking back from adults; hostile, aggressive behavior; extreme fear or withdrawal; behavior that's destructive of property or the self; verbal abuse; or out-of-control behavior. None of these means that abuse has definitely occurred, but all are warning signals to get more information. Children who are abused physically are frequently also abused psychologically—subjected to chronic humiliation, belittling, and/or ridicule. The most urgent need of children who have been physically abused is for physical safety. These kids also need to know that adults will believe and protect them, that the abuse wasn't their fault, that this happens to other kids too, and that it's possible for things to get better.

See also *The Mad Family Gets Their Mads Out* (Chapter 5), which suggests ways for kids to cope when someone bigger starts to hurt them. See *A Terrible Thing Happened* and *The Tin Forest* (Chapter 33) for stories that are helpful in traumatic situations, including child abuse.

Daisy **by E. Sandy Powell. Illus. by Peter J. Thornton.**
40 pages Carolrhoda, 1991.
This story is a good choice for children whose abuse leads to feeling alone and blaming themselves. Daisy is psychologically and physically abused by her single father, who uses alcohol problematically. She copes admirably using make-believe and drawing; her father taunts her cruelly about this and forbids it. His brutal physical abuse escalates, and he orders her not to tell anyone how she got bruised. After disclosing her abuse to the school principal, who reassures her that it isn't her fault, Daisy is placed in a foster home. At the end of the story, she dares to draw herself for the first time. This story lets abused children know that this happens to other kids, that it isn't the child's fault, and that it's possible to tell, find safety, and begin to feel good about yourself.

Ages: 8–13   **Cultural context:** Multicultural
Main character's cultural background: European-American

Don't Hurt Me, Mama **by Muriel Stanek.**
Illus. by Helen Cogancherry. 32 pages Whitman, 1983.
When abusing parents get the help they need, things can be better for the child. A girl's single mother seems sad and rejects the girl's attempts to connect with her. Mama drinks too much and hits the girl, who feels scared, lonely, and helpless. Noticing that the girl seems troubled, her teacher sends her to the school nurse, who understands that she's been abused, tells her it isn't her fault, and arranges for a social worker to see Mama. After apologizing to the girl, Mama explains how the social worker will help. At the end of the story, the girl

is well cared for, and Mama no longer hits her and starts to respond to her attempts at connection. This story offers children empathy with the experience of physical abuse and hope that there are caring adults who can make things better. It should only be used when hopes for an ending like this are realistic.

Ages: 5–9   **Cultural context:** Multicultural

Main character's cultural background: European-American

Robin's Story: Physical Abuse and Seeing the Doctor **by Deborah Anderson and Martha Finne.**
Illus. by Jeanette Swofford. 47 pages Dillon, 1986.
Although abusing parents often tell children to keep abuse a secret, when kids tell, both parent and child can get the help they need. When Robin's mom is angry, she throws a cookie tin at Robin, causing a serious cut. She tells Robin to lie about it. Robin initially does, but a gentle school social worker helps her disclose the truth and refers Robin to a caring physician. Both the social worker and physician report the abuse to Children's Protective Services, and both follow up with Robin. Robin's mom gets the assistance she needs and is no longer abusing Robin a year later. An afterword for kids defines physical abuse and distinguishes it from discipline, offering children ideas about where to find help. An afterword for adults summarizes signs of physical abuse, encourages adults to help children report it, and gives suggestions about what to do if a child does report abuse. A useful tool for educating, Robin's story shows kids that by reporting physical abuse, they can be safe.

Ages: 7–11   **Cultural context:** Multicultural

Main character's cultural background: European-American

A Tale Worth Telling **by Linda Sky Grossman.**
Illus. by Petra Bockus. 26 pages Second Story, 2002.
This rhyming story emphasizes the importance of disclosing physical abuse. When David is at a new school, his classmate, Niron, notices that his arm is injured, but David asks him not to tell anyone. He's already tried to tell his sister and his dad, and they wouldn't listen. Niron persists, causing David to tell him that their soccer coach abused

him verbally and grabbed his arm. Niron believes David and urges him to find help. He suggests they confide in the school custodian, whom Niron trusts. The custodian helps David to tell his father, and David is finally heard. With a helpful note for grown-ups included, this story will encourage kids to keep telling about abuse until they find someone who will help.

Ages: 4–8   **Cultural context:** Multicultural
Main character's cultural background: European-American

SEXUAL ABUSE

Sexual abuse means sexual behaviors with a child, where the offender is in a position of power or authority, is much older than the child (including older children), or uses force or trickery. *Sexual behaviors* include both sexual contact and other behaviors such as child pornography, exhibitionism, and voyeurism. Child sexual abuse is most often committed by nonrelatives who are known to the child, but is also sometimes committed by relatives and strangers. Because these sexual behaviors are developmentally inappropriate for children, and as a result are confusing (the child usually senses that something is wrong, and at the same time is told that this means he/she is "special" and/or has pleasurable sexual sensations) and because abusers may demand that the activity be kept secret and/or threaten the child or those close to her/him, sexual abuse often leads to emotional and relationship problems. Children who have been sexually abused may show an unusual interest in or avoidance of sexuality, say that something's wrong with their bodies or with their private parts, avoid a specific person, develop secretiveness, depression, sleep problems, withdrawal, aggression, or callous disregard for others. Again, none of these means that a child has definitely been abused, but all are warning signals that deserve further investigation. When children have been sexually abused, they need you to listen calmly and nonjudgmentally, take them seriously, and reassure them that they did the right thing by telling, that it wasn't their fault, and that you'll keep them safe.

See also *The Mad Family Gets Their Mads Out* (Chapter 5), which advises kids to call the Child Abuse Hotline if someone touches them in a way that they don't like. See *A Terrible Thing Happened* and *The Tin Forest* (Chapter 33) for stories that are helpful in traumatic situations, including child abuse.

Chilly Stomach by Jeannette Caines.
Illus. by Pat Cummings. 32 pages Harper & Row, 1986.

If someone does anything to a child that feels sexually suggestive, it's important for the child to tell so that he/she can be protected. When Sandy's Uncle Jim tickles her, hugs her, or kisses her on the lips, she feels uncomfortable—she gets a "chilly stomach." Sandy feels good when her parents kiss her, and her friend, Jill, feels good when *her* uncle hugs and kisses her. Sandy avoids Uncle Jim whenever she can, and eventually tells Jill about her discomfort. Jill encourages Sandy to tell her parents and says she's going to tell her own parents. Sandy's afraid that her parents won't believe her, or will reject her, but by the end of the story she's determined that they know. Although the story ends there, before Sandy tells her parents, its distinction between touches that feel good and touches that feel creepy, and Sandy's decision to tell, will encourage children in similar situations to disclose their concerns.

Ages: 4–7   **Cultural context:** Multicultural
Main character's cultural background: European-American

Laurie Tells by Linda Lowery. Illus. by John Eric Karpinski.
40 pages Carolrhoda, 1994.

When children disclose sexual abuse and aren't believed, it's important to keep telling. Laurie describes her feelings about two years of sexual abuse by her father: pain, grief, betrayal, anger. She tells her mother about the abuse, but Mom just tells her not to get carried away by her imagination. It's another year before Laurie finally finds the courage to tell her aunt. Aunt Jan believes her, assures her that it's not her fault, and promises that she'll keep loving her and that her father won't abuse her any more. Laurie feels safe tucked into the bed in Aunt Jan's guest room. The language used to describe the abuse is not explicit, but it is clear. An afterword to children explains that most fathers don't abuse their children and most mothers do believe them, and encourages children to tell if this has happened to them.

Presenting empathy with the painful feelings around sexual abuse, this story gives strong support for telling an adult who can help.

Ages: 9–14   **Cultural context:** European-American

Margaret's Story: Sexual Abuse and Going to Court
by Deborah Anderson and Martha Finne.
Illus. by Jeanette Swofford. 47 pages Dillon, 1986.
When sexual abuse leads to a trial, children sometimes have to testify. Margaret tells of being sexually abused by an adult male neighbor. The offender orders her not to tell, but she tells her mom. Her parents are supportive and immediately report the abuse to police. Margaret is scared and cries, especially when it's time to testify in court. Her mom comforts Margaret, reminding her that she's brave and capable, and she's finally able to go into the courtroom. After having given her testimony, she acknowledges that it was scary, but she's glad to have done it, and it felt good to have told the truth. This book also includes a didactic section on sexual abuse, suggestions for confidants, a glossary, and a note to adults. For children who have to give court testimony about sexual abuse, this story will be helpful because it shows that others have been through it with positive outcomes and because it acknowledges the difficult feelings involved.

Ages: 7–11   **Cultural context:** Multicultural
Main character's cultural background: African-American

No More Secrets for Me **by Oralee Wachter.**
Illus. by Jane Aaron. 48 pages Little, Brown, 1983.
In four stories, children find ways to cope with sexually abusive situations. Two stories involve a feeling that something isn't right (a boy's babysitter insists on drying him after a bath and doesn't knock before coming into the bathroom; an adult hangs around the video arcade, offers a girl more money to play, sits too close, and tries to keep her from leaving) and two are more explicitly abusive (a camp counselor tells a boy to undress for a "game", threatening to get him in trouble if he refuses; a girl's stepfather touches her private parts at bedtime and insists that she promise not to tell). Each child listens to his/her instincts, tells a supportive adult, and gets help. An introduction ex-

plains the difference between acceptable and unacceptable touches. With its diverse cross-section of examples, these stories will help children to trust themselves, recognize dangerous situations, and know what to do to stay safe.

Ages: 7–12   **Cultural context:** European-American

Sam Speaks Out **by Linda Sky Grossman.**
Illus. by Petra Bockus. 26 pages Second Story, 2002.
When children have difficulty disclosing sexual abuse, they sometimes act out in aggressive behavior toward other kids or pets, as Sam does in this rhyming story. Sam has to stay in his room for some "thinking time" after teasing his dog. But he has something he wants to tell his friend Charlene: a neighbor boy tickled him, wrestled him to the floor, and touched him in a "yucky" way. The boy wouldn't stop when Sam said no, and he told Sam to keep it a secret. But Sam realizes that secrets that hurt someone shouldn't be kept. Charlene believes and supports Sam, recalling her mother's advice that your body isn't for other people to play with. She brings her mom to Sam's house, and in their presence, Sam tells his mom what happened. Sam's mom praises his courage and promises to help. A note for grown-ups is included. Sam's experience will help children feel safe disclosing sexual abuse.

Ages: 4–8   **Cultural context:** Multicultural
Main character's cultural background: European-American

Tears of Joy **by Barbara J. Behm. Illus. by Ellen Anderson.**
32 pages Way Word, 1999.
It's important for children who have been sexually abused to tell someone who can help keep them safe. Carly, a happy, loving child, suddenly becomes sad and scared, and won't talk to anyone. Her teacher brings her to Miss Mitchell, the school counselor. Carly plays with Miss Mitchell's toys, and she even laughs. When Miss Mitchell, using the voice of a horse puppet, encourages Carly to talk about her sadness, she cries and cries, telling Miss Mitchell that her daddy has been touching her private parts. Miss Mitchell praises Carly's courage and emphasizes how important it is for sad or scared children to

keep talking until someone believes them. Reassuring Carly that her father's behavior isn't her fault, Miss Mitchell promises to help keep Carly safe. An afterword for adults is included. This story will help children feel safe in disclosing sexual abuse, an important first step in healing.

Ages: 4–8　　**Cultural context:** Multicultural
Main character's cultural background: European-American

EXPOSURE TO SPOUSAL OR PARTNER ABUSE

Violence between parents is terrifying and confusing. Children often understand, at some level, that a violent parent is out of control and may try desperately to control him or her, even to the point of blaming themselves for their parent's behavior. Many children will have deep feelings of anger, shame, and/or fear, difficulty concentrating and/or will show aggressive behavior. Adding to children's confusion, frustration, and lack of control, adults—even those who are victimized—may tell children that the abuse isn't serious, when it's clear to the child that it is. Children who witness violence between their parents need to be safe, to know that violence is inappropriate, to learn constructive ways to express anger and other feelings, to care for themselves, to have their mixed feelings about an abusing parent respected, and to know that the violence isn't their fault.

　　See also *The Mad Family Gets Their Mads Out* (Chapter 5), which acknowledges the angry, scared, and confused feelings kids have when their parents fight, and advises them to take care of themselves by reminding themselves that fights between adults are an adult problem. See *A Terrible Thing Happened* and *The Tin Forest* (Chapter 33) for stories that are helpful in traumatic situations, including witnessing partner violence.

A Family That Fights by Sharon Chesler Bernstein.
Illus. by Karen Ritz. 32 pages Whitman, 1991.
Children who witness violence between their parents need to know that they're not alone. In the family in this story, when the parents dis-

agree, or when Dad's in a bad mood, he hits Mom. Dad is "a grown-up
. . . [who] has not learned to express his angry feelings in a grown-up
way." The children have feelings and experiences common in this situation: fear, shame, difficulty concentrating, wishes to get away, trying
to keep Dad from hitting by being "good," trying to get the younger
kids to be "good," telling Dad to stop hurting Mom, planning to get
revenge on Dad when they're bigger, and hitting other children. When
Mom tells the oldest child not to worry about the violence, he feels
angry and invalidated. The author states clearly that the children are
not to blame for the violence, and she includes a list of coping strategies for kids and parents and a preface for adults. In the context of an
empathic story, this book offers positive suggestions for children who
witness partner violence and don't know how to proceed.

Ages: 6–10   **Cultural context:** European-American

A Safe Place **by Maxine Trottier. Illus. by Judith Friedman.
24 pages Whitman, 1997.**
In some situations of partner violence, children leave with a parent
to stay at a shelter. Emily recalls how her daddy hit her mama, and
how she tried to be good in the hope that that would stop their fights.
She recalls how her mother brought her to a shelter during the night.
Although she's frightened at first, she comes to experience the shelter as a safe place, and works through some of her feelings about her
father's violence there. As the story ends, Emily and Mama are leaving
the shelter to live in a new apartment, away from Daddy. With an
honest look at life in a partner violence shelter, this story provides
empathy and hope for a positive future.

Ages: 4–8   **Cultural context:** Multicultural
Main character's cultural background: European-American

*Something Is Wrong at My House: A Book About Parent's
Fighting* **by Diane Davis. Illus. by Marina Megale. 40 pages
Parenting, 1984.**
When children witness violence between their parents, it's important
for them to be safe. Each two-page spread in this book contains two
versions of the text: a simpler version for younger children on one page
and, on the facing page, a more elaborate version for older children.

A child tells that his parents fight. Scared and angry, he feels like picking on younger kids and pets, doesn't get along with teachers or classmates, doesn't do schoolwork, and steals at school. (This book is probably best for children who already show these kinds of behaviors). The child describes ways to cope with anger and to feel better. In the older kids' version, neither the child's mother nor his neighbor takes him seriously, but his teacher listens and suggests agencies that might help. The story ends by affirming the child's worth and the legitimacy of his needs. An introduction for adults is included. This book offers empathy, positive coping strategies, and resources for children who witness violence between their parents, along with an important message about persisting in searching for an adult who'll listen.

Ages: 3–10   **Cultural context:** Multicultural

Main character's cultural background: European-American

References

Bernstein, Joanne, and Rudman, Masha Kabakow. (1989). *Books to Help Children Cope With Separation and Loss: An Annotated Bibliography*, vol. 3. New York: R. R. Bowker.

Doll, Beth and Doll, Carol. (1997). *Bibliotherapy With Young People: Librarians and Mental Health Professionals Working Together*. Englewood, CO: Libraries Unlimited.

Finkelhor, David. (1994). Current information on the scope and nature of child sexual abuse. *The Future of Children, 4,* 31–53.

Grindler, Martha C., Stratton, Beverly D., and McKenna, Michael. (1997). *The Right Book, The Right Time: Helping Children Cope*. Boston: Allyn and Bacon.

Hearne, Betsy and Stevenson, Deborah. (2000). *Choosing Books for Children: A Commonsense Guide*. Urbana, Il: University of Chicago Press.

Schonfeld, David J. (2001). *In the Aftermath of Crisis: Parents' Guide to Talking With Children About Death*. National Center for Children Exposed to Violence. Available: http://www.nccev.org/pdfs/children_death.pdf.

Shapiro, Lawrence E. (2001). *"Will They Fly a Plane Into Our House?" How to Talk to Children About Terrorism*. Play2Grow, LLC and Childswork/Childsplay, LLC. Available: http://www.guidancechannel.com/talkingterrorism.pdf.

Singer, Dorothy G. (1993). *Playing for Their Lives: Helping Troubled Children Through Play Therapy*. New York: Free Press.

Singer, Dorothy G. and Singer, Jerome L. (2001). *Make-Believe: Games and Activities for Imaginative Play*. Washington, D.C.: Magination.

Trelease, Jim. (2001). *The Read-Aloud Handbook* (5th edition). New York: Penguin.

Author Index

Illustrator Index

Title Index

Topic Index

About the Author

Jacqueline Golding, Ph.D. is a psychologist in private practice in Pleasanton, California who works with children, teens, and adults. A graduate of Yale University, Dr. Golding earned her Ph.D. in psychology at the University of California, Los Angeles and completed a post-doctoral fellowship at the Central Contra Costa County Child, Adolescent, and Family Mental Health Service in Concord, California. She holds an appointment as Adjunct Professor at the University of California, San Francisco. Dr. Golding, a Fellow of the American Psychological Association, has published over 100 articles in scientific and professional journals on topics such as trauma, depression, and cultural issues in mental health. She lives in northern California with her family, and in her free time enjoys hiking and photography.